Vinod Acharya
Nietzsche's Meta-Existentialism

M000239567

Monographien und Texte zur Nietzsche-Forschung

Begründet von
Mazzino Montinari
Wolfgang Müller-Lauter
Heinz Wenzel

Herausgegeben von
Günter Abel, Berlin
Werner Stegmaier, Greifswald

Band 65

Vinod Acharya

Nietzsche's Meta-Existentialism

—

DE GRUYTER

ISBN 978-3-11-048178-5
e-ISBN 978-3-11-031275-1
ISSN 1862-1260

Library of Congress Cataloging-in-Publication data
A CIP catalog record for this book has been applied for at the Library of Congress.

Bibliographic information published by the Deutsche Nationalbibliothek
The Deutsche Nationalbibliothek lists this publication in the Deutsche Nationalbibliografie;
detailed bibliographic data are available in the Internet at http://dnb.dnb.de.

© 2014 Walter de Gruyter GmbH, Berlin/Boston
Typesetting: PTP-Berlin Protago-TₑX-Production GmbH, Berlin
Printing: Hubert & Co. GmbH & Co. KG, Göttingen
♾ Printed on acid-free paper
Printed in Germany

www.degruyter.com

Acknowledgements

Many people have contributed to my development as a philosopher. First and foremost, I thank my parents for helping me cultivate the taste for a certain kind of freedom and the impulse to pursue new and unexplored tasks, without which I would not have ventured into philosophy. I would also like to thank Michael Gelven and Ted Kisiel, my teachers at Northern Illinois University, who introduced me to Continental philosophy, and helped me navigate my way through the complex terrain of Western philosophy. As this book is adapted from my Ph.D. dissertation, I am grateful to my dissertation committee members at Rice University for their invaluable advice and support. I would like to thank Christian Emden for his encouragement and friendship. I owe a special debt of gratitude to Dan Conway. I have profited immensely from our conversations on Nietzsche. I appreciate very much both the positive feedback and the constructive criticisms that I have received from Dan at various stages of this work. I also thank him for his enthusiasm and for his confidence in my project. I am most indebted to Steve Crowell for his guidance, unflinching encouragement and understanding without which this project would not have been possible. Steve's comments on the manuscript spurred me to think critically about my ideas and arguments, and to make crucial revisions. I thank Steve for his support over the years and for his belief in my philosophical abilities. This work benefited significantly from my stay in Freiburg, Germany in 2009–2010, thanks to a DAAD research grant. Thanks to Andreas Urs Sommer, Gitta Fehrenbach and Philipp Fehrenbach for their friendship and hospitality in Freiburg. I also wish to thank the Humanities Research Center at Rice for supporting my research through a Dissertation Writing Fellowship for the academic year 2010–11. Lastly, I profoundly thank Summer. Summer's loving enthusiasm for my work, her cheerful spirit, her keen eye for clarity and details, her openness to new ideas, her ability to entertain conflicting perspectives while maintaining her objectivity and composure, and her passion for travelling have deeply contributed to the realization of this work.

Portions of the fourth chapter of this book were originally published as, "Nobility and Decadence: The Vulnerabilities of Nietzsche's Strong Type," *PhaenEx* 7.1 (2012): 130–161. I gratefully acknowledge the permission to use this article.

Abbreviations

Abbreviations of Nietzsche's texts are as follows:

AOM	*Assorted Opinions and Maxims*
BGE	*Beyond Good and Evil*
BT	*The Birth of Tragedy.* "Attempt" denotes the 1886 Preface, titled "Attempt at Self-Criticism." "Foreword" denotes the 1872 Preface, titled "Foreword to Richard Wagner."
CW	*The Case of Wagner*
D	*Daybreak*
DS	*David Strauss*
EH	*Ecce Homo.* The four major divisions of this text are indicated by abbreviations of their titles: "Wise," "Clever," "Books," and "Destiny." The subsections of "Books" that discuss Nietzsche's individual works are indicated by shortened titles of these works.
GM	*On the Genealogy of Morality.* Roman numerals indicate the essay number.
GS	*The Gay Science*
HH I	*Human, All Too Human,* Vol. I
HL	*On the Uses and Disadvantages of History for Life*
KGW	*Werke. Kritische Gesamtausgabe*
KSA	*Sämtliche Werke. Kritische Studienausgabe*
Philosopher	"The Philosopher: Reflections on the Struggle Between Art and Knowledge"
Philosophy in the Tragic Age	*Philosophy in the Tragic Age of the Greeks*
SE	*Schopenhauer as Educator*
The Struggle	"The Struggle between Science and Wisdom"
TI	*Twilight of the Idols.* The eleven major divisions of this text are indicated by abbreviations of their titles: "Maxims," "Socrates," "Reason," "Real World," "Morality," "Errors," "Improvers," "Germans," "Expeditions," "Ancients," and "Hammer."
On Truth and Lies	"On Truth and Lies in a Nonmoral Sense"
WS	*The Wanderer and His Shadow*
Z	*Thus Spoke Zarathustra.* Roman numerals indicate the part number, followed by the section number and a sub-section number, if any. The Prologue at the beginning of the book is indicated by "Prologue" followed by the section number.

Abbreviation of Kierkegaard's text is as follows:

Postscript	*Concluding Unscientific Postscript to Philosophical Fragments*

Note on sources

In citing Nietzsche's published works, I have used the above acronyms followed by the appropriate section number, designated by Arabic numerals. Nietzsche's Prefaces are indicated with a "Preface" after the book's acronym, followed by the section number of the Preface. All quotes appear in English. In some instances, I have quoted the original German from the critical edition of Nietzsche's collected works (KSA) in addition to the English translation. In such cases, references to KSA indicate the volume number followed by the page number.

In citing Nietzsche's *Nachlaß* of the 1860s and 1870s, I have used the title of the corresponding essay or compilation in English followed by the relevant page number. These unpublished writings include, "Homer on Competition," "The Greek State," "The Pre-Platonic Philosophers," "The Philosopher as Cultural Physician," "The Dionysiac World View," "Philosophy in the Tragic Age of the Greeks," "The Struggle between Science and Wisdom," "The Philosopher: Reflections on the Struggle Between Art and Knowledge," and "On Truth and Lies in a Nonmoral Sense." Only in citing the last four selections, I have used abbreviated versions of the titles (I have indicated these abbreviated titles above), while I have employed the full titles for the rest.

Finally, I have used the critical editions of Nietzsche's collected works (KSA or KGW) to refer to the compilation of Nietzsche's *Nachlaß* of the 1880s, which was published as the anthology, *Der Wille zur Macht*. References to KSA and KGW provide the corresponding volume number (and part number for KGW), followed by the relevant fragment number and any relevant aphorism. I have referred to Walter Kaufmann's English translation (*The Will to Power*) in quoting this unpublished material.

Any deviations from the consulted English translations are duly noted in the text.

Contents

Acknowledgements —— **v**

Abbreviations —— **vii**

Introduction —— **1**

Chapter One
Nietzsche's meta-existentialism —— **18**

Chapter Two
Meta-existentialism and Nietzsche's critique of metaphysics —— **43**

Chapter Three
Will to power: existence and the qualitative aspect of power —— **79**

Chapter Four
Nobility and decadence: the vulnerabilities of Nietzsche's strong type —— **106**

Chapter Five
Greek glory and decadence: a case study —— **138**

Conclusion —— **180**

Bibliography —— **183**

Index —— **189**

Introduction

Synopsis

The purpose of this study is to present a methodological framework to interpret Nietzsche's philosophy. My claim is that Nietzsche is best read as an "existential" thinker, however in a sense that is radically different from how existentialism (whether attributed to Nietzsche or not) is usually understood. In clarifying Nietzsche's peculiar version of existentialism, this work aims to provide the methodological foundations of his thought. It does not directly deal with the details of the multifaceted critical evaluations of morality, science, art, religion, culture, etc. that run throughout Nietzsche's writings, although one may use the interpretation presented here as the lens with which to approach these evaluations.

Accordingly, this study seeks to accomplish two main objectives. First, it provides a new existential interpretation of Nietzsche's philosophy. Second, it aims to undertake a thorough investigation of Nietzsche's critique of metaphysics. However, these two objectives are not unrelated to each other. The existential interpretation I offer necessitates an inquiry into Nietzsche's critical assessment of metaphysics, and at the same time, the latter presupposes an existential understanding of Nietzsche's thought. To reflect this mutual relation between Nietzsche's existentialism and his critique of metaphysics, I call the former, "meta-existentialism."

In simple terms, existential philosophy primarily emphasizes the meaning of human existence. According to the established view, the basic argument of existential thinkers (such as Kierkegaard, Dostoevsky, Nietzsche, Camus, Jaspers, Heidegger and Sartre) is that "objective" categories of religion, morality, science and traditional philosophy (such as reason, mind, body, matter, force, causality, virtue, guilt, sin, salvation, duty, etc.) are either insufficient or inappropriate to interpret the meaning of human existence. These categories tend to conceive of human beings as either substances or things with particular physical or mental properties, or as beings who have a rational purpose or a preset goal (whether these purposes or goals are understood in terms of religious or moral norms).[1] The existentialists tend to argue that such objective approaches are unsuitable to understand human existence, since the latter does not have a preset meaning or essence, like inanimate objects do. In the formulation of Sartre, human "existence comes before its essence," and therefore, "man first exists: he materializes in the world, encounters himself, and only afterward defines himself ... to begin with he is nothing ... he will be what he makes of himself."[2] Each individual simply *is*; only

---

[1] See Steven Crowell, "Existentialism," *The Stanford Encyclopedia of Philosophy*, ed. Edward N. Zalta, Winter 2010 Edition http://plato.stanford.edu/archives/win2010/entries/existentialism/. Also see Walter Kaufmann, ed. *Existentialism: From Dostoevsky to Sartre* (New York: Meridian Books, 1956).

[2] Jean-Paul Sartre, *Existentialism is a Humanism*, trans. Carol Macomber (New Haven: Yale University Press, 2007) 22.

subsequently, he or she creatively determines meaning through the process of existing. The meaning of the individual's existence is fluid and always subject to re-interpretation. Hence Sartre emphasizes "subjective existence" and defines "subjectivism" as the "freedom of the individual subject to choose what he will be."[3]

Further, it is not simply that the objective categories are inappropriate in themselves, but the use of them reflects impersonal and abstract conceptions of human life. It is not merely a question of *what* categories one uses to philosophize, but *how* one philosophizes that is crucial. Hence existentialism argues for a fundamental re-orientation in our approach, where the starting point of philosophical reflection must be the individual's existence in the world. This does not mean that we should think of human existence in terms of subjects encountering objects in the world, because this latter conception, too, implies reified notions of subject and object, in addition to an impersonal approach. What it does mean is that the existential notion of subjectivity can be elucidated only by emphasizing themes like passion, inwardness, appropriation, decision, authenticity, freedom, death and anxiety, as well as a deeply passionate and a personally involved style of philosophizing.

It is apparent, then, from the existential point of view, that there is a tension between the objective and subjective (existential) modes of inquiries. However, in typical existential interpretations there is not only a tension, but an opposition between these two kinds of approaches, such that, for example, it would not be possible for one to undertake a personal, existential investigation into the meaning of one's existence, while at the same time engaging in a speculative, metaphysical inquiry into the nature of all reality. I isolate metaphysics because it is the quintessential example of an objective approach and of an impersonal, abstract form of thinking (at least, according to one of the earliest pioneers of existential thought, Kierkegaard, and his interpretation of Hegelian philosophy). Metaphysical objectivity reduces human reality to one of the realities in the world, which needs to be apprehended, even if it is granted that human reality is, to a certain degree, a special or a privileged one. This view that a personal, individualistic mode of philosophizing is necessarily at odds with systematic philosophy and metaphysical thought, has been adopted by commentators such as Kaufmann, Jaspers, Fink and Solomon to argue that Nietzsche is an existential thinker, in a similar sense as Kierkegaard is an existentialist.[4]

However, I shall argue that although the above view of existentialism may be true with regard to Kierkegaard, it is too restrictive and limited with respect to Nietzsche, since it requires that we set aside or bracket the issue of Nietzsche's relation to metaphysics in order to view him as existentialist. Nietzsche's specific version of existentialism can be understood only by thoroughly investigating his critique of metaphysics. I will begin with, what I call the "existential distinction," which is the central distinction made by any existential philosophy between objective thinking (or objectivity)

---

3 Sartre, *Existentialism* 23.
4 See Kaufmann, *Existentialism* 11–12.

and subjective thinking (or subjectivity). Through an analysis of one of Kierkegaard's most famous pseudonymous works, *Concluding Unscientific Postscript*, I will show that the existential distinction is by its very nature conceptually ambiguous and unstable. The ambiguity and the instability consist in the fact that this distinction inevitably collapses back on itself, undermining the very conceptual grounds on which it was found. That is, in order to expound the realm of existence and subjectivity, the existential philosopher must rely on a contrasting, objective perspective. But once the existential realm is explicated, we learn that complete abstraction from existence is absolutely impossible for the existing subject, and that the so-called objectivity is only a differential variation within the subjective. The tension between these two conditions implies the inevitable ambiguity of the existential distinction. Therefore the goal of the existential philosopher is not to dispose of the ambiguity, but rather to affirm it.

However, this affirmation is not possible for an approach that posits an opposition between a passionate, subjective thinking and a purely abstract, objective thinking, since this opposition contradicts the finding that objectivity and subjectivity, from the existential point of view, vary differentially with respect to each other. The reason why Kierkegaard's pseudonym, Climacus, is unable to radically affirm the existential distinction, is that he begins his critique of Hegel by opposing his existential philosophy to Hegel's purely speculative metaphysics, even though, later in his argument, he concedes that there is nothing like purely abstract objectivity to imply that all objectivity is a variation within subjectivity.

The ambiguity of the existential distinction can be radically affirmed by a philosophical approach, which recognizes only a differential relation between objectivity and subjectivity, without the aid of an opposition between existential thinking and objective metaphysics. I claim that this approach is at the very basis of Nietzsche's philosophy, especially the mature phase of his thought, which begins in 1878 with the publication of the first volume of *Human, All-Too-Human*. Nietzsche grasps the fundamental implication of drawing the existential distinction, which is that this distinction is never set once and for all. Instability belongs to its very nature, since it tends to collapse back on itself, undermining the very grounds on which it was established. Hence there is an ever-renewed necessity to redraw this distinction. Nietzsche's existentialism, I argue, is able to undertake this repetitive process, and thus confront and affirm the instability of the existential distinction, precisely because it conceives of subjectivity and objectivity not as opposite concepts, but rather as thoroughly differential terms engaged in a mutually interpretative interplay. His existential approach does not directly explicate the realm of existence by first setting up an opposition against pure objectivity, but rather it interprets existence in a radically *indirect* manner, through the continuously evolving subjective and objective perspectives. In this way, it develops to the fullest the very meaning of making the existential distinction, thus justifying the term "meta-existentialism." It endlessly meditates on the implications of subjecting the existential distinction to its own conditions. Thus Nietzsche's existential philosophy has a "meta" aspect at its very core.

Nietzsche's meta-existentialism makes the typical existential position foundational, and then develops to the maximum all the implications of this position. Doing so is necessitated by the ambiguity of the existential distinction itself. Only by assuming the "meta" stance can one fully justify the implicit claims of existentialism. The basic methodological tenets of existentialism essentially entail the meta-existential position. However, this transformation into a meta-existential stance implies significant methodological differences. For instance, in Nietzsche's approach, the usual emphasis on the individual subject and his or her subjective becoming takes a backseat; the individual's subjective existence is not the absolute reference point of existential reflection, as it is for writers like Kierkegaard. Nietzsche has a more dynamic and richer conception of the subject since, for him, the subjective sphere constantly wanes and grows in its continuous interaction with the objective sphere. That is, it is not only that the subject constantly appropriates the objective sphere (the realm of science, history, religion, etc.), but also that the objective sphere constitutes the subject in such a way that the neat demarcation between an individual subject and the world is no longer possible. The spheres of subject and object constantly shift boundaries through mutual interpretations of one another.

This does not mean that Nietzsche abandons the personal style of philosophizing characteristic of existentialism to adopt an abstract, systematic form of thought. I agree with writers such as Solomon and Jaspers that Nietzsche's passionate form of philosophizing is indeed inseparable from the content of his arguments. At the same time, however, Nietzsche's meta-existentialism implies a much more drastically "indirect" style than that of Kierkegaard. However, this work will not explore these stylistic aspects in great detail, as it will focus more on the radicalness of the methodological aspects of meta-existentialism through a detailed consideration of Nietzsche's relation to metaphysics.

Nietzsche's critique of metaphysics is directly implicated by his existential approach. For Nietzsche, the fundamental characteristic of a metaphysical evaluation is that it posits oppositional schemas, whether these oppositions are between a so-called objective thinking and subjective thinking, or between a "real" and an "apparent" world, or between "truth" and "falsity." The primary emphasis is on the positing of the oppositional structure itself, and not on the two terms that are involved in the opposition, or on that term in the opposition which metaphysics values more (say, the real world) than the other term (the apparent world). Metaphysical thought, according to Nietzsche, sees oppositions where there are only differences in degrees. And the setting up of oppositions goes hand-in-hand with, what Nietzsche calls, the denial of existence or life. Denial of life, therefore, is another fundamental trait of metaphysics. In other words, metaphysical evaluations deny life not because they set up a real world in opposition to the apparent world (the world of life, nature and our existence), as some commentators argue. On the contrary, the positing of a real world may be a symptom of a prior life-denying evaluation.

This implies that, in his attack against metaphysics, Nietzsche does not posit his own set of oppositions. Put more radically, he does not begin his critique by initially conceding that metaphysics opposes a real world to an apparent world, or the truthful world to the world of falsity and illusions, in order to either reverse these oppositions or to reduce the oppositional terms to differential ones. Rather, in keeping with his meta-existential approach, he begins straightaway with a differential discourse. In doing so, Nietzsche's intent is not to avoid undertaking a critique of the oppositional terms of metaphysics, since he does this precisely by interpreting them as differential subjective and objective terms engaged in a mutual struggle. Nevertheless, his primary intention is to target the very *source* of the metaphysical-oppositional structure, the source of the life-denying evaluation.

This brings us to one of the central problems to be tackled in this study: Nietzsche's concept of "will to power" and its relation to metaphysics. In my interpretation, the theory of will to power is a meta-existential theory, which provides an interpretation of the very essence of existence. I will also discuss, what I term, the "qualitative" dimension of the will to power, which is the clue to unraveling the source of metaphysical oppositions. Particularly, this qualitative aspect takes us to the most basic distinction of Nietzsche's philosophy, which is the typological distinction between a strong will and a weak will. While the former will is a life-affirming one, the latter is the life-denying one.

However, I shall argue that although this typological distinction can be made, this distinction is not a pure or a fixed one. Nietzsche's complex analysis illustrates that these types of wills, as they are manifest in cultures and individuals, undergo transformations during the course of history, often sharing many traits. I will consider the problem of decadence, specifically the decadence of the strong type of will, to show that Nietzsche's analysis implies a "topological" continuity between the two types of wills, which forbids a strict distinction between them. In other words, although there are indeed two distinct types of wills for Nietzsche, it is not possible to determine, unequivocally, what particular quality it is about the strong or the weak type that allows them to affirm or deny life. The upshot of this argument is that, ultimately, the quality of the will to power as the source of metaphysical oppositions remains ever-elusive. Nietzsche delivers a thoroughly ambiguous critique of metaphysics in accordance with his meta-existential approach. The ambiguity of his critique means that Nietzsche neither simply overcomes the metaphysical tradition, nor does he remain stuck within its confines. Rather, he provides an open-ended criticism of it. An ever-renewed encounter with and critique of metaphysics is an indispensible aspect of his meta-existentialism. Thus my interpretation addresses one of the most frequently debated issues in Nietzsche scholarship: the precise relation of Nietzsche's thought to the metaphysical tradition.

In order to further situate my project, I will now briefly discuss three groups of Nietzsche commentators, not including the existential interpreters mentioned above. Although the reading offered here shares some affinities with each of these three groups of scholars, I will point out some of the important divergences between my approach and theirs, especially with regard to the issue of metaphysics. The reader must bear in mind that, keeping in line with the focus on methodological issues in this work, my appraisal of the following commentators will focus less on the details of their respective Nietzsche interpretations and more on the methodological commitments guiding their readings.

Three groups of interpreters

The Externalists

The first group is represented by those interpreters who argue that Nietzsche is a metaphysical thinker. For these commentators, it is necessary to set aside Nietzsche's colorful language, his metaphorical word-plays, and his rhetorical exaggerations, so as to get at the "real" content of his thought (for example, his concept of truth, his interpretation of being as will to power and eternal recurrence, and his interpretation of nihilism). In this way, they locate Nietzsche within the mainstream philosophical tradition. Here I include Heidegger and more contemporary commentators like Danto, although Danto is not so explicitly concerned with the nature and limits of metaphysics in general as is Heidegger.

I call these metaphysical interpreters of Nietzsche, "externalists," because they evaluate the significance of Nietzsche's works and his criticism of metaphysics *externally*, that is, from a point of view that uses standards of evaluation external to the intentions of Nietzsche's own writings. For these interpreters, what a philosophical theory should do and what standards of truth a philosophical theory should comply with are somehow given external to the internal content of a philosopher's philosophy. Danto, for example, argues that "Nietzsche's is a philosophy of Nihilism," which, while denying that there is any order or essence to this world, still posits its own essence about the world with its concept of "Will-to-Power"; trapped in this self-contradiction, Nietzsche "too has his metaphysics."[5] Danto uses the criterion of self-contradiction to attribute to Nietzsche a metaphysics of nihilism, while ignoring, for example, the idea that, in Nietzsche, such self-contradictions might have a stylistic import designed precisely to counteract the reader's preconceptions about the kind of incongruities in which a philosopher can legitimately engage. Hence Danto reads Nietzsche's concept of will to power much too "literally" than what its originator intended.

Although Heidegger is guilty of similar charges as Danto, his interpretation of Nietzsche is most relevant for my arguments, mainly because he had the most sophis-

---

5 Arthur C. Danto, *Nietzsche as Philosopher* (New York: Columbia University Press, 2005) 62.

ticated analysis of metaphysics among all of Nietzsche's commentators. Heidegger had a clearly developed conception of a philosophy of being in addition to a hermeneutical interpretation of the history of Western thought, which he used not only as the external standards to evaluate Nietzsche's philosophy, but also to inform his own efforts to carry out a destruction of metaphysics in order to go beyond it. For Heidegger, a philosophical theory worthy of this name should say something definitive about the essence and existence of beings as a whole, or the "being of beings." This theory, then, will constitute the philosopher's basic "guiding" thought or question (*Leitfrage*), according to which the specifics of his or her philosophy would be worked out.[6] According to Heidegger, the failure to go beyond the level of the guiding question of the being of beings, in order to ask the "grounding" question (*Grundfrage*) of philosophy (that is, the question of being itself ("what is being?")), is the most fundamental feature of all metaphysical thought.[7] Every great philosopher from Plato to Nietzsche is guilty of this fallacy, and therefore, the history of Western philosophy is the history of metaphysics. In accordance with the guiding question, the metaphysical conception of *truth*, for Heidegger, is the "correspondence" between a thing and reality, or the "correctness" of the representation of "*what* beings are and *how* they are" according to their inner essence.[8] In other words, truth involves perceiving something *as* that very thing and not as something else.

Heidegger applies these external criteria in order to argue that Nietzsche is a metaphysician who endeavors to overcome the metaphysics of Platonism, but only manages to "invert" it, confirming the Platonic tradition all the more.[9] For Heidegger, the will to power is Nietzsche's metaphysical interpretation of the being of all beings.[10] Whereas in Platonism the real, supersensible world (the supersensuous), as the world of being, is valued higher in comparison to the sensible world (the sensuous) of becoming, change and appearances, Nietzsche's will to power reverses this order of preference. It affirms the sensible world in opposition to the supersensible world. It rejects truth, but its rejection is only apparent, as when Nietzsche's "inversion is fully executed, the sensuous becomes being proper, i.e. the true, i.e. truth. The truth is the sensuous."[11] One is in truth, when one recognizes the sensible world as such and affirms it in one's thought and evaluations.

To affirm beings as whole through will to power, Nietzsche must arrest or fixate the continuous flow of becoming.[12] And for the latter, he must go *beyond* (or over and

---

6 Martin Heidegger, *Nietzsche*, vol. I, trans. David Farrell Krell (San Francisco: Harper & Row, 1979) 67–68.

7 Heidegger, *Nietzsche* I: 67.

8 Martin Heidegger, *Nietzsche*, vol. III, trans. Joan Stambaugh, David Farrell Krell and Frank A. Capuzzi (San Francisco: Harper & Row, 1987) 34.

9 *Nietzsche* I: 160.

10 *Nietzsche* III: 193–200.

11 *Nietzsche* I: 154.

12 *Nietzsche* III: 211.

above) the realm of beings to access the being of beings. Hence affirmation of becoming is meta-physical. Only through such a "permanentizing of becoming" is the truth of becoming secured.[13] According to Heidegger, it is Nietzsche's idea of the "eternal return of the same" which achieves this permanence (*Beständigkeit*) of becoming. I suggest that this emphasis on the going-beyond indicates another sense in which Heidegger's reading is externalistic. It is not merely that he is imposing external standards of being and truth to evaluate Nietzsche's philosophy, but also that, for him, Nietzsche himself is committed to a sort of "external" (meta)perspective precisely in order to metaphysically affirm will to power as the truth of beings.

Heidegger's interpretation could be analyzed at many levels, and I cannot do full justice to it in this work. However, I will argue that the most crucial aspect of his reading is that it ascribes to Nietzsche an *oppositional* schema, and this is what fundamentally allows Heidegger to claim Nietzsche as a metaphysician. Heidegger does this when he argues that, for Nietzsche, the metaphysical nature of Platonism consists in opposing the real world to the apparent world. Nietzsche's critique of Platonism begins with the recognition of this opposition. But here, Heidegger's emphasis is on the types of worlds ("*this* world is opposed to *that* world") which are opposed to each other, but *not* on the oppositional schema itself. This, I argue, is tantamount to attributing an oppositional structure to Nietzsche's own critique. According to the Heideggerian reading, the only thing Nietzsche's critique can now achieve is a mere reversal of the Platonic opposition. Nietzsche ends up with his own set of oppositions just as much as the metaphysics of Platonism.

My central argument is that in his critique of metaphysics, Nietzsche attacks precisely the oppositional schema itself, and not one of the terms involved in the opposition. Since the ascription of an oppositional structure to Nietzsche is the central feature of all metaphysical interpretation, I will challenge this ascription at various points in my argument.

To be sure, at many points in his lectures, Heidegger complicates and problematizes Nietzsche's position. For instance, when he discusses Nietzsche's summation of the history of philosophy in "The History of an Error" in *Twilight of the Idols*, Heidegger pays specific attention to Nietzsche's account of the final stage of this history. Here Nietzsche writes, "We have abolished the real world: what world is left? The apparent world perhaps? ... But no! *with the real world we have also abolished the apparent world!*" (TI Real World). Heidegger interprets this to mean that Nietzsche rejects the very opposition between a real or supersensuous world and an apparent or sensuous world, since this opposition belongs to the history of Platonism. The "overturning of Platonism and the ultimate twist out of it" cannot consist in the mere reversal of the terms that constitute its hierarchy or in the abolition of all hierarchy.[14] Instead Hei-

---

13 *Nietzsche* III: 213–215. Heidegger argues that Nietzsche's idea of "eternal return of the same" achieves this permanence of becoming.
14 *Nietzsche* I: 208–209.

degger claims that what Nietzsche was looking for was "a new interpretation of the sensuous on the basis of a new hierarchy of the sensuous and the supersensuous."[15] This new hierarchy implies that the old "ordering *structure* must be changed."[16] To what extent Nietzsche succeeds in "overcoming" Platonism so understood and to what extent not, these are "necessary critical questions" which are fundamental for Heidegger's reading of Nietzsche.[17]

Heidegger's account of the new sensuousness leads him to consider what Nietzsche means by "art." I cannot go into the details of Heidegger's explication here, but the upshot of his argument is that even though Nietzsche apparently rejects the Platonic notions of truth and being associated with the higher value accorded to the supersensuous world, Nietzsche's new, transfiguring conception of art still maintains a sense of the metaphysical conception of truth as "harmony with the actual," where the "actual" has the qualities of becoming and semblance, instead of being and permanence.[18] This allows Nietzsche to undertake a criticism of those weak evaluations, which deny life by favoring being instead of becoming. The affirmation of these qualities of becoming and semblance amounts to an affirmation of life. This affirmation involves a "permanentizing of becoming into presence [*Anwesenheit*]" as the supreme will to power.[19] Through this reading, Heidegger views Nietzsche as the last philosopher in the tradition of modern philosophy inaugurated by Descartes, whose metaphysics of "subjectivity" provides a fundamental solution to the question of being of beings through an interpretation of the metaphysical "subject."[20] Nietzsche's metaphysics still holds on to an interpretation of truth and being, despite his claims to the contrary, where now the being of beings would be the becoming of the new sensuous world, which he affirms. It is through Nietzsche that the "consummation of Western metaphysics" is achieved as the extreme consequence of the history of Platonism.[21]

---

15 *Nietzsche* I: 209.

16 *Nietzsche* I: 209. Similarly, Heidegger argues that "morality" has a metaphysical meaning for Nietzsche insofar as it means "positing an ideal, indeed with the signification that the ideal, as the supersensuous grounded in the Ideas, is the standard for the sensuous, whereas the sensuous counts as the lesser, the valueless, hence something to be fought and exterminated" (*Nietzsche* III: 133). Therefore Heidegger understands the title of Nietzsche's work, *Beyond Good and Evil*, to announce the latter's "immoralism," which removes itself from the "moral" distinction that grounds all metaphysics, and denies the hierarchy of values posited by it.

17 *Nietzsche* I: 210.

18 *Nietzsche* III: 125–126.

19 *Nietzsche* III: 156.

20 See Martin Heidegger, *Nietzsche*, vol. IV, trans. Frank A. Capuzzi (San Francisco: Harper & Row, 1982) 123–149.

21 *Nietzsche* III: 157.

The Internalists

This group is comprised of mostly French poststructuralist readers of Nietzsche. However, the writers I am describing as the "internalists" by no means represent the complex and varied landscape of poststructuralist philosophers inspired by Nietzsche. And I also do not wish to undermine the enormous differences in the details of the Nietzsche interpretations of Haar, Kofman, Blondel, Derrida and Müller-Lauter.[22] Nevertheless, these authors have a common agenda against Heidegger's reading of Nietzsche,[23] which as Blondel puts it, is blind to "the interpretative nature of the body and the genealogical question."[24] Challenging the Heideggerian metaphysical reading is precisely what is common to thinkers as diverse as Blondel, Haar, Kofman, Derrida and Müller-Lauter. For the internalists, it is important to emphasize the various elements of Nietzsche's philosophy – such as, the genealogical method, the irreducibility and the primacy of interpretation, the interpretative nature of the body, and the metaphorical nature of the will to power – that are suppressed by the Heideggerian reductive reading. These partly linguistic, partly stylistic dimensions are not mere aesthetic adornments, but have deep *philosophical* import which must be taken into account, even if this means that we must welcome a new way of doing philosophy and a new art of interpreting the world.[25] It is crucial to heed to the originality of Nietzsche's project, and not impose on the latter, from without, the forms of metaphysical thought and conceptual language. In other words, these commentators insist that we must evaluate Nietzsche's relation to philosophy or metaphysics according to standards that are *internal* to his own writings.

For Müller-Lauter, it is necessary to be faithful to Nietzsche's text in order to bring out precisely the "real contradictions" in his philosophy, which interpretations like those of Heidegger suppress "in favor of an uncontradictory foundation" that is not "elaborated or even considered by Nietzsche himself."[26] According to Haar, one must consider the question of the "overcoming of metaphysics" anew, not by imposing this question upon Nietzsche "from the outside" as Heidegger did, but from the point of

---

22 For an excellent treatment of Nietzsche's influence on postmodern French philosophy, see Alan Schrift, *Nietzsche's French Legacy: A Genealogy of Poststructuralism* (New York: Routledge, 1995) and also, Alan Schrift, *Nietzsche and the Question of Interpretation: Between Hermeneutics and Deconstruction* (New York: Routledge, 1990).
23 One could also include Gilles Deleuze in this group. His interpretation of Nietzsche could be read as anti-Heideggerian, although he does not explicitly formulate it in this way.
24 Eric Blondel, *Nietzsche: The Body and Culture*, trans. Seán Hand (Stanford: Stanford University Press, 1991) 5.
25 For instance, see Sarah Kofman, *Nietzsche and Metaphor*, trans. Duncan Lange (Stanford: Stanford University Press, 1993) 3–4.
26 Wolfgang Müller-Lauter, *Nietzsche: His Philosophy of Contradictions and the Contradictions of His Philosophy*, trans. David J. Parent (Urbana and Chicago: University of Illinois Press, 1999) 3.

view of Nietzsche's own reflections.[27] And for Kofman and Blondel, it is essential to emphasize the irreducible primacy of metaphor and interpretation, instead of reducing Nietzsche's philosophy to a few key concepts as Heidegger does, since the reduction indicates a forgetting of the basic metaphorical nature of all concepts. However, the accusation of committing violence to Nietzsche's text is in itself not a devastating objection against Heidegger, precisely since the standard of a supposed fidelity to a philosophical text cannot be the yardstick for determining the success or failure of a reading, not only for Heidegger, but also for Nietzsche. And these poststructuralist writers, who highlight the fundamentally interpretative aspect in Nietzsche's thought, must especially concede this point.

However, there is a more important sense in which the above-mentioned commentators could be called internalists. It is not just the case that the standards of evaluation of Nietzsche's philosophy should be internal to that philosophy, but also that Nietzsche himself should be seen as providing an internal or immanent critique of metaphysics. We acknowledge this when we note that the absolute primacy of interpretation and perspectivism implied by the concept of will to power yields a non-foundational interpretation of the sensible world. In such a world, the metaphysical principle of identity does not hold unconditional validity. What we have instead is an interpretative play of differences, which moves entirely within the realm of immanence without "transcending" to the world of being. For the internalists, this implies that Nietzsche's philosophy leads to tropes that exceed the limits of metaphysical discourse. It breaks open the confines of metaphysical thought, and hence overcomes the latter.[28] Derrida, Blondel and Haar make this point explicitly by noting that the Nietzschean internal critique begins by first acknowledging the oppositions of metaphysics (real versus apparent world, truth versus falsity etc.), submitting to it, but only in order to reverse the hierarchy of oppositions. At this stage, the internal critique looks very similar to Heidegger's interpretation. However, the internalists argue further that, in the next stage of his critique, Nietzsche retracts the initial submission in such a way that the very schema of metaphysical opposition is annulled and replaced by a non-conceptual interpretative play of differences.[29]

Although I agree that Nietzsche's will to power yields something like a non-foundational interplay of differences rather than opposites, I will argue, nevertheless, that the internalist account does not quite escape the Heideggerian reading insofar as it maintains that Nietzsche begins by first acknowledging or recognizing the hierarchy of metaphysical oppositions. Therefore their account does attribute, at least initially, an oppositional schema to Nietzsche. The internalists are similar to Heidegger to the

---

27 Michel Haar, *Nietzsche and Metaphysics*, trans. Michael Gendre (Albany: State University of New York Press, 1996) ix.

28 See Haar ix–xiii, 1–5. Also, see Kofman 120–121 and Blondel 5.

29 See Blondel 23–27, 36. Also, see Jacques Derrida, *Positions*, trans. Alan Bass (Chicago: University of Chicago Press, 1981) 41–44.

extent that they too fail to realize that Nietzsche immediately attacks the oppositional structure itself, as he targets the source of this structure. When we tackle this latter issue directly, we grasp that Nietzsche neither remains merely confined within metaphysical boundaries nor does he simply overcome them. Thus my strategy will be to play the Heideggerian interpretation against the internalist one, in order to reveal the ways in which my reading differs from the interpretations of both these groups of interpreters. Accordingly, I will be revisiting the externalist and internalist readings at various junctures in this book.

The naturalists

The third camp is represented by the current-wave of Anglo-American commentators, who interpret Nietzsche's philosophy under the banner of "naturalism." Particularly, I have in mind the works of Cox, Janaway, Schacht, Leiter, Clark, Hill and Richardson. Many of these interpreters attribute a roughly naturalistic-scientific view of the world to Nietzsche, arguing that he sought to provide *true* causal explanations of moral phenomena in ways that do not conflict with science or our best empirical theories. Leiter, for example, understands Nietzsche's naturalism as a kind of "methodological naturalism."[30] The latter is the doctrine that philosophy should be continuous with empirical inquiry in the sciences or it should follow the method of the empirical sciences. Accordingly, Leiter seems to assume that Nietzsche's philosophy takes the natural, organic world and a human being's psychological type as "natural facts" (he calls the latter, "type-facts"), beyond all perspectival interpretations. In Leiter's view, a typical Nietzschean form of argument runs as follows: "a person's theoretical beliefs are best explained in terms of his moral beliefs; and his moral beliefs are best explained in terms of natural facts about the type of person he is (i.e., in terms of type-facts)."[31] Firstly, I am not sure why Leiter insists that what type a person is a "fact." In what sense is a type a "fact" for Nietzsche? Is it because what a type a human being belongs to is a fixed or given data waiting to be revealed (which would be a highly dubious claim for Nietzsche, if not a metaphysical one)? And why is it a "natural fact"? Is it a natural fact because it belongs to "nature"? But what is nature for Nietzsche? It is surely not something simply given as if it was some metaphysical or ultimate ground that is self-evident and obvious to everyone. If Nietzsche remarks that his goal is to "translate man back in to nature," and if commentators claim Nietzsche to be a naturalist based on such quotations (as Leiter does), then, at least, they need to present a thorough investigation into the Nietzschean idea of nature and

---

30 Brian Leiter, *Nietzsche on Morality* (New York: Routledge, 2002) 6.
31 Leiter 7.

its metaphysical import, instead of using this term as a metaphor for a self-evident concept that would be apparent to everyone who reads Nietzsche.[32]

In any case it is evident that such "realism" about nature mostly ignores or under-plays the relevance of the constitutive power of interpretative acts significantly distorts Nietzsche philosophy. In other words, at the very least, naturalistic readings seem to be undermined by vital "aesthetic" dimensions of Nietzsche's thinking, such as the primacy of interpretations and perspectivism, and the highly metaphorical, "personal" style of his writings. These dimensions appear to be incompatible with the objectivity and truth-seeking ideals of scientific inquiry. The force of the objections, in Nietzsche's works, to a purely objective enquiry is so compelling that it has prompted some writers, like Nehamas, to resort to purely aesthetic interpretations.[33] Such interpretations compromise the substantive features of Nietzsche's criticism by reductively reading all of his polemic as nothing more than the exemplifications of the becoming of the Nietzsche's own personal self. Pure aesthetic commentaries perceive, at the ultimate core of Nietzsche's criticisms, a kind of "private" insight or an artistic inspiration to which only Nietzsche (and perhaps some kindred spirits) have access.

Such commentaries have, however, become unpopular among current scholars. Instead, one of the outstanding research projects in present-day Nietzsche scholar-ship is to integrate the naturalistic elements of Nietzsche's thought with its aesthetic elements. Writers like Cox, Clark, Janaway and Acampora have tried to show that Nietzsche's naturalism is properly understood only when it is seen to complement and presuppose important aesthetic dimensions of his philosophy. The latter dimen-sions either refer to the primacy and irreducibility of interpretations and perspectival truths (Cox),[34] or to the co-fundamentality of the "value drive" along with the "truth drive" (Clark),[35] or to the "literary, personal, affectively engaged style of [Nietzsche's] inquiry" (Janaway),[36] or to the significance of art for science (Acampora).[37] Although I sympathize with the intentions of these interpretative attempts, I maintain that the integration of the two elements in question will be successful only if we abandon

---

[32] One move that naturalistic interpreters are known to adopt is to claim that nature is whatever it is that our best empirical theories posit as existing. But this unequivocally positive appraisal of empirical or scientific theories is very un-Nietzschean at its core. Nietzsche's evaluation of science is complicated and multi-dimensional, and he repeatedly points out (especially in his later works) the metaphysical and moral underpinnings of science and its theories. For example, see §§23–28 of the Third Essay of GM, where Nietzsche emphasizes that science is the most spiritualized product of the ascetic ideal since it still has faith in truth.

[33] Alexander Nehamas, *Nietzsche: Life as Literature* (Harvard University Press, 1985).

[34] Christoph Cox, *Nietzsche: Naturalism and Interpretation* (University of California Press, 1999).

[35] Maudemarie Clark and David Dudrick, "Naturalisms in *Beyond Good and Evil*," in *A Companion to Nietzsche*, ed. Keith Ansell-Pearson (Oxford: Blackwell, 2006) 148–167.

[36] Christopher Janaway, "Naturalism and Genealogy," in *A Companion to Nietzsche*, ed. Keith Ansell-Pearson (Oxford: Blackwell, 2006) 340.

[37] Christa Davis Acampora, "Naturalism and Nietzsche's Moral Psychology," in *A Companion to Ni-etzsche*, ed. Keith Ansell-Pearson (Oxford: Blackwell, 2006) 314–333.

viewing Nietzsche's philosophy solely or primarily through either the naturalistic lens or through the aesthetic lens. There must be a fundamental reorientation.

The basic problem with the naturalist approach is the lack of real concern for the issue of metaphysics in Nietzsche. Naturalist interpretations, unlike the externalist and internalist ones, tend to emphasize the epistemological dimensions more than the metaphysical ones. Nevertheless, they betray the underlying metaphysical commitments of their interpretations, even as they insist that Nietzsche is a sort of "postmetaphysical," "naturalist" thinker.[38] This becomes clear when we observe that the naturalists must attribute a view of truth to Nietzsche precisely in order to claim him as a naturalist. Clark is a case in point. At the outset of her study, she makes her methodological decision apparent that in contrast to the poststructuralist or the deconstructionist reading, she intends to "separate sharply Nietzsche's critique of metaphysics and his denial of truth."[39] For Clark, this separation implies that "Nietzsche rejects metaphysics and eventually overcomes it in his own work, but that he ultimately affirms the existence of truths, and therefore does not undermine his own theory when he claims truths for his positions."[40] This move, typical of naturalistic commentaries, involves positing a realm of truths that is supposedly not metaphysical, where metaphysical truth is defined as "correspondence to the thing-in-itself."[41] These naturalistic, non-metaphysical truths involve truth claims about "history, philosophy, the ascetic ideal and the affirmation of life" which Nietzsche apparently does make.[42]

However, I find this notion of non-metaphysical truths unconvincing, if not ultimately incoherent. If one operates with a more fundamental and all-encompassing concept of metaphysics and truth as Nietzsche and Heidegger do as opposed to an epistemological variant of a Kantian concept of truth (as "correspondence to the thing-in-itself"), then one must acknowledge that metaphysics and truth stand or fall together. This is why, after pointing out that science too first needs a "metaphysical faith," a philosophical presupposition, in order for it to acquire a direction, a meaning and method, Nietzsche goes on to emphasize that henceforth science itself *"requires justification"* (although Nietzsche insists that such justification may not be forthcoming); and since as science too has faith in truth, "the will to truth itself requires justification" (GM III 24). Therefore, insofar as the naturalistic interpretation does intend to retain and attribute a notion of truth to Nietzsche, it *does* ascribe to him a meta-

---

38 For instance, see Cox 6.

39 Maudemarie Clark, *Nietzsche on Truth and Philosophy* (Cambridge: Cambridge University Press) 21.

40 Clark, *Nietzsche* 21.

41 Clark, *Nietzsche* 21.

42 Clark, *Nietzsche* 21. Similarly in his book, Hill too uses something like a neo-Kantian notion of truth as correspondence with thing-in-itself to free up a naturalistic philosophy (which Hill ascribes to Nietzsche) that denies the thing-in-itself, although this philosophy apparently employs a "transcendental realism about space and time." See R. Kevin Hill, *Nietzsche's Critiques: The Kantian Foundations of his Thought* (Oxford: Oxford University Press, 2003) 133.

physical position, just like Heidegger's reading does. The naturalistic reading, at best, turns out to be a covert externalist one. However, in the end, the confusion of holding on to a post-metaphysical, yet "naturalistic" or "scientific" notion of truth only shows the failure of the naturalists to truly engage with Nietzsche's critique of metaphysics, a failure of which Heidegger is not guilty.

Chapter outline

This book is divided into five chapters. The first two chapters present the details of Nietzsche's meta-existential approach from a methodological point of view, and also demonstrate that this approach necessarily entails his critique of metaphysics. The last three chapters deal directly with Nietzsche's evaluation of metaphysics, especially with regard to his critique of the source of the oppositional structures of metaphysics. The breakdown of each chapter is as follows:

Chapter One begins with a brief summary of the popular existential accounts of Nietzsche, which read him as a passionate, individualist type of philosopher with a personal style. Methodologically, I ground this popular account in the existential distinction, which is the distinction between objectivity and subjectivity. I trace the existential distinction back to *Concluding Unscientific Postscript*, where Kierkegaard's pseudonym, Climacus, draws this distinction as the essential mark of his existential philosophy. By analyzing Climacus' distinction between "direct" and "indirect communication," I show that the ambiguity inherent in this distinction reflects the necessary ambiguity and instability of the existential distinction. My primary criticism against Climacus' approach will be that the method by which he draws the existential distinction does not allow him to radically affirm this ambiguity. This will allow me to make the transition to meta-existentialism. Instead of an oppositional beginning, Nietzsche's meta-existential philosophy begins straightaway with a differential interpretation of the subjective and objective. The first chapter concludes by exploring how this meta-existential approach allows Nietzsche to carry out all the implications of the existential distinction, and thus to thoroughly affirm the ambiguity inherent in this distinction.

In Chapter Two, I explore the specifics of Nietzsche's meta-existential method by differentiating between the central term "existence" on the hand, and the interpretative-differential concepts of "subjectivity" and "objectivity" on the other. I argue that Nietzsche does not arrive at the concept of existence through a prior opposition, but corresponding to his radically indirect approach, he treats existence as the ultimate presupposition of his thought. Accordingly, he provides continuous interpretations of existence through the evolving subjective and objective perspectives. Further, through a reading of Nietzsche's concept of the "body," I reveal that both the subjective and objective perspectives are necessary and indispensible from the point of view of a life-form's conditions of preservation and growth. Nietzsche does not unequivocally prefer the subjective to the objective interpretative term (or vice versa), as both these terms are expressions of the "will to power." Based on this, I shall argue that Nietzsche's critique of metaphysics cannot consist in a mere reversal of the oppositional hierarchy between the objective (real world) and the subjective terms (apparent world), but rather it targets the very source of the oppositional structure, as the origin of metaphysics and its life-denying evaluations.

Chapter Three presents a detailed exposition of Nietzsche's concept of will to power, with the aim of isolating its qualitative dimension, which holds the clue for determining the source of metaphysical oppositions. This analysis will lead us to the most basic distinction of Nietzsche's philosophy, which is that between the life-affirming strong type of will and the life-negating weak type of will. Nevertheless, I argue that we cannot unambiguously isolate that unique quality of the will to power, which is "behind" a particular type's life-denying or life-affirmation evaluation. Against the different groups of interpreters, I claim that, for Nietzsche, these two types are not pure or fixed types, but they undergo radical transformations, at times even sharing many characteristics. There is a topological continuity and a gray area of transition between the two types, which forbids a clear-cut distinction between them. The final two chapters carry out this argument in depth through a consideration of the problem of decadence of the strong type.

Chapter Four undertakes an investigation of the strong type's decadence at a more general level. My argument will be that the dominance of the weak type in history presupposes the prior disintegration of the strong type on its own terms. Only the latter process makes possible the birth of a new weak type that governs the future course of history. Relying on Nietzsche's various analyses of the noble type, I shall isolate four typical characteristics of this type. These traits not only make the strong type what it is, but they also show the various ways in which this type could be vulnerable to decadence. The very activity and strength of the strong type may result in the decadence of this type. Thus the analysis of these traits reveals a gray area of continuity between the two types, in which the strong type disintegrates leading to the birth of a new weak type that is different from the previous weak types. The threshold point of decadence, then, will bring us closer to grasping the source of life-denying evaluations.

With the arguments of Chapter Four in the background, Chapter Five presents a detailed case study of the decadence of the noble Hellenic culture. This chapter demonstrates that the very superior health of the Greek culture results in its decadence. Based on Nietzsche insights into this culture in his early writings, I analyze its glory and splendor in terms of three signposts: Greek state, art and philosophy. While the former two are more unequivocal expressions of Greek strength, pre-Platonic philosophy has a thoroughly ambiguous meaning, since it is both an expression of the highest strength of the Greeks and also of the beginning of their decline. I shall argue that these two expressions are sharply juxtaposed within the domain of pre-Platonic philosophy, revealing that gray area in the topological scale where the distinction between strength and weakness appears indiscernible. Given this irreducible ambiguity, I claim that the threshold point of Greek decadence is necessarily elusive, in the sense that one cannot interpret this point as clearly belonging either to the strong Hellenic type or to a weak Socratic type, as the latter type itself depends on the prior decadence of the former type. Therefore the source of metaphysical oppositions, of life-denying evaluations, remains elusive. This reveals the ultimate ambiguity of Nietzsche's critique of metaphysics, which is itself grounded in his meta-existential approach.

Chapter One
Nietzsche's meta-existentialism

Nietzsche as an existentialist: the popular account

There have been many attempts to interpret Nietzsche as an existential philosopher. Karl Jaspers, Eugen Fink, Walter Kaufmann, and in more recent years, Bernd Magnus and Robert Solomon have sought to portray Nietzsche as an existential thinker. Jaspers sees Nietzsche's philosophy as sharing many tenets with that of another prominent existentialist, Kierkegaard,[43] while Kaufmann[44] and Solomon[45] see parallels between Nietzsche's philosophy and those of Kierkegaard, Sartre and Camus. Such existentialist readings, however, have gone out of fashion, and have been replaced by the French postmodernist appropriations of Nietzsche and the naturalist interpretations among Anglo-American writers. Against the current grain, I want to reclaim Nietzsche as an existential philosopher. However, my use of the term "existentialism" is significantly different from that of the earlier interpreters. In my inquiry, I seek to understand Nietzsche's existentialism from the point of view of his critique of metaphysics. It is precisely a sensitivity to this latter issue that is missing in the construal of the earlier existentialist commentators, resulting in a view of existentialism which is limited and unfaithful to Nietzsche's originality and depth. The main tendency among them is to understand Nietzsche's existentialism as a call to engage in one's own philosophy in a "personal" manner. As Kaufmann observes, the common feature of all existentialism, including Nietzsche's, is a kind of "perfervid individualism."[46] It consists of a passionate, personally-engaged style of philosophizing that gives an honest assessment of a human being's place in the world, especially the modern world. Existentialism is primarily concerned with the meaning of individual existence, and not with abstract accounts about the nature of reality, society, culture and morality. Existentialists like Nietzsche and Kierkegaard, according to this account, celebrate "individual existence to the exclusion of all sorts of abstract theories and notions in favor of the passions of life."[47] A passionate disdain for abstraction is essential to bring out the loss of meaning and homelessness of modern humanity. Existentialism, then, is a label for revolt against traditional, systematic philosophy: "The refusal to belong to any school of thought, the repudiation of the adequacy of any body of beliefs whatever,

---

43 See Karl Jaspers, "Existenzphilosophie," in *Existentialism: From Dostoevsky to Sartre*, ed. Walter Kaufmann (New York: Meridian Books, 1956) 158–183.
44 *Existentialism* 20–21.
45 Robert Solomon, *Living with Nietzsche: What the Great "Immoralist" Has to Teach Us* (Oxford: Oxford University Press, 2003) 120, 176–177.
46 *Existentialism* 11.
47 Solomon, *Living with Nietzsche* 176.

and especially of systems, and a marked dissatisfaction of traditional philosophy as superficial, academic and remote from life – that is the heart of existentialism."[48]

I agree with the above characterization of existentialism, and also with the classification of Nietzsche as an existential thinker based on these grounds. I also think that the comparison of Nietzsche to Kierkegaard is not unfounded, even if it is true that no other thinker philosophized with the deep fervor and the brutal intellectual honesty with which Nietzsche wrote and philosophized. Each of his works stands as a testament to his own personal self-overcoming, in addition to being a document expressing profound insights into the modern human condition, its genealogical history and its future possibilities. He experimented with multifarious styles of expression, often speaking in manifold voices and tones, and communicating ambivalent emotions. Even in his earliest published works, one can note that the *kinds* of problems he considered worth pursuing, and also the passionate way in which he approached these problems, were "existential." For example, the fundamental problem that triggers Nietzsche's investigation into Greek tragedy in *The Birth of Tragedy* is that of suffering. He was deeply moved by this issue, as he considered suffering an inescapable condition of existence. Nietzsche admired Schopenhauer precisely because he saw in his "educator" a great sensitivity to the problem of suffering, to which Schopenhauer apparently provides a solution through his version of "European Buddhism."

Nietzsche's essential point of entry into philosophy was not some abstract epistemological one, like Kant's, about the scope and limits of human knowledge, or an aesthetic one about various art-forms and their order of hierarchy, or some cultural curiosity that amounted to a romantic longing for the greatness of Ancient Greece. It was rather a concrete problem of existence (or of what Nietzsche calls "life") and existential suffering that motivated him. As he notes in his later preface to his first book, what he had dared to achieve in this "reckless" book is *"to look at science through the prism of the artist, but also to look at art through the prism of life"* (BT Attempt 2). Because Nietzsche, like Kierkegaard (or Kierkegaard's pseudonym Johannes Climacus, as we shall see below), conceives life or existence as essentially a process of "becoming," "contradiction," and "strife," he sees suffering as the fundamental and inescapable characteristic of existence. Hence Nietzsche operates with the view that existence is not justified in itself and so the question of how the Ancient Greeks justified "existence [*Dasein*] and the world eternally" guides his interpretation of Greek tragedy. Indeed, his conclusion was that only through their highest art form, tragedy – that is, only as an *"aesthetic phenomenon"* – that the Greeks justified existence (BT 5). His "artist's metaphysics" read the "primordial unity" itself as "eternally suffering and contradictory" (BT 4); and the Greeks, because they had a "unique gift for *suffering*" and "sensitivity to suffering," could find in themselves the power to justify and affirm existence (BT 3). In his later preface to *The Birth of Tragedy*, he writes that this

---

48 Kaufmann, *Existentialism* 12.

"profoundly personal" work tackled a complex, ambiguous problem of whether there could be a "pessimism of *strength*," a suffering due to "overflowing health, from an *abundance* of existence" (like the Hellenes experienced), or whether all pessimism or suffering is a sign of decline, weakness and "debilitated instincts" (BT Attempt 1). For Nietzsche, this ambiguity associated with the problem of suffering implies the "great question mark over the value of existence" (BT Attempt 1).

The *Untimely Meditations* pick up and follow through a set of themes that one may term "existential." In these essays, Nietzsche calls for the authentic (spiritual) development of the "individual" in an age, which he deems more and more to be degenerate. Just as Kierkegaard's pseudonym, Climacus, in the *Concluding Unscientific Postscript* laments the "abstractly many-sided" nature of the "present age,"[49] Nietzsche too, in the first *Meditation* on David Strauss, raves against the decadent tastes of German culture and its "cultural philistinism" (DS 2). This theme is deepened in the second *Meditation*, in his critique of the historical culture of modernity, where he investigates the different "disadvantages" from the perspective of "life" that a "Hegelian" age, oversaturated with history and with objective and universal education, will encumber. He protests against how life is made sick by the "dehumanized and mechanical grinding of gears, the 'impersonality' of the laborer" (EH The Untimely Ones 1). Nietzsche makes the shrewd observation that the modern human being believes herself to be a latecomer on the world's stage due to the weight of history on her; the world has become an "exhibition" for her, and she is the "strolling spectator" (HL 5). One grave consequence of excessive history is that the "individual" has lost and destroyed her instincts; she has grown fainthearted and unsure, and she no longer believes in herself. "Individuality" itself "has withdrawn within" (HL 5). What the modern human is or does on the outside and how he appears on the surface, completely betrays what he is inside. He is like the Hegelian scholar who operates from the lofty eternal viewpoint, always ready to synthesize any instance of thinking with being, but is nevertheless as petty and ignoble as an office clerk who lusts after a promotion. His outward actions betray his inward existence: the "how" of his existence is incongruous to "what" he appears to be. (As we shall see below, this critique of historical culture and Hegelianism is very similar to Climacus' critique of the same in the *Postscript*).

Nietzsche, therefore, makes the existential call apparent: "To what end the 'world' exists, to what end 'mankind' exists, ought not to concern us at all for the moment ... on the other hand, do ask yourself why you, the individual, exist" (HL 9). His positive interest lies in asking whether there could be an un-historical fertile patch in the present or in the future times, which would allow for the flourishing of the individual again, and through the individual, the re-birth of a new philosophy and culture. For this purpose, he even inquires into what role history itself, the realm

---

49 Søren Kierkegaard, *Concluding Unscientific Postscript to Philosophical Fragments*, trans. Howard V. Hong and Edna H. Hong (Princeton: Princeton University Press, 1992) 349.

of the objective, could positively play. Untimeliness of the thinker and his existential-ism go hand-in-hand: both Nietzsche and Kierkegaard were untimely men, who were primarily concerned with a new beginning for the individual and for philosophy after the devouring machinery of speculative philosophy and Hegelianism has swallowed them both. Both were keen observers of the virtues and vices of their age. As Jaspers notes, "Such [existential] thinking is grounded in the Existenz of Kierkegaard and Nietzsche insofar as it belongs to their age in a distinctive way ... [they] experience[d] this epoch to the end in their own natures, to be it completely in order to overcome it."[50] In this way, they both sought "authentic Existenz."[51]

It is precisely from the point of view of the authentic cultivation of the individual in modernity that Nietzsche, in the third *Meditation*, looks up to Schopenhauer as an educator. Nietzsche admired Schopenhauer as a writer, who had virtues essential to be a philosopher of modernity: virtues such as "honesty," "cheerfulness that really cheers" (which is a sign of a "victor" and conqueror, and not that cheerfulness of Strauss, which "compromises our time and the people in it") and "steadfastness" (SE 2). Nietzsche also thought that Schopenhauer's pessimism – which is an extreme consequence of the cultural bankruptcy of modernity – was useful in driving the modern culture into despair regarding itself, which would be a necessary step for any future genuine culture. Nietzsche sought in the philosopher a "model," an exemplar, who did not just write books, but who *lived* his philosophy, and who supplied an example by his life (SE 3).[52] The honest philosopher would have a genuine *relation* in his existence to "what" he professes in his philosophy, to its objective content. "Isolation" and "despair of truth" also belong to the lot of the Schopenhauerian philosopher, in whom the drive for truth is always geared towards asking only the following question: "what is existence worth as such?" (SE 3). The genuine philosopher seeks to overcome his age by resting his eye "upon existence," and by determining its "value anew" (SE 3). Thus he inaugurates a new cultural and philosophical beginning.[53] Such a new culture would foster the production of individual great human beings – whether in the form of philosophers, artists or saints – as its greatest exemplars and justifications. The important question is always "how can your life, the individual life, receive the highest value, the deepest significance?" (SE 6). The third *Meditation*, therefore, is a testament to the "hardest self-love, self-discipline ... as pointers to a higher concept of culture" (EH The Untimely Ones 1).

---

50 Jaspers, "Existenzphilosophie" 166.
51 Jaspers, "Existenzphilosophie" 166.
52 Nietzsche writes that, "The only critique of a philosophy that is possible [is to see] whether one can live in accordance with it" (SE 8).
53 I note that this central task that Nietzsche ascribes to the philosopher in the third *Meditation* remains mostly unchanged even in his final works. Nietzsche introduces this task in the existential context and spirit of the *Meditations*.

In all of these earlier works, some existential theme or the other is fundamentally dictating Nietzsche's inquiries, not just in terms of the kind of problems he takes to be important (like that of suffering), but also in terms of his personal, concrete and individualistic attitude towards these problems. Nietzsche's existentialism may be compared to that of Climacus in *Postscript*, in its emphasis on individual existence and freedom, on the objective meaninglessness of history without the subject's appropriation, on the relation between the philosopher's own existence and "what" the objective content of her philosophy is, and on the personally-engaged style of philosophy. And these Kierkegaardian aspects of Nietzsche's existentialism do not vanish in his later works, as writers like Jaspers and Kaufmann have noted. Some of the major themes of his later philosophy like his critique of metaphysics, morality and the problem of nihilism, and his approach to these themes show his existential bent. For example, in *The Gay Science*, Nietzsche observes how crucial a personal approach is for the philosopher: "The lack of personality takes revenge ... It makes the most telling difference whether a thinker has a personal relationship to his problems and finds in them his destiny, his distress, and his greatest happiness, or an 'impersonal' one" (GS 345). Starting from *Human, All-Too-Human*, and armed with a personally-involved approach, Nietzsche declares war on metaphysics, morality and religious thought that puts an emphasis on "another" world, a "supersensible" world or the world of "being," in order to deny "life," or "this" earthly "sensible" world of "becoming" (HH I 8, 9, 16). He writes for the sake of the individual "free spirits" who have enough strength in them to continuously switch between the scientific and artistic perspectives of evaluations, and thus affirm the sensuality of life.

In the later works, in providing his genealogical account of morality, Nietzsche reads the history of Platonic-Christian morality as that dominated by the "*ressentiment*" morality of the "weak," the "herd" or the "sick" type of human being who is unable to affirm life, thus continuing and deepening his critique of European culture. He interprets this history as extending to modernity, which has produced the "sickest" human being. But he also interprets modernity as the era of "nihilism" or the "death of God" due to which the highest values have come to devaluate themselves (GS 125). Nihilism is the extreme consequence of the "truthfulness" preached by Platonic-Christian morality, such that, paradoxically, this very truthfulness has come to undermine a naïve belief in God or "other-wordly" values. Truthfulness has dislodged the ground beneath it, hurling humanity into a world of chaos and meaninglessness. Nietzsche, however, sees a future for the free individual given the condition of nihilism. Now, for the first time, it may be possible for the free individuals to muster enough strength and creativity to re-evaluate all the previous values of morality – "beyond good and evil" – and set up a new order of rank based on the affirmation of life in all its possibilities. The creative individual or the "overhuman" (*Übermensch*) creates new values, not by appealing to some pre-existing "objective" or "transcendent" values, but by artistic "self-creation" or by "giving style to one's character" (GS 290). In free self-creation, the individual brings his variegated, and often contradictory, impulses and passions (which in the modern man remains scattered) under the rule of a single governing instinct that concretely affirms existence.

In the above summary of the popular existential account of Nietzsche's philosophy, some commentators focus more on the problem of nihilism, and others, like Solomon and "aesthetic" interpreters like Alexander Nehamas, concentrate on the themes of authentic or artistic "self-creation" of the individual. I do not think these accounts are incorrect. On the contrary, I do think it is very important to emphasize these classical existential themes with respect to Nietzsche's philosophy, and also to recognize the kinship between Nietzsche and thinkers like Kierkegaard based on these themes. However, at the same time, I argue that this popular understanding of existentialism brings out only a restricted aspect of Nietzsche's complex philosophy. I maintain that it is not *radical enough* to embrace the complete breadth and depth of his thought. We can appreciate the full extent to which Nietzsche is an existentialist only when we inquire into his relation to metaphysics. This investigation will lead to a new understanding of Nietzsche's existentialism, which I call "meta-existentialism."

The tendency among the previous existential commentators (similar to that among the naturalistic interpreters) is to set aside the issue of metaphysics in order to claim Nietzsche as a post-metaphysical thinker, or to remain indifferent to this issue. Metaphysics would then belong to the realm of impersonal and "bloodless abstraction," something for which Nietzsche's concrete, passionate life-philosophy has nothing but disdain.[54] But this view of metaphysics is naïve, along with the very opposition between "bloodless abstraction" and "existential concretion," at least with respect to Nietzsche, as I shall argue. Solomon is a case in point. He urges us to read Nietzsche from the "existential point of view," that is, "*personally*," as a "provocative writer who means to transform the way we view our lives."[55] Any other way of reading him, for example as a "prophet, a social critic... a physician, an ideologue... a cranky moralist..." is "distinctively *impersonal*."[56] Solomon does not include in this list "metaphysician" or "anti-metaphysician," but one might as well include these titles, insofar as they too deal only with "abstract and impersonal conceptions of meaning and human life."[57]

What is interesting to observe in this characterization of existentialism is that the positive emphasis is on *how* one ought to read Nietzsche; but surprisingly, on the

---

54 I should note here that Jaspers and especially Fink are more sensitive to the question of Nietzsche's relation to metaphysics than the other existential authors. See Karl Jaspers, *Nietzsche: An Introduction to the Understanding of His Philosophical Activity,* trans. Charles F. Wallraff and Frederick J. Schmitz (Baltimore: The Johns Hopkins University Press, 1997) and Eugen Fink, *Nietzsche's Philosophy*, trans. Goetz Richter (New York: Continuum, 2003). I will indicate below some of the important ways in which my approach is different from theirs.

55 *Living with Nietzsche* 12.

56 *Living with Nietzsche* 12.

57 *Living with Nietzsche* 176.

negative side, this principle that one must read him "personally" has an implication about *what* one should not read him as. This is quite odd. I agree that Nietzsche is a personal thinker, and Solomon's suggestion as to "how" one must read him; but whence comes the inference about "what" he must not be read as? Does reading Nietzsche personally necessarily imply that one cannot take his critique of morality or metaphysics seriously? Can we not read Nietzsche personally and still, in a personal spirit, consider his criticism of metaphysics? Does an existential reading of Nietzsche automatically preclude a serious consideration about his relation to metaphysics or rather does it presuppose it? In what follows, I will suggest that an inquiry into Nietzsche's relation to metaphysics is indeed indispensible for an understanding of his version of existentialism.

The disposition among existential interpreters is to view existentialism at odds with the conceptual language of metaphysics. They imply an "either/or": either existentialism or metaphysics. Fink, for instance, remarks that in *Thus Spoke Zarathustra*, Nietzsche "sidesteps the issue [of overcoming metaphysics] and chooses an existential expression"; indeed, existentialism is exactly the "sign of a profound conceptual need."[58] Unlike Solomon, however, Fink does seriously consider Nietzsche's relation to metaphysics, but his analysis, like Heidegger's, is an "external" one. Accordingly, he imposes the problem of metaphysics on Nietzsche from "outside," as it were, since the non-conceptual existential expression of Nietzsche's own highest thought, according to Fink, precludes a direct confrontation with metaphysics. Like Heidegger, Fink conceives metaphysics as the thought concerning the essence of "being of beings" – an understanding of metaphysics not found in Nietzsche – and employs this external criterion to assess the limits of Nietzsche's philosophy. So the implication seems to be that there could be no question of a consideration of Nietzsche's critique of metaphysics internally, that is, from the point of view of his own texts, which is *at the same time*, an existential reading of Nietzsche.[59] In contrast, I suggest that Nietzsche provides an internal critique of metaphysics, which is *also* an existential critique. Indeed, for him, these two aspects are inseparable, and this is what marks the unique status of Nietzsche in philosophy. Therefore we need a new account of Nietzsche's existentialism.

We begin to appreciate Nietzsche's new kind of existentialism if we contrast him to Kierkegaard with regard to how they respectively take up and explicate what I call the "existential distinction." I take this distinction to be the central aspect of any existential philosophy, and I define it as the distinction between "subjective thinking" and "objective thinking" or that between "subjectivity" and "objectivity" (or some version thereof). We have already encountered a variant of this distinction –

---

58 Fink 107.
59 This point also holds true with respect to the internalists who, contra Heideggerian interpretations, focus on Nietzsche's internal and immanent critique of metaphysics, but they reject the existential interpretation of Nietzsche.

between "personal" and "impersonal" ways of reading Nietzsche or ways of doing philosophy – above. Indeed, the existential distinction can be originally traced back to Kierkegaard's pseudonym, Climacus, as the very hallmark of the latter's existential philosophy, which he articulates in *Postscript*, specifically through the contrast he draws between "indirect" and "direct communication." In what follows, I will critically analyze this latter distinction to argue that it is, at bottom, *ambiguous*. I argue that this ambiguity must be understood as an essential aspect of Climacus' existential method, and it reflects the *necessary* ambiguity of the existential distinction itself. The ambiguity implies that the existential distinction inevitably collapses back on itself, undermining the very conceptual grounds on which it was found. Conceptually, the fundamental philosophical position I will be attributing to Nietzsche may be viewed as an existential methodology that is developed through a radicalization of Climacus' version of existentialism. I call the resultant existential position, meta-existentialism. Specifically, Nietzsche's meta-existential approach, instead of attempting to eliminate (or cover up) the ambiguity or the instability of the existential distinction, uniquely affirms it in multifarious ways through an ever-renewed process of redrawing this very distinction, a feat which Kierkegaard's Climacus fails to achieve. Thus it develops to the fullest the very meaning of the existential distinction. In doing so, I argue that Nietzsche's meta-existentialism necessarily invokes and intertwines with his critique of metaphysics. I will explain these claims later. We must first discuss Climacus' contrast between direct and indirect communication.

Indirect versus direct communication: the three stages of Climacus' argument

Kierkegaard's *Postscript*, written under the pseudonym Johannes Climacus, is widely acknowledged as one of the founding texts of existentialism.[60] In this work, Climacus discusses the idea of indirect communication as a crucial aspect of his existential philosophy, and contrasts it to direct communication, which he associates with the "objective" and "abstract" Hegelian philosophy. There has been plentiful discussion in recent literature about the ambiguous status of this distinction between direct and indirect communication, and what this ambiguity implies. Vanessa Rumble, for instance, has argued that a "sustained ambiguity" is "central to the practice" of Kierkegaard's indirect communication and it calls attention to the "multiplicity of possible readings of a work and the reader's activity in appropriating it."[61] Edward Mooney argues that "Rather than two distinct categories of communication, there is a

---

60 For example, see Merold Westphal, *Becoming a Self: A Reading of Kierkegaard's Concluding Unscientific Postscript* (West Lafayette: Purdue University Press, 1996) 3.
61 Vanessa Rumble, "To Be as No-One: Kierkegaard and Climacus on the Art of Indirect Communication," *International Journal of Philosophical Studies* 3.2 (1995): 312.

continuum and overlap" to suggest that this distinction is entirely context-sensitive;[62] but instead of following through on this discovery and interpreting what this means for Climacus' existential method as a whole, he confounds himself by still maintaining that there are unequivocal instances of "direct" communication involving pure content or "information-transfers."[63] In response to this, Jamie Turnbull questions the very idea that appealing to ambiguity would yield a satisfactory account of indirect communication, while arguing that a dominantly theological interpretation will do justice to Kierkegaard's paradoxical claims about his own project.[64] Others, like Stephen Evans[65] and John Lippitt,[66] suggest that Climacus' indirect communication must be understood through ambiguous literary tactics like irony or the comical, although they do not directly mention ambiguity itself. In this section, while arguing that Climacus' distinction between indirect and direct communication is indeed fundamentally ambiguous, I suggest, in contrast to these commentators, that the *type* of ambiguity is reflective of that of the basic distinction between "subjective thinking" (or "subjectivity") and "objective thinking" (or "objectivity") which is the central existential distinction that Climacus makes in the *Postscript* in his polemic against Hegel. This ambiguity, instead of being a negative feature, which one must avoid, is the essential mark of any existential philosophy. The only criticism, then, which I will bring out against Climacus is that his methodology does not allow him to radically *affirm* this ambiguity, given its point of departure.

I will identify three stages in Climacus' argument against direct communication and his endorsement of indirect communication. At the first stage, he sets up the "purely objective" speculative Hegelian thinking and the direct communication that corresponds to it as being *completely* "indifferent" to the "existence" of the "subjective individual"[67] as they focus exclusively on the "result" and the "external."[68] In this completely abstract mode, the individual "really becomes objective" as she goes astray in the infinity of reflection, and then she loses more and more the "decision of subjectivity."[69] The Hegelian systematic idea is "subject-object ... Objectively understood, thinking is pure thinking, which just as abstractly-objectively corresponds to

---

62 Edward F. Mooney, *On Søren Kierkegaard: Dialogue, Polemics, Lost Intimacy, and Time* (Hampshire: Ashgate, 2007) 208.

63 Mooney 203. Such transfers, remarks Mooney, do not involve the "ruffling [of] subjectivity's feathers" (206).

64 Jamie Turnbull, "Kierkegaard, Indirect Communication and Ambiguity," *The Heythrop Journal* 50.1 (2009): 13–22.

65 C. Stephen Evans, *Kierkegaard's "Fragments" and "Postscript": The Religious Philosophy of Johannes Climacus* (New Jersey: Humanities Press, 1983).

66 John Lippitt, "Illusion and Satire in Kierkegaard's *Postscript*," *Continental Philosophy Review* 32 (1999): 451–466.

67 *Postscript* 193.

68 *Postscript* 135.

69 *Postscript* 116.

its object, which in turn is therefore itself ... This objective thinking has *no relation* to the existing subjectivity."[70] Climacus calls speculative philosophy's fascination with being an observer of existence, "unethical."[71] Corresponding to pure objective thinking is "direct communication,"[72] which involves mere reporting or expression of a "truth" already secured once and for all in the identity of thinking and being. The focus in such communication is solely on the conceptual or objective content of "what" is said: "*Objectively the emphasis is on what is said*."[73] Climacus uses the example of his own excessively scholarly-historical age, in which one believes that if one has a bookish knowledge about Christianity, and if one appears knowledgeable on the outside, one possesses the truth, even though one does not have any *personal* or *internal* relation to Christianity. If such a person "reforms an entire age through his zeal and teaching, he confounds his existence" since "his own form of existence is not adequate to his teaching."[74] The basic charge against direct communication is that its form contradicts or does not correspond to its content or external expression, as is evident when it presents the ethical in "paragraphs and [glibly] by rote."[75]

In *opposition* to this, the ethical person is introduced in the second stage of the argument as somebody who is only concerned with developing herself to the utmost, inwardly and subjectively. The key to Climacus' argument is his notions of "existence" and the "subjective." Existence is a "process of becoming,"[76] which is the unfolding or unraveling of eternity in time. Climacus calls it the "prodigious contradiction" that the eternal becomes, that it "comes into existence."[77] Existence is not synthesized into the infinite, but it is the child begotten by "the infinite and the finite, the eternal and the temporal" and for this reason it is "continually striving."[78] The process of becoming never finishes *in* existence to present the eternal to the existing person. For this reason, it is impossible to completely conceptualize existence by presenting it to the categories of thought as a finished, rigidified "object" like speculative philosophy claims to do. Existence always maintains a space of indeterminability; in antithesis to the "system," which is the conclusiveness that combines, existence "is the spacing that holds apart."[79] Climacus' notion of existence introduces a "separation,"[80] a gap between all those poles of reflection that the Hegelian system had synthesized. It

---

70 *Postscript* 123, emphasis added.
71 *Postscript* 135.
72 *Postscript* 74–75.
73 *Postscript* 202.
74 *Postscript* 137.
75 *Postscript* 153.
76 *Postscript* 80.
77 *Postscript* 82.
78 *Postscript* 92.
79 *Postscript* 118.
80 *Postscript* 123.

spaces out "subject from object, thought from being."[81] This absolute distinction that existence introduces between the subjective and the objective is the existential distinction. It is a dynamic distinction that implies an elusive gap, which is not present as a static object. Hence it is not *directly* accessible to thought.

Given this, there could only be a subjective access to the realm of existence, since only the individual subject as existing can keep thought and being apart, separated "one from the other," and thus affirm the existential distinction.[82] Only in and through the process of the subject's existing is its meaning accessible to that subject in a distinctive and personal way. Even regarding the meaning and truth of historical events, there is an "objective uncertainty."[83] For example, the significance of the birth and life of Jesus is not pre-determined for the existing subject, however much knowledge the subject has about these events; what meaning this event will have for the subject is continuously determined by the subject in her existence. Such meanings are suspended, which await the inward appropriation of the existing subject.[84] What is decisive is "that the individual relates himself to a something *in such a way* that his relation is in truth a God-relation."[85] Meaning is a relational term, and in this sense, subjectively, the "truth" is in the "how" of the action or the statement: "*subjectively the emphasis is on how it is said*" as opposed to the "what."[86]

Corresponding to subjective truth, Climacus argues for an "indirect" or "artistic" communication. While objective thinking "invests everything in the result," subjective thinking "invests everything in the process of becoming and omits the result."[87] In contrast to the abstract thinker, the existing individual, who develops herself subjectively, is primarily interested in her own thinking, and she exists in this thinking, rendering it concrete. In doing so, she *could* perhaps "produce a great effect in the external world, but this would not occupy [her] at all," since for the subjective individual the external "means nothing either *pro* or *contra*."[88] The ethical individual is solely and infinitely concerned with the inward becoming of her subjectivity, but is indifferent to the external sphere, which is purely accidental. For her, the "results are nothing but junk."[89] Indirect communication involves two stages corresponding to the two stages of subjective reflection: first, there is the proper expression of the thought in words, and the second reflection captures the "intrinsic relation of the communi-

---

81 *Postscript* 123.
82 *Postscript* 192.
83 *Postscript* 204.
84 Other key notions which Climacus associates with the process of "becoming a subject" are "interestedness," "passion," "decision" and "possession." But we will not analyze these notions in great detail here.
85 *Postscript* 199.
86 *Postscript* 202.
87 *Postscript* 73.
88 *Postscript* 135–136.
89 *Postscript* 242.

cation to the communicator and renders the existing communicator's own relation to the idea."[90] The second stage is the "form" of the communication, which direct communication ignores. Art and self-control are essential for indirect communication to be successful, which would ensure that the subject communicates his thought while at the same time preserving his own inwardness of existence. They would guarantee "inwardness" and "secrecy" appropriate to the communication of subjective truths.[91] Thus through indirect communication the subjective individual communicates in a form that conforms to his existence. It is apparent to see that this argument, which specifies the appropriateness of indirect communication for the subjective individual, is based on an opposition to and inversion of direct communication and objective thinking that takes more interest in the external and the result.

However, in the third stage of Climacus' argument, things appear more ambiguous. The opposition between direct and indirect communication proves to be untenable, if the subjective individual and her indirect communication are seen to be not *completely* indifferent to the external after all. Consider Climacus' comments about Socrates, whom the former regards as the model existential philosopher. Climacus notes that the outward appearance of Socrates was "ugly": he had "clumsy feet, and ... bumps on his forehead and other places."[92] But Socrates, in the role of a teacher, was "pleased with his advantageous appearance" precisely because he wanted to create the "repulsion of opposition" in his students, through which he wanted to communicate that the "learner essentially has himself to deal with."[93] This repulsion is the *effect* Socrates consciously wanted to create on the external world. His repulsive appearance was used to keep the "learner at a distance" so that the learner would not aim for a "direct relation to the teacher" in a bid to completely identify himself with the latter, and therefore forget his own subjectivity.[94] However, we must note that *what* his external appearance was, was not a matter of complete indifference for Socrates. So it is exaggerated and misleading for Climacus to say that the "results are junk" and that between thought and action there is no "difference at all in content"[95] but only in the form.[96] For, the specific form does determine inwardly to an extent the particular content or external expression that is adequate to it. The Socratic case

---

90 *Postscript* 76.

91 *Postscript* 77–78. Secrecy reflects two facts: first, that subjective truth is a dynamic consequence of the subject's becoming, which is still taking shape and transforming. Hence, one cannot just say "everything"; Second, given that subjective truth means "appropriation," to understand this truth, one must have "appropriated" this truth oneself in one's own personal existence. This truth would remain "a secret for everyone who is not through himself doubly reflected in the same way" (79).

92 *Postscript* 248.

93 *Postscript* 248–249. This is related to Socrates' idea of irony.

94 *Postscript* 248–249.

95 *Postscript* 340.

96 Evans also makes a similar point about the interest Climacus' ethical individual might have about the results of his communication or action. He writes, "if the individual is truly earnestly attempting

shows that precisely in order to effectively communicate in an indirect way, Socrates had to use his outward appearance to his own advantage; he could not have settled for any arbitrary external expression of his inwardness. This is so since, presumably, the form of his inwardness does in turn depend, to an extent, on his ability to efficiently express it outwardly. Hence indirect communication implies not only that the form is adequate to the teaching or the content of expression, but also that the latter is somewhat adequate to the form. The form of existence is still most vital, but the outward content or the result is not a matter of total indifference.

If this is true, then the whole opposition between direct and indirect communication appears unsustainable. For, the subjective individual who communicates indirectly still has an interest in the content or the effect she has on the external world, precisely because she knows that her inward subjectivity in turn is affected by her external relations and deeds.[97] Presumably, Socrates' inward subjectivity would have been affected if he had failed to communicate his teaching in an effectively indirect manner by creating a "repulsion of opposition" in his students. All this suggests that there is a more *dynamic exchange* between the inner and the outer, which Climacus is not always ready to acknowledge.

Furthermore, we could equally question Climacus' initial depiction of "pure objectivity" as something that is completely indifferent to the inward form of existence. Climacus himself notes that one cannot read off directly the "absence of inwardness" in another person's thinking or reflection.[98] But to claim that Hegelian thinking completely abstracts from existence, and is entirely indifferent to the inward form, as Climacus does in the first stage of his argument, is to precisely presuppose a "direct" access to the "absence of inwardness" that supposedly plagues Hegelian metaphysics. If the latter is some sort of "pure thinking," then it cannot be itself read off and presented "purely objectively." This is what it means to take seriously the proposition that existentially the truth is in the "how" of what is said. Just as it is not necessary that, if a person has an immense historical knowledge of Christianity, she will automatically fail to subjectively appropriate its truth, it is also not necessary that Hegelian objective thinking entails a complete absence of inwardness. How exactly does Climacus know that Hegel's concepts of pure thinking and pure being amount to a *total* disregard for existence? Could we not read Hegelian thought symptomatically

---

to accomplish something, he is attempting to achieve results of some type ... and in that sense, 'cares about the result'" (Evans 79).

97 Although Evans draws very different conclusions than the ones I will make here, he expresses a similar criticism against Climacus: "What Climacus fails to see or at least fails to give sufficient notice to, is that even though subjectivity is not reducible to these outer [] activities, it is only recognizable through these outer expressions ... Inwardness is in turn influenced by, and is acquired in the context of, these outward relations" (Evans 284).

98 *Postscript* 244.

as an expression of a certain "subjective" condition that has already incorporated existence in a particularly idiosyncratic way?[99]

In fact, this is what Climacus does in the third stage of his argument. He calls it the "remarkable quality" of existence that an "existing person exists whether he wants to or not."[100] Even if it is the case that developing one's subjectivity is an achievement that "cannot be done without passion,"[101] it is nevertheless true that one who thinks abstractly still exists. One major consequence Climacus draws from this observation is that complete abstraction from existence is impossible, and hence the so-called "pure objective thinking" is a "phantom."[102] Such thinking can begin only with the presupposition of an existing subject with its own peculiar kind of (subjective) reflection.[103] The beginning of the system could be achieved only by halting this reflection as required by abstraction. But reflection is infinite; it does not stop on its own, since it reflects the endless movement of the subject's becoming. However, it is possible to "momentarily" abstract from reflection, through a subjective "leap,"[104] although at such moments the subject "pays his debt to existence by existing nevertheless."[105] Abstraction "disregard[s] existence but still maintains a relation to it."[106] Thus Climacus unveils the earth-bound origins of objective thinking, and reveals its *real* "subjective" meaning. He thereby provides a subjective interpretation of objective thought. Through this interpretation, he treats "pure objectivity" and its claims as mere surface symptoms, which dissimulate the subjective truth that lie beneath the surface.

This procedure, I argue, is very much consistent with Climacus' existential method, since making the existential distinction obliges him to expose the folly behind an objective thinking which claims to have subsumed all subjectivity within it, by showing the absolute fundamentality of the subjective realm for existence which cannot be subsumed. In accordance with this procedure of reclaiming the objective sphere, Climacus observes that all abstract thinking in relation to "all existence-issues [is] a trial in the comic" and that "pure thinking" is a "psychological oddity, an admirable kind of ingenuity in joining and constructing in a fantastic medium: pure being."[107] His often-repeated explanation for this oddity is that the abstract thinker

---

99 Mooney rightly notes that the ambiguity of indirect communication implies an interpretative uncertainty: "What seems to be direct communication from a sender's side of a communication may be received as such; but it *may*, in some circumstance, evoke another's subjectivity in such a way that it functions, from the standpoint of the receiver, as an *indirect* transfer" (Mooney 210). However, Mooney fails to follows through the implications of this uncertainty for Climacus' existentialism.
100 *Postscript* 120.
101 *Postscript* 311.
102 *Postscript* 314.
103 *Postscript* 112.
104 *Postscript* 115–116.
105 *Postscript* 191.
106 *Postscript* 313. Therefore, like reflection, the act of abstraction is also infinite.
107 *Postscript* 304.

is "absentminded,"[108] because of which he is "thoughtlessly unaware of the relation that abstraction still continually has to that from which it abstracts."[109] Thus, in the end, "objective thinking" is revealed to be a kind of distorted, inauthentic subjectivity infected with forgetfulness.

However, this only proves what we hinted above that there is no strict opposition between direct and indirect communication, since there is nothing like a complete and pure direct communication, in which the external expression does not bear *any* intrinsic relation to the form of the existence of the communicator. The purely abstract thinker is still an existing human being. The ambiguity of the distinction between the two sorts of communication implies that instead of an opposition, we have something like a *differential continuum* with variations in degrees. That is, in any human communication, whether by an "objective" or a "subjective" thinker, attention is paid both to the internal form and the external expression: *there is only "indirect" communication*, just as there is only a "subjective" reflection for the thinker, and any "objective" attempt at thinking, however abstract, is merely a variation within subjectivity. Subjectivity, being the most basic feature of an existing human being, cannot be completely imperiled through abstraction.[110] This is what drawing the existential distinction implies, since it shows the absolute fundamentality of the inward subjective form of the communicator, even if the latter is an abstract philosopher. There simply is no "pure objective thinking." Thus the ambiguity of the distinction between direct and indirect communication reflects the ambiguity of the distinction between objectivity and subjectivity.

The ambiguity of the existential distinction and the limitations of Climacus' existential method

But the subjective and the existential interpretation of objective thinking comes only at the final stage of Climacus' argument. So why did he initially begin with a "purely objective" interpretation of speculative philosophy, and thereby contradict his later finding that no such purely objective interpretation is possible? Why did he set up the counterfactual idea of "pure abstract thinking" and ascribe this idea to Hegelianism, only to later use his existential method to knock this idea down as chimerical? These

---

108 See *Postscript,* 145–146, 192, 227.

109 *Postscript* 314. At times, Climacus traces this absentmindedness itself back to modern age's excessive fascination and "constant association with world history," which corrupts the thinker (*Postscript* 146).

110 For Rumble, this implies the redundancy of Climacus' theory of communication: "In the final analysis, however, no form of communication can either insure or preclude the subject's self-conscious exercise of freedom [which Rumble takes to be the basic principle of all subjectivity]. Climacus' theory of communication [is] oddly redundant, as though it would safeguard an aspect of human existence which cannot be jeopardized" (Rumble 313).

are vital *methodological* questions, which take us to the heart of Climacus' existential method. Climacus himself concedes that it is a deliberate move on his part to embark on such a beginning: "By beginning straightaway with ethical categories against the objective tendency, one does wrong and fails to hit the mark, because one has nothing in common with the attacked. But by remaining within the metaphysical, one can employ the comic."[111] Remaining within the metaphysical, he begins with a "direct" reading of the objective, and so initially concedes to Hegelianism, precisely in order to argue against the latter. This "contradiction" in Climacus' procedure, I maintain, takes us to the heart of the ambiguity in the distinction between objectivity (direct communication) and subjectivity (indirect communication). It points to the "meta" problem in which the critical philosopher finds herself: in drawing the limits to (subjective) thinking, she oversteps the very limits which are being drawn. This ambiguity cannot be explained away by referring to the importance of Climacus' use of irony or the comic, however true, since what is at stake here is a deeper question about his existential method.[112]

I argue that Climacus is compelled to begin by remaining within the metaphysical precisely because of one of the implications of the existential distinction. Existence, if we recall, never *is* as a fixed thing, since this would presuppose that existence is finished and the point of eternity has been encountered. Because existence implies a space of indeterminability, the elusive gap between subject and object invoked by the existential distinction cannot be directly accessed. Hence to clarify this gap, Climacus resorted to positing an idealized concept of the object as "pure object," which is totally abstracted from all becoming. Only in opposition to this concept, he could explicate his notions of existence and subjectivity, which have nothing to do with the complete abstraction of pure objectivity. The existential distinction is initially established with the help of an argument that opposes "subjective" existence to "objective" thinking. But once these existential notions are clarified, Climacus switches to the subjective viewpoint, and in accordance with *another* implication of the existential distinction, he calls attention to the inescapable existential ground of the subject from which the subject cannot abstract completely. His argument concludes by implying that any kind of thinking is in truth a variant of subjective thinking, since all thinking involves movement, contradiction and becoming, and hence presupposes existence. This brings out the most primary *meaning* of drawing the existential distinction. However,

---

111 *Postscript* 124.

112 An explanation of the ambiguity that refers to the centrality of the comic for Climacus would not be entirely wrong, and would actually be very much in tune with the intentions of Kierkegaard's pseudonym, Climcaus, in the *Philosophical Fragments* and the *Postscript*. As Climacus himself admits, he is "neither a religious speaker nor a religious person, but just a humorous, imaginatively constructing psychologist" (*Postscript* 483). Nevertheless, I want to push Climacus on this issue by denying him his refuge in the comic in order to test the limitations of his existential approach. This would not be altogether against Climacus' wishes. For, as Climacus remarks, "the presence of irony does not necessarily mean that [] earnestness is excluded" (*Postscript* 277, footnote).

the existential gap is not annulled now through a subsumption of the objective within the subjective because there is no such subsumption; rather, the objective is read as a variation within the subjective – an inauthentic or absentminded one – and it is seen to vary differentially with respect to the subjective. Such a reading preserves and affirms the separation between the subject and the object.

The above two implications together reveal the *necessary* ambiguity involved in making the existential distinction: on the one hand, the latter distinction means that the existential gap is not directly determinable, thus requiring the setting up of a contrasting objective viewpoint to explicate this gap; on the other hand, it emphasizes the absolute existential ground of the subject, thus claiming the objective as a differential variation within the subjective. For Climacus, this ambiguity means that he had to use an oppositional discourse to explicate the existential distinction, which, when explicated undermines the very oppositional discourse on which it was founded. The meaning of the existential distinction he discovers overtakes the method he uses to discover it. It therefore appears that his argument against Hegelian objective thinking collapses back on itself when the meaning of the existential distinction is applied back to Climacus' own "purely objective" interpretation of objectivity. Thus the existential distinction is seen to stand on an unstable conceptual ground. Hence we should ask if the condition that the existential gap cannot be directly explicated *necessitates* the initial positing of a purely objective interpretation of objectivity. Could one not instead, *right at the outset*, read Hegelianism symptomatically as an expression of a certain "subjective" or "existential" condition, relying on Climacus' own teaching that, for a subject, one's own existence and "the principle of contradiction [have] absolute validity"?[113]

The issue is which constraint is more binding methodologically: whether initially to adopt a purely objective interpretation of objectivity, or to concede straightaway that there is no such thing as a purely objective thinking that has completely abstracted from existence. I argue that it is the latter constraint which is more binding, and it corresponds to the primary meaning of the existential distinction. Yielding to it at the expense of the former constraint would result in a new existential approach, which allows for a more radical affirmation of the "indirect" method by opening up the possibility of a differential interplay between subjectivity and objectivity. This approach would not even admit that there is some sort of "direct" or "purely abstract thinking," but rather it would operate thoroughly indirectly from the beginning, acknowledging that the subjective and the objective are – precisely because of the fundamental meaning of the existential distinction – concepts that are more mutually implicative than what Climacus recognized.[114] For this reason, it would entail a much more devastating critique of Hegel, since in carrying out this critique one would not even

---

113 *Postscript* 315.
114 At the end of his book, Evans hints at this point when he writes, "The relation between subjectivity and objectivity is more 'dialectical' than Climacus suggests" (Evans 284). Evans notes that in his

initially corroborate the Hegelian-metaphysical position, as Climacus' method does. Furthermore, such an approach would not imply that the existential distinction could be explicated directly or that the ambiguity of this distinction would be overcome. On the contrary, this thorough-going indirect method would affirm the ambiguity by allowing for an ever-renewed process of *repeating* or *redrawing* the existential distinction. I call this new kind of existentialism, "meta-existentialism," and I argue that it is at the very foundation of Nietzsche's philosophy.

Nietzsche's meta-existentialism

Nietzsche had little more than a passing acquaintance with Kierkegaard's writings. Thomas Brobjer, who has documented Nietzsche's knowledge of Kierkegaard, writes that Nietzsche had a "reasonable knowledge of Kierkegaard's thinking and writing," although he "never read any full text by Kierkegaard."[115] Nietzsche's knowledge of Kierkegaard was derived from Hans Lassen Martensen's book, *Die christliche Ethik*, which Nietzsche read in 1880, and which frequently quotes Kierkegaard, while treating him as an ethical individualist.[116] Other treatments of Kierkegaard's thinking, which Nietzsche read in the 1870s and 1880s, include some works by Georg Brandes and Harald Höffding.[117] In sum, Brobjer notes that Nietzsche read about fifty pages of various accounts of Kierkegaard's philosophy, including about five full pages of quotations from Kierkegaard.[118]

   Although this may not count as a significant or a direct influence of Kierkegaard's thought on Nietzsche, it must not prevent us from a making a conceptual connection between the two philosophers. My argument is that Nietzsche arrives at his version of existentialism through a response to the above problems in Climacus' existentialism. Nietzsche's basic approach, especially in his middle and later works, involves working out to the fullest the very meaning of drawing the existential distinction, thus radically affirming its ambiguity. I will explain what I mean by this. In Climacus' argument the existential distinction has an ambiguous status, which he does not anticipate or respond to, given that he initially posits a "metaphysical" and a purely

---

later writings (such as *Practice in Christianity*), Kierkegaard recognizes this shortcoming in Climacus' approach (284).

115 Thomas H. Brobjer, *Nietzsche's Philosophical Context: An Intellectual Biography* (Urbana and Chicago: University of Illinois Press, 2008) 75.

116 Brobjer 74–75.

117 Brobjer 75.

118 Brobjer 75. Also, in a letter to Georg Brandes, dated February 19, 1888, Nietzsche, who was stationed in Nizza at the time, mentions that during his next trip to Germany he plans to "study the psychological problem of Kierkegaard," although, unfortunately for Nietzsche's readers, this plan never came to fruition. See *Selected Letters of Friedrich Nietzsche*, trans. Christopher Middleton (Indianapolis: Hackett, 1996), 285.

objective interpretation of objectivity – and thus an oppositional discourse – in order to draw the existential distinction. We must recognize that the ambiguity necessarily belongs to the existential distinction itself as its essential feature, and it is not a consequence of Climacus' oppositional discourse. The latter only compromises his ability to affirm the ambiguity drastically.

It is precisely on this issue that Nietzsche's existentialism differs. Nietzsche's answer to this ambiguity is not to get rid of it, but to face up to it, celebrating and multiplying the different ways in which it can manifest itself, such that the existential distinction becomes more fluid and elusive than in Climacus. The crucial difference to note is which of the two implications of the existential distinction (that together constitute its ambiguity) does Nietzsche take to be more fundamental methodologically: whether the fact that the existential distinction cannot be explicated "directly" or whether that the "objective" and the "subjective" vary only differentially with respect to each other. For Nietzsche, I argue, it is the latter implication that is more primary (although he does not fail to duly pay attention to the former one), such that his critical philosophy begins straightaway with a differential interplay between the subjective and the objective, whereas Climacus only catches a glimpse of the latter implication at the end of his argument. Moreover, in Climacus' argument the existential distinction appears to stand on an unstable conceptual ground because these two implications are, as it were, set in conflict against each other because of the way he draws this distinction. Existentialism, as a philosophical principle, appears untenable. In other words, his final discovery that objectivity is only a variation within subjectivity, and hence varies only in terms of degrees with respect to the latter, undermines his own initial methodological decision to set up the objective as "pure objectivity" devoid of all subjectivity. He interpreted objectivity as "pure objectivity," and hence posited an oppositional discourse, precisely as a response to the first implication that the existential distinction cannot be accessed directly. Again, Nietzsche's method does not do away with the instability itself by making a "foundational" ground out of the existential distinction. Rather, it disposes of the *particular kind* of instability that is characteristic of Climacus' approach by affirming straightaway the differential subject-object relation. This move clearly bases the instability solely on the direct inaccessibility of the existential distinction.

However, both the ambiguity and the instability of the existential distinction can be affirmed only by way of repeating or redrawing this distinction again and again. Repetition is possible since both subjectivity and objectivity are now understood to vary differentially. Because of the differential interpretation, it is possible to anticipate the conceptual instability of making the existential distinction, and to be "better prepared," so to speak, to cope with its ambiguity. By beginning straightaway either with a subjective interpretation of the objective or vice versa – and not making any pretensions about directly explicating the existential gap – and then subsequently clarifying the notion of existence by drawing the existential distinction, one could then go on to repeat this exercise again from another perspective. In *Postscript*, Climacus could not embark on this repetitive process precisely due to his oppositional beginning, because of which he finds himself trapped within his own creative findings. I maintain that Nietzsche's meta-existentialism succeeds where Climacus' approach fails. It emerges as the only viable form of existentialism which can positively affirm the two implications of drawing the existential distinction outlined above, namely: a) the existential gap cannot be directly conceptualized; b) there is nothing like a "pure objectivity" since it is impossible to completely abstract from existence. Any claim to objectivity can be interpreted as a variation within the subjective, an interpretation which still maintains the "separation" of existence. The subjective and the objective differ only in terms of degrees; there is solely a differential relation between them. In addition, the meta-existential approach can meet a *third* implication that c) the existential distinction inevitably stands on a precarious ground, which calls for the distinction to be drawn again and again. By meeting all of these three conditions Nietzsche's version of existentialism works out to the fullest the very meaning of drawing the existential distinction. Thus it responds to the "meta" problem that plagued Climacus' existentialism.

This is the *first* sense in which the term "meta-existentialism" is justified. Nietzsche's meta-existentialist position takes a step back from the typical existentialist position, and then develops to the maximum all the implications of this position. Nietzsche's approach is a result of applying the implications of the existential distinction back on the conditions that make it possible, which leads to another new instance of this distinction, and so on. It is an endless meditation on the implications of subjecting the existential distinction to its own conditions. The most important innovation, which makes it possible for him to undertake this process in a repetitive manner, is his tacit but consistent refusal to recognize anything like a "pure objectivity" or "metaphysics" or "speculative thought" that stands in *opposition* to existential thinking. These elements are interpreted within the differential fabric of existence right from the outset, with the subjective and the objective terms involved in a continuous mutually implicative interplay.

Climacus went astray at the beginning with an idealized concept of "pure objectivity," which in effect he equated to (Hegelian) metaphysics, before he began his existential critique of it. Because of this, his existentialism, which greatly employs irony and the comic, does not really get past a merely *polemical* stance against metaphysics, as it fails to genuinely see the differential subject-object relation. And therefore it is really not in a position to confront objectivity and metaphysics head-on. It is not enough to say that Climacus never wanted to confront metaphysics, but rather he just intended to call metaphysics itself into question as something irrelevant for an individual's religious or ethical concerns. The reason is that if he intended to do only the latter, he cannot justify his decision to begin by remaining within the metaphysical; that is, he cannot be parasitic on metaphysics, if he wants to call the whole of metaphysics itself into question. The simple appeal to irony is insufficient, since it opts for a convenient way out of this quandary. Rather, we must acknowledge that Climacus' choice of an oppositional starting point betrays the insincerity of his investigation. Or, in other words, he cannot simply choose to bring metaphysics itself into question without contradicting himself. He must necessarily confront it directly, which is what Nietzsche does.

Nietzsche does not equate the metaphysical tendency exclusively either to the "objective" or to the "subjective" tendency. Neither does he equate metaphysics to one of the terms of other traditional binaries in philosophy, such as "mind" in mind/body or "truth" in truth/error or "being" in being/becoming. The point is to avoid the oppositional structure as such, and thereby *release* metaphysics from the very structure of oppositions through an existential critique of it. Therefore in *Beyond Good and Evil*, Nietzsche characterizes traditional philosophy and metaphysics by its essential tendency to posit "oppositions of values": "The fundamental belief of metaphysicians is the *belief in oppositions of values* [*Der Grundglaube der Metaphysiker ist der Glaube an die Gegensätze der Werthe*]" (BGE 2; KSA 5, 16). Metaphysics believes in and conceives fundamentally only oppositions. Nietzsche provides various other formulations of metaphysics in several places, and we will analyze some of them below, but I take the above definition to be the most decisive one.[119]

One major consequence of this definition is that any attempted critique of metaphysics that cannot avoid setting up its own set of oppositions is itself very much embroiled within metaphysics. "Oppositions" convey the sense that the two terms in conflict have been set up in such a way that one of the terms – mostly the one which is accorded the higher value by the metaphysician – has an origin or an essential meaning that is not infiltrated or corrupted by the opposite term. For example, in Plato's *Republic* Socrates suggests that the good cannot be defined as pleasure since there can also be bad pleasures, and he goes on to argue that the good is not being, but "something yet beyond being, superior to it in rank and power" just like the sun is responsible for the "coming-to-be, growth and nourishment" of things in the visible world, without "itself coming to be."[120] And in *Phaedo*, Socrates argues that the body is "mortal, multiform, unintelligible, soluble, and never consistently the same," and therefore, the soul is pure and most like "divine, deathless, intelligible, uniform, indissoluble, always the same in itself" when it guards itself against the corruptions of the body.[121] Similarly for Descartes, the mind as the thinking thing or the *ego cogito* is something that absolutely cannot be doubted, and hence it provides the foundation for all knowledge (*ego cogito ergo sum* "is necessarily true every time I utter it or

---

119 Both in his earliest mature works and in his final works, Nietzsche continues to maintain the necessary relation between oppositional discourse and metaphysics. See, for example, HH I 1; BGE 2, 24; TI Real World; and KSA 12, 9[107], KSA 12, 9[91].
120 Plato, *Republic*, trans. C.D.C. Reeve (Indianapolis: Hackett, 2004) 200, 205.
121 Plato, *Phaedo* in *Five Dialogues*, trans. G.M.A Grube (Indianapolis: Hackett, 2002) 118.

conceive it in my mind"[122]), whereas the body and the senses, as sources of error and deception can and must be doubted; and for Schopenhauer, the "will to live" as the "thing in itself is imperishable," whereas the phenomenal world of temporality and perishability is the realm of "continual becoming without being."[123]Nietzsche sums it by writing that the metaphysician conceives "truth" and "noumena" to be not corrupted by the intrusion of the "mad chaos of confusion and desire," which belongs to the lowly world of "error" and "phenomena" (BGE 3).

I argue that Nietzsche's existentialism, which avoids setting up an oppositional discourse, is not only able to critique metaphysics head-on, but it *necessarily* does so, given that it enacts the primary meaning of the existential distinction, which is to reduce oppositions to variations in degrees by engaging in a thorough differential discourse. Ultimately, in Nietzsche, Climacus' discovery that the objective is a variation within the subjective gets elevated to the general principle that oppositions must be reduced to variations in degrees. Therefore Nietzsche's existentialism necessarily involves a confrontation with and critique of metaphysics, which is the *second* reason why I term his approach, "meta-existentialism."

Nietzsche's meta-existentialism improves upon Climacus' approach because it does not rely on any opposition, including that between objectivity and subjectivity, in order to elucidate the meaning of existence. Instead of exaggeratedly beginning with a "pure objectivity" with which its opposite, the newly demarcated "subjectivity," has nothing in common, Nietzsche begins straightaway with a critical interpretation of "objectivity" that is already couched in "subjective" terms, thereby leading to an instance of an interpretation of existence as the gap between the objective and subjective terms. This process is repeated, but from the converse perspective, where "subjectivity" is interpreted anew from the "objective" stance. This entire process is repeated again and again leading to ever anew interpretations of existence. Thus instead of an opposition that crumbles under its own postulation, in meta-existentialism we have a mutual interpretation, a mutual struggle and interdependence, and a *perspectival* interplay between the subjective and the objective terms. In this dynamic interaction, the existential distinction is alternatively determined and explicated from the two evolving viewpoints, but of course, there is no question of anything like "complete," "objective" or "direct" determination.

In the next chapter, we will see more concretely how the mutually interpretative struggle between the subjective and objective terms proceeds. I should further note here that in the transformation from the oppositional to the differential structure, Climacus' particularly strong emphasis on the individual subject and her ethical task of "becoming subjective" takes a backseat. For Climacus, the access to the realm of existence and becoming is only through the becoming of the individual subject's

---

122 René Descartes, *Meditations on First Philosophy*, trans. Donald A. Cress (Indianapolis: Hackett, 1993) 18.
123 Arthur Schopenhauer, *Essays and Aphorisms*, trans. R.J. Hollingdale (London: Penguin, 1970) 51.

existence: "The process of becoming is the thinker's very existence."[124] Existence is not a subject-independent category, but neither does the subject idealistically "thinks up" or "create" existence. Each individual accesses existence in her own unique way through inwardly appropriating the objective manifestations of existence. And this task, for Climacus, is an ethical and a religious one to be performed with uncompromising determination and seriousness. In this context, Climacus (and Kierkegaard in his other pseudonymous works) often opposes the single individual's existence to the universal category of crowd, society or humankind, and highlights how the "particular" is in "truth" while the "crowd" is in "untruth."

We have already noted that Nietzsche, like Kierkegaard's Climacus, emphasizes the authenticity of the individual existence and his freedom as opposed to the decadence of the "herd" or the modern "last man." In his mature works, he conceives of the strong authentic individual as the "free spirit," and, finally, as the *Übermensch*, the self-stylized individual, who, in the wake of the death of God, creates the very principles he lives by, along with the standards by which one should evaluate these principles. The freedom of the strong individual is vital, especially in the wake of Western nihilism and the death of God, which makes it impossible for the individual to discover preset meanings. The individual is challenged to invent meaning rather than simply discover it. But at the same time, Nietzsche's very complex portrait of the strong individual also calls attention to masks, self-deceptions and irresponsibility as equally essential ingredients in the creative process of the strong type. Nietzsche's free spirit has the ability to play, to lose herself in some frivolity or the other from time to time, to inauthentically and self-deceptively place her trust in the herd as part of the nourishment required for self-creation. Contradictory impulses in conflict constitute the strong type of individual who endeavors to bring these impulses under one governing instinct. To be sure, Climacus' style also has elements of the comic and the ironic, but I suggest that, for him, these elements belong to the "aesthetic" or the imaginative realm of "possibility" of the authentic ethical and religious individual, but not to the latter's "actuality," which is this individual's primary concern.[125]

What allows for Nietzsche's much richer conception of the individual, the battlefield of extraordinarily large number of conflicting impulses, is his readiness to make the individual subject *vulnerable* to configurations (such has history, culture, religion, society, etc.) that belong to the "objective" world, just as the individual influ-

---

124 *Postscript* 91.

125 See *Postscript* 314–330 for a discussion of the differences between (aesthetic) "possibility" and (ethical or religious) "actuality." I am basing my argument on Climacus' view that "aesthetically and intellectually ideality [as actuality] is possibility" (325). Evans also makes a similar point about Climacus' role as a "humorist" and an "experimental psychologist" (Evans 21–24). Further, Climacus himself, describing his personality, says the following: "I am neither a religious speaker nor a religious person, but just a humorous, imaginatively constructing psychologist ... It is just for this reason that I know that the comic is excluded in religious suffering, that it [the latter] is inaccessible to the comic" (*Postscript* 483).

ences and molds these configurations. For this reason, Nietzsche has a broader, more dynamic conception of the subject, but this does not make him any less of an existential thinker; it only enriches his existentialism. For example, it matters absolutely which historical time period and which culture – whether Greek, Roman or Oriental – a heroic individual lived in to understand his particular subjective greatness, just as this culture itself is specifically defined through the greatness of its individuals. Nietzsche's historical philosophy thus ensures that there is a continuous mutual exchange between the subject and the objective domains. This is in contrast to Climacus' individual, who is the site of an absolute beginning, for whom the objective or the external has only an accidental significance, in contrast to her own ethical relation to God, which alone has an absolute significance. We are not dealing with an insignificant difference here, since it again shows that Nietzsche is not operating with a strictly oppositional structure between the subject and the object. And this fact is in the end the reason, why, in Nietzsche's writings, the theme of the self-creation of the free individual, which although a persistent one, is not always the most important theme. At times, it even takes a backseat to other arguments regarding the very nature of objective thought, including those of metaphysics, science, art, psychology and history. In a sense, Climacus' emphasis on the primary significance of the individual's becoming subjective and his oppositional discourse go hand-in-hand. Nietzsche, on the other hand, relieves himself of this partnership.

Instead of an individual subject appropriating the uncertainties of the objective world, Nietzsche has, as his starting point, a perspectival interplay between "subject-like" and "object-like" terms in continuous mutual interpretation. He writes about the absolute primacy of interpretation and perspectivism in a much-quoted passage: "No, facts is precisely what there is not, only interpretations" (KSA 12, 7[60]). Nietzsche's philosophical analysis oscillates between such subjective and objective terms, and in doing so, it clarifies and provides an interpretation of existence as the medium between them. In other words, Nietzsche would agree with the Sartrean existential call that "subjectivity must be our point of departure"[126] when he asks about the objective character of things, whether this character is "not [] merely a difference of degree within the subjective ... that the objective is only a false concept of a genus and an antithesis within the subjective" (KSA 12, 9[40]). However, he would be quick to also emphasize an additional point that "The 'subject' [itself] is not something given, it is something added and invented..." (KSA 12, 7[60]). Existence is not specifically tied to the narrow conception of the individual's becoming, precisely because of the direct inaccessibility of the existential gap, which entails that neither the subject nor the object is accessible as a basic fact. Even the idea of the "individual subject" would not be accessible purely, simply and directly.

---

126 Sartre, *Existentialism* 22.

In Nietzsche's analysis, the mutual interpretations and the evolving struggle between the subject and the object are themselves *prior* to any delineation of them as pure object and subject for metaphysical-oppositional purposes. Therefore it is incorrect for Heidegger to argue that Nietzsche has a "metaphysics of subjectivity," whose basic solution to the question of the being of all beings lies in an interpretation of the metaphysical "subject."[127] This is so since the Heideggerian reading overlooks the essentially interpretative and differential quality of the interaction between the subject and the object, instead favoring a fixed notion of "subject" as the underlying essence of all being. For Nietzsche, the evolving struggle yields subject-like and object-like terms that serve as temporary place-holders in the interpretative process, but they yield no fixed poles of subjectivity and objectivity.

Our next task is to provide the conceptual framework to further concretize our analysis of Nietzsche's meta-existentialism. In Chapter Two, I will differentiate between the central concept "existence" on the one hand, and the mutually interpretative concepts of "subjective" and "objective" on the other. I will discuss Nietzsche's definition and use of the term "existence" in his works, and also the implication of this use for his *style* of philosophizing. Further, through an examination of some of Nietzsche's published and unpublished writings, I will demonstrate the nature of the differential interaction between the subjective and the objective terms, and how Nietzsche's account of this interaction reflects his meta-existential approach. These considerations will finally lead us to the topic of Nietzsche's critique of metaphysics.

---

127 See Martin Heidegger, "The Word of Nietzsche: 'God is Dead'" in *The Question Concerning Technology and Other Essays*, trans. William Lovitt (New York: Harper & Row, 1977) 88–90. Also, see Heidegger, *Nietzsche* IV: 123–149. The Heideggerian reading places Nietzsche as the last philosopher in the tradition of modern philosophy beginning with Descartes, which is characterized by various metaphysical interpretations of "subjectivity." I will return to Heidegger at various junctures throughout this work, and from different perspectives, to argue against his metaphysical account of Nietzsche.

Chapter Two
Meta-existentialism and Nietzsche's critique of metaphysics

Existence and the existential mode of philosophizing

Existence emerges as the ultimate presupposition of Nietzsche's philosophy, since what existence is cannot be directly conceptualized. Nor can the realm of existence be first discovered by means of an opposition to pure objectivity. If this could be done, it would mean that there is a more basic realm other than and beyond existence. Nietzsche always already treats existence (and the existential distinction) as "given" in some sense, but not as something that is simply there as the unquestionable ground or "being" like Plato's "idea" or Kant's "noumena." Existence in Nietzsche's meta-existentialist philosophy occupies a status that is between these two extremes.[128]

However, this does not mean that we can simply attribute to existence the property of "this-worldly becoming" in opposition to that of "other-worldly being" accepting Nietzsche's own contrast regarding this matter at face-value, as many commentators tend to do.[129] Christoph Cox, for example, who is admittedly not interested so much in the concept of existence, but in giving a naturalistic account of Nietzsche, invokes this fundamental contrast nevertheless, and interprets the "sensible," "natural," "this" world as the "actual" world we are acquainted with, in order to claim Nietzsche as a naturalist.[130] It is evident that Cox appeals to some sort of "direct" reading of one's experience of the "actual" world, which is hard to understand, given Cox's recognition of the primacy of interpretation and perspectivism.

I maintain that, for Nietzsche, existence is a dynamic gap presupposed by the various binaries recognized in traditional philosophy – including "becoming" and "being" – where each term of each binary is in constant strife with the other term. Therefore existence cannot be defined using one of the terms of a binary, since if one ventures to do this (as Cox does), one would set up a faulty opposition between the terms in strife, which betrays the existential separation between the terms. I suggest, instead, that the notion of existence is that of *indirection* itself: if existence can be explicated at all, it is only indirectly through various "perspectival" (*perspectivische*) points (GS 374), which the mutual interpretations of the objective and subjective

---

128 Although I cannot explicate this in detail here, the term "existence" may be compared to Derrida's notion of "difference" which he defines as the "non-full, non-simple, structured and differentiating origin of differences." See Jacques Derrida, "Différance," in *Margins of Philosophy*, trans. Alan Bass (University of Chicago Press, 1982) 11.

129 Nietzsche invokes this central contrast at many places in his texts. See for instance, HH I 1–10, 16, 222; GS 344, 354; BGE 2; TI Reason, TI Real World; KSA 12, 9[91], KSA 12, 9[60], KSA 13, 14[168].

130 Cox 87.

terms in strife offer. Nietzsche does say that existence or the world has the quality of "becoming,"[131] but I argue that here becoming is not a concept opposed to "pure being" or to the quality of "being" that belongs to the "supersensible world."[132] Neither is it a concept that Nietzsche explicates by making it synonymous with the individual subject's becoming. In fact, he does not even conceive existence as "human life" in general or "organic life." The sense of the term existence is extended to include both organic and inorganic worlds, as Nietzsche argues that the entire opposition between organic and inorganic is a "prejudice," as there is the "will to power in every combination of forces," both organic and inorganic (KSA 11, 36[21]). In our usual sense of the term, death is opposed to life, but Nietzsche's concept of existence envisages a continuum between the living and the dead, where the "living is only a form of what is dead, and a very rare form" (GS 109).

Existence corresponds to the whirl and flux of "becoming," of what Nietzsche calls "will to power." Nietzsche most frequently employs the term *"Dasein"* for existence in both his published and unpublished writings.[133] His often-used term "life" (*Leben*) is only a "unique case" within "existence" – that pertaining to the organic world – and therefore, he writes, "one must justify all existence [*Dasein*] and not only life – the justifying principle is one that explains life, too" (KSA 12, 9[13]). In his critique of religion, morality, history and other constructs of the organic world, Nietzsche uses "life" to mean the same thing as "existence." For example, he uses the phrase "affirmation of existence"[134] interchangeably with "affirmation of life,"[135] and "value of life"[136] is synonymous with "value of existence."[137] Generally, the word "life" has the same methodological implications as "existence," and they can be used interchangeably, except when it is necessary to emphasize the limited scope of "life."

On the one hand, existence is the presupposition for all interpretation of existence: "Being – we have no idea of it apart from the idea of 'living' – How can anything dead 'be'?" (KSA 12, 2[172]). On the other hand, this presupposition of existence is not simply present as a fact; it is clarified and understood only through the evolving interpretations of the subjective and objective perspectives. Existence (and therefore, life) interprets by existing and exists by interpreting; these two aspects of existence cannot be made independent of each other: "life itself is *essentially* a process of appropriation, injuring, overpowering the alien and the weaker, oppressing ... incor-

---

131 KSA 12, 2[149–152], KSA 13, 11[72], KSA 11, 38[12].
132 We will return to the issue of existential becoming in the next chapter on the will to power.
133 Important uses of *Dasein* in the published works are to be found in BT Attempt 1, 5; BT 5; GS 1, 357, 373, 374; Z Prologue 3; Z I 12, 15; Z II 13, 20; Z III 13; BGE 262; and TI Errors 8. However, in an important section (section 6) in the chapter, "'Reason' in Philosophy," in TI, Nietzsche uses the term *"Realität"* to refer to existence.
134 TI Reason 6.
135 TI Ancients 5.
136 TI Morality 5.
137 GS Preface 2.

porating [and] exploiting" (BGE 259). These processes are different ways of "interpreting," and therefore interpretation should not be seen as just some cognitive activity. Understood thus, interpretation goes hand-in-hand with the method that meditates on existence in a differential manner without the aid of oppositional structures and facts. Interpretation cannot encounter existence as a finished product for contemplation or appropriation. Through interpretation existence interprets itself.

Consider again the three implications of the existential distinction. With respect to the first implication, we have the condition that the existential gap can neither be directly conceptualized, nor assimilated or synthesized into a higher unity. This lends elusiveness to existence. It means that any attempt to interpret or bridge the gap will be essentially incomplete. The differential-interpretative nature of the exchange between the subjective and objective terms brings this incompletion out only too clearly. In other words, each subject-like or object-like interpretation is fundamentally incomplete; none of these interpretations produce a final, definitive point of view. Or, from the perspective of these interpretative terms, the given quality of existence and the existential gap appear as an "excess" that cannot be completely assimilated; it appears as though there is always something "more" to be incorporated.

Next, if each interpretative term is incomplete, it implies that each subjective interpretation is already dependent on an objective interpretation and vice versa. Thus an excessiveness of the existential gap implies the quality of *lack* about each interpretative attempt. This captures the fact that interpretations are fundamentally carried out by "perspectives" which are essentially lacking. Each perspectival interpretative attempt depends on, anticipates and leads into an interpretation from the contrary perspective. This is the nature of the differential interpretative exchange (which is the second implication) between the subjective and objective perspectives, which I will explore in the next section of this chapter.

Finally, because of the duality of excess and lack, there is always a renewed impulse for the interpretative process to repeat itself anew, as if it were compelled to find a completion, which it never will find. In this sense, the excessive quality of existence implies the ambiguity and instability of the existential distinction. Thus meta-existentialism captures and develops to the fullest all three implications of the existential distinction. And it does so without recourse to a direct or oppositional stance, since the kind of interpretations it provides, either from a subjective or an objective point of view situates itself in the ongoing self-interpretative movement of existence. Nietzsche's meta-existentialism does not exclusively try to isolate the existential gap as such in a direct manner, but "shows" this gap "performatively" through the multiple perspectival interpretations it offers. Hence Nietzsche's methodology is more "indirect" than Climacus', revealing its ability to thoroughly affirm the excessive quality of existence.

Existence as presupposition, existence's excess and Nietzsche's radically indirect method together anticipate the existential *style* with which Nietzsche philosophizes, which I will discuss in the remainder of this section. As indicated in chapter one, starting with his earliest works (and I would include here even his unpublished writings and lectures on Ancient Greek art and philosophy), the kind of problems he considers important and his approach to these problems are personal and concretely existential. However, given that existence is the ultimate presupposition of his philosophy, the personal style of Nietzsche's philosophizing assumes a peculiar form, which I describe as a style of *radical indirection*. He never abandons this unique style, even in his final works.

We appreciate the uniqueness of his indirect, existential style by first noting the *way* in which Nietzsche gains entry into philosophy. His style of philosophizing does not clearly (or categorically) distinguish between existence on the one hand and philosophical inquiry on the other, as if the former was a distinct object of reality for contemplation. This is in contrast to other philosophers like Plato, Kant, Hegel or Kierkegaard, who begin their philosophy by positing a distinct realm of "forms" or "noumena" or "pure objectivity" as distinct from human knowledge, "phenomena" or "subjectivity," even if only to argue that the latter cannot or can access the former, or that the latter reveals the redundancy or the unreality of the former. In contrast, Nietzsche does not enter the personal mode of philosophizing by surveying other modes such as the "third-person" or "objective" approach, and then opposing his style to the latter. Like Climacus' "stylist" who is "never finished with something," but who picks up where he left off, bringing the "most ordinary expression ... into existence with newborn originality,"[138] Nietzsche too, consistent with an interpretative philosophy, picks up and continues the train of various ongoing interpretations always already occurring at the "practical" level of life, without falling into abstraction. He breathes life into philosophy, by *philosophizing* life: life and thought are inextricably intertwined for him, as are practice and theory, which allows him to transform an ordinary expression into an original one. As he writes in a discarded draft originally intended to be included in *Ecce Homo*, "I speak only of what I have lived through, not merely what I have thought through; the opposition of thinking and life is lacking in my case. My 'theory' grows out of my 'practice'" (340).[139] What Jaspers has written applies to Nietzsche: "philosophy is practice ... a theoretical attitude towards it becomes real only in the living appropriation of its contents from the texts."[140]

What makes possible Nietzsche's radically indirect style, which does not clearly differentiate between life and philosophy, between practice and theory, is precisely the reliance on the ultimate givenness and the excessive quality of existence. Unlike Climacus, who first acknowledges the Hegelian pure objective philosophy as such and then polemically (and ironically) opposes his existential philosophy against it,

---

138 Kierkegaard, *Postscript* 86.
139 This reference is to the page number in the Kaufmann edition, rather than to the chapter and section number.
140 Jaspers, "Existenzphilosophie" 134.

Nietzsche always already begins with the existential mode, since he takes existence to be prior to any objective or subjective interpretations. Only subsequently does he goes on to read the history of philosophy, the past philosophers, morality, culture, religion, science, art and history from within this existential perspective, alternating differentially between the subjective and the objective viewpoints. Through such an interpretative practice, he re-translates all of these things back into the prism of life. This achievement is possible only for a philosopher who never questions the continuity between life and thinking, but who also acknowledges the dynamic separation between them.

It is as if Nietzsche takes up and responds to the challenge posed to philosophy by the Kierkegaard-inspired Wittgenstein, who in effect argued that philosophical thought is necessarily abstract, and a result of "confusions," since philosophical problems arise only when one abstracts away from how "language" functions at the level of the concrete reality of life and "forms of life."[141] There can be no legitimate philosophical problems, and so Wittgenstein – both early and late – sought to draw a clear distinction between "philosophy" and "life," and keep them separate in order to clear up the confusion, and lay philosophy to rest.[142] In spirit, I think Nietzsche would agree with this critique of philosophy from the perspective of life; *but at the same time*, if philosophy *could* encroach upon life, life too equally encroaches upon philosophy. In other words, for Nietzsche, objects that belong to the realm of life, such as culture, history, religion, science and artists are not "confusion-free"; they too have their philosophical and moral prejudices and dispositions that have their own meanings and claims on life. And these prejudices or problems never simply work themselves out, as Wittgenstein tends to believe. Life-forms and their prejudices need to be criticized too, just as much as the philosophical or moral or artistic tendency that strays away from or "denies" life. Nietzsche's writings, then, carry out a critique of both these fronts: philosophy and life. There cannot be a clear boundary or demarcation between an "objective philosophy" and a "subjective life"; there must be an interminable exchange between them. Only by tracing this exchange, do his writings illustrate a living philosophy and say the unsayable.

---

141 Ludwig Wittgenstein, *Philosophical Investigations*, trans. G.E.M. Anscombe (Oxford: Blackwell, 2001) 41–44, 75. In section 38, Wittgenstein writes that "philosophical problems arise when language *goes on holiday*." Also, in section 111, Wittgenstein notes that "[philosophical] problems aris[e] through a misinterpretation of our forms of language."

142 See his earlier work: Ludwig Wittgenstein, *Tractatus Logico-Phiolosophicus*, trans. D.F. Pears and B.F. McGuinness (London: Routledge & Kegan Paul, 1974). Especially in his Preface, Wittgenstein claims that his work, which draws "a limit to thought," has found "the final solutions [to philosophical] problems" which arise due to a misunderstanding of the "logic of our language." In the later work, *Philosophical Investigations*, although his method of criticism drastically alters, his negative attitude towards philosophy remains the same in essential aspects. For example, he writes in section 133 that he aims for "*complete* clarity," which is attained only when "philosophical problems ... *completely* disappear."

To be sure Nietzsche, like Kierkegaard, does acknowledge the dilemma the existential philosopher faces regarding the style of her communication. The latter cannot just write for anybody and everybody. She must choose her reader. Therefore Nietzsche, beginning with his earliest works, experimented with various styles including longer essays, aphorisms, quasi-fictional narratives, masks and exaggerated rhetoric. He was well aware that, "Ultimately, nobody can get more out of things, including books, than he already knows. For what one lacks access to from experience one will have no ear" (EH Books 1). This has led scholars like Jaspers to conclude that Nietzsche, too, like Kierkegaard, adopted "indirect communication."[143] Jaspers emphasizes that Nietzsche is forced to use "even contradictions as indirect indicators" in order to express the "existential appeal to the essential truth born by essential life."[144]

However true the above observation is, one must also notice that Nietzsche never really recognizes that there could be anything like a direct communication. Again, this point testifies to the radical indirection of his existential style. For instance, as a reader of Plato or Schopenhauer or Kant (or even Hegel), he spontaneously interprets their arguments in an indirect manner. That is, for example, as a "psychologist" he interprets their theories, not literally or directly, but only as *symptoms* of a certain kind of "life" – "affirmative" or "negative"[145] – closely paying attention to "signs, the tempo of signs, the gestures" (EH Books 4). Nietzsche does not primarily evaluate these thinkers based on the success or failure of their arguments. Nor does he pause to acknowledge an objective, direct communication by a writer to oppose his own style of writing to it. To put it another way, Nietzsche demonstrates an indirect style not just in communicating or expressing his own views, but also in his reading of other philosophers' views. From the outset, his thoughts and writings move *within* the existential sphere, actively interpreting the subjective nature of objectivity or vice versa. It is from such a specifically existential, deeply indirect point of view, that he encounters the problems posed by other philosophers, interpreting them as signs of ascending or descending life. Hence all the idiosyncratic interpretations of Nietzsche's philosophy, for example, his definition of the philosopher in his early Greek lectures as the "man of keenest taste" (*Philosophy in the Tragic Age* 43) or his characterization of Socrates

---

143 Jaspers, "Existenzphilosophie" 165.

144 Jaspers, *Nietzsche* 190.

145 "Affirmation" and "denial" of life (as corresponding to two different types of life – ascending / strong and descending/ weak) are notions that are absolutely central to Nietzsche's thought, and also to the interpretation put forward in this study. Nietzsche remarks in *Ecce Homo* that "the fundamental conception" of his greatest work, *Thus Spoke Zarathustra*, is the "idea of the eternal recurrence [which is] the highest formula of affirmation" (EH Zarathustra 1). In simple terms, affirmation of life involves saying "yes" to life in all its manifestations, and the denial of life is the "will to *negate* life" (BGE 259). Although we will not get into an analysis of the idea of "eternal recurrence," we will return to these notions of affirmation and denial of life in the following chapters as they become crucial, especially to the methodological arguments pertaining to the problem of metaphysics.

and Plato as "symptoms of decay" (TI Socrates 2), or his reading of Kant's philosophy as merely a clandestine way to justify the moral realm when the metaphysical wanderings of reason have already come under attack by the scientific naturalism of the 18th century French *Philosophes* (AOM 27; D Preface 2).

Because Nietzsche takes the sphere of life, from the very outset, to be the sole sphere of reflection and criticism, he is able to afford a lot of freedom – corresponding to the "exceptionally large" multiplicity of "inward states" that resides in him – for the kind of unabashed "experimentation" (with multiple images, masks and tones) that his writings epitomize (EH Books 4). Hence Nietzsche claims that his writings exhibit "the most multifarious art of style" (EH Books 4). For him, there simply is no "objective" style, no "Good style *in itself* – [which is] a pure folly, a mere 'idealism', on a level with the ... 'thing in itself'" (EH Books 4).[146] From this point of view, I dare suggest that Nietzsche would regard even Kierkegaard as a kind of "idealist" (as he considered Socrates to be, the philosopher famous for not having written anything) because he had a fear of direct and literal communication, philosophizing as he was in the shadow of Hegel. For Nietzsche, even the opposition between direct and indirect communication would be too "purist," too "moralistic." Nietzsche meets all the three implications that are really at stake in Climacus' existential distinction without the aid of an opposition between direct and indirect communication. Straightaway he takes a plunge into the existential sphere, thereby making his communication drastically indirect. Once this plunge is taken, he is free to confront and experiment with even the so-called "direct" language of conceptual thought as one of the various styles at his disposal.

Further, hand-in-hand with Nietzsche's style that takes existence or life to be the ultimate presupposition, is the readiness with which he takes the problems of "morality" and "values" to be the basic problems of philosophy.[147] By "morality" he does not mean some "practical" philosophy of actions or knowledge of what is good and bad. Nor does this term primarily mean a *"sense for custom"* (D 19) or the decadent Platonic-Christian morality, or even something like "ethics" in the Kierkegaardian sense of an inward, passionate, authentic existence of the individual. For Nietzsche,

---

146 Derrida also emphasizes the plurality of Nietzsche's style. See Jacques Derrida, "The Ends of Man," in *Margins of Philosophy*, trans. Alan Bass (Chicago: University of Chicago Press, 1982), 135. For Nietzsche, the multifariousness of style is essentially linked to the plurality of truth ("there are many kinds of 'truths', and consequently there is no truth" (KSA 11, 34[230])). Conversely, his rejection of the truth in itself goes hand-in-hand with his denial of the style in itself. One could read these complementary notions of truth and style into the question of "woman," especially with regard to the Preface of *Beyond Good and Evil*, which begins with the rhetorical question: "Suppose that truth is a woman – and why not?" For a provocative discussion of these themes of woman, style and truth in Nietzsche, see Jacques Derrida, *Spurs: Nietzsche's Styles*, trans. Barbara Harlow (Chicago: University of Chicago Press, 1978).

147 Nietzsche writes in a "Note" at the end of the first essay of GM: "the philosopher has to solve the *problem of values* and [] he has to decide on the *hierarchy of values*."

morality is "a system of evaluations that partially coincides with the conditions of a creature's life" (KGW VII/4, 34[264]). And evaluations or values are a particular type of life's "conditions of preservation and growth" within the flux of existence's becoming (KSA 12, 9[38]). Evaluations are always made from a particular perspective, whether this is of an individual, a community, a race, a state, a church, a faith, or a culture. There is no choice: every form of life *must* live by evaluating, setting up its nook and corner, its articles of faith, and its values and morals, in order not only to preserve itself, but also so that it can grow and create itself. Since life is a process of appropriating, overpowering, incorporating and exploiting, the basic trait of life is its necessity to *"always overcome itself"* (Z II 12). When we establish values, it is "life itself [which] evaluates through us" (TI Morality 5).

Given this, it is plain to see why one cannot gain a perspective from "outside" life to evaluate life itself, for all evaluations happen "under the inspiration and from the perspective of life" (TI Morality 5). Morality is, therefore, a symptom and a *"sign language of the affects,"* and it betrays the kind of life – ascending or descending – that interprets through it (BGE 187). One cannot simply abandon the realm of existence and the tension created by the existential gap in favor of a disinterested knowledge of life. Neither can one abandon the realm of existence, even if momentarily, to state that such disinterested knowledge is impossible. Knowledge is not a passive acquisition that results due to mere "observation," but it is a product of active creation as a specific form of appropriation, incorporation and overpowering. Evaluation is more basic than knowledge or any epistemological stance, since knowledge itself is one of the tools at disposal for the sake of life-preservation and growth (GS 110). Therefore Nietzsche's philosophy automatically takes any attempt to "know" life from "outside" as a symptom of certain kinds of life, either of a declining or of an ascending life. Either way, he begins immediately with a subjective interpretation of this purposed objectivity.

The above account of Nietzsche's style of radical indirection is not meant to be exhaustive. My intention is only to indicate how this style is unique compared to the indirect form of communication of existentialists like Kierkegaard, how it complements the excessive quality of existence, and how it results from Nietzsche's treating the realm of existence as the ultimate presupposition. The issue of style in Nietzsche is a rich and a complex topic which is at the center of his distinctive existential approach, and one to which I cannot do justice in this work. My focus will be more on the methodological aspects of his meta-existentialism, which will lead us directly to the issue of his relation to metaphysics. With this goal in mind, we must next proceed to consider the nature of the differential interplay between the subjective and objective perspectives. The above discussion has made apparent that the latter process complements existence's excessive quality and also Nietzsche's radically indirect approach. If Nietzsche's philosophy begins indirectly by taking existence as its basic presupposition, then the ambiguity of the existential distinction is accentuated and heightened through the perspectival interplay of interpretations between the subjective and the objective viewpoints. In the next chapter, we will return to Nietzsche's notion of existence, but again, from a methodological point of view, when we consider the concept of "will to power" and the connection between this concept to Nietzsche's ideas of affirmation and denial of life.

The interpretative interplay between the subjective and the objective

The excessive quality of existence implies that it cannot be hermetically sealed and offered as a unit or a finished product for understanding or appropriation. Its essential incompleteness means that there is always something more to be unraveled. Hence any "pure" concepts – either those of objectivity or subjectivity – are unsuitable for existential reflection, since they presuppose the completion of existence, as Climacus maintains, with respect to the Hegelian concepts. But there is also an intricate link between pure concepts and conceptual opposites, since as Nietzsche argues, the setting up of opposites serves the purpose of valuing one of the oppositional terms more than the other, such that the preferred term appears "purer," un-infiltrated by its opposite (BGE 2). Therefore, conversely, there is an intricate link between the excessive quality of existence and a differential-interpretative structure: the former necessitates the latter. This structure deals only with "impure" terms: objective terms are always inevitably interpreted by subjective terms and vice versa. Climacus sees this only partly, when he reclaims the domain of objectivity as a variant of subjectivity, but he does not make this inter-relation a methodological principle. Impure terms signify, on the one hand, the impossibility of completely reducing (or "sublating" in the Hegelian sense) one type of term to the other; the existential distinction is decisive and indispensible. On the other hand, they signify that these terms cannot be totally independent of each other either, and that they form two mutually interdependent perspectives. We must discuss below the nature of the dynamic interaction between the two types of terms.

I begin by emphasizing that this differential-interpretative exchange represents an irreducible duality *within* existence. What I mean is that because existence is the presupposition, which cannot be directly determined or appropriated by any single viewpoint, we have a duality of interpretations in mutual conflict and dependency, which continuously determines existence. However, it is not as if, with respect to these two (subjective and objective) interpretative viewpoints, we can "add up" their individual viewpoints so as to produce a unitary interpretation adequate to capture existence. This is why it must be emphasized that there is always a mutual conflict, a struggle between the subjective and the objective interpretations. The duality maintains and affirms the original excessive quality of existence, and so this dual framework can never be adequate to existence. A subjective or objective interpretation either over-determines or under-determines existence. This means there is always a play between an excess on the one hand and a lack on the other. Nietzsche suggests that the interpretative play takes the basic forms of "obedience" and "commanding" as "forms of struggle" (KSA 11, 36[22]). But it is also not the case that the subjective term perfectly complements the objective term. The mutual conflict between the two viewpoints implies a certain discordance between the two such that the existential gap is never bridged, and the excessive quality is never overcome.

We can better appreciate the above arguments once we recognize that the subjective and objective viewpoints are not necessarily or primarily theoretical points of view that the critical philosopher may take. Above all, they are manifestations of existence; they are the *transformations* that existence itself undergoes through which existence interprets itself. These transformations determine all the forms of life, the entire organic and the inorganic world. However, it should not be supposed that existence is like the Kantian noumena lurking behind its phenomenal transformations, since existence (as will to power) is no such "thing-in-itself," "substance" or "fact" for Nietzsche, terms which have an ontological status independent of their multiple perspectival interpretations. We shall return to this point in the next chapter.

The subject-like and object-like states are basic tendencies in existence, serving as temporary place-holders in the evolving self-interpretation of existence. But in spite of the moving interpretations and perspectival play, the meanings of the objective and subjective terms are not arbitrary. There are particular sets of meanings or salient features that are ascribable to both types of terms. For Nietzsche, the tendency towards objective states is the basic tendency in existence towards fixation, completion, rigidification, constancy, truth, being, and so on. In Nietzsche's interpretation and critique of philosophy, the typical terms that assume some or all of these tendencies are "soul," "consciousness," "supersensible," etc. The tendency towards the subjective states, on the other hand, is the basic tendency in existence towards change, semblance, error, becoming,[148] and so on. Typical terms that signify some or all of these meanings are the complementary terms to the objective ones such as "body," "instincts," "sensible," etc. The crucial point is that these two types of terms, for Nietzsche, are not opposites. They are terms in a dynamic, differential struggle. And as we shall see, Nietzsche does not favor one over the other, for instance, subjective becoming over objective being.

Heidegger, who wanted to claim Nietzsche as a "metaphysician of subjectivity," insisted on a reading which conceived of these objective and subjective terms as opposites, in order to attribute to Nietzsche a metaphysical conception of "truth" as "harmony with the actual."[149] As a reversal of Platonism, Nietzsche's metaphysics

---

148 I note here that the subjective tendency towards "becoming" is not the same as the character of existence as "becoming," which I have argued above cannot be derived through an opposition to "being." This is not to suggest that the subjective tendency towards becoming derives its meaning through an opposition to the objective tendency towards being. But, as we shall see below, existence's becoming is the source of *both* subjective becoming and objective being.
149 Heidegger, *Nietzsche* III: 126–127.

interprets the "actual" to have the subjective qualities of becoming and semblance, instead of being and permanence. So the affirmation of these qualities amounts to an affirmation of life. But, as I will argue below, this is a simplification and misrepresentation of Nietzsche's thinking. The subjective terms are not unequivocally affirmative of life, just as the objective ones do not unambiguously deny life. For as Nietzsche remarks, the will to posit "being," "reason" and "truth" is the "will to be master over the multiplicity of sensations" (KSA 12, 9[89]); and being so, it has the same basic creative, life-enhancing quality, which Nietzsche, at other times, attributes to the artist's ability to celebrate semblance and error. The key here is to comprehend the thoroughly dynamic nature of the interpretative play between the subjective and the objective, as well as, to recognize how these terms lead into each other, and, at occasions, lead to an overlap of meanings.

In order to substantiate the above arguments, I will consider some important sections in the unpublished notes of the 1880s, which are relevant for our discussion of the subjective-objective interaction. I begin with Nietzsche's description of "life" as a "multiplicity of forces, connected by a common mode of nutrition" (KSA 10, 24[14]). A multiplicity of forces forms a *relative* unity through organization and co-operation when a single dominant drive or force comes to subjugate other forces, which also have the lust to rule. The ruling force interprets the subjugated forces by forming a political structure, by setting up an "order of rank and division of labor as the conditions that make possible the whole and its parts" (KSA 11, 40[21]). Nietzsche calls this political structure, "body [*Körper*]," which has its own "perspective" as a "complex form of specificity" (KSA 13, 14[186]). Each perspective or viewpoint – whether described as subjective or objective – "strives to become master over all space and extend its force" (KSA 13, 14[186]). In cases where a dominating force is unable to subjugate a drive to obey the command of its regime, it could leave this drive out of its unit, in order to continue preserving the relative stability of the unit. In other scenarios, where it can transform a weaker force into its functionary without destroying the latter, it seeks to form a new alliance (KSA 12, 9[98]). Or, when there is another equally strong force that is also seeking to control the regime, the currently dominating force seeks to "conspire together [with the other force] for power," therefore forming a new sort of union (KSA 13, 14[186]). In this sense, appropriation, vanquishing, incorporation, subjugation, disintegration, assimilation, exploitation and overpowering are various means of interpretation, which is "itself a means of becoming master of something" (KSA 12, 2[148]).

It must be stressed that the unity that constitutes an interpretative perspective is only a relative one, not an absolute or an unconditional one. The unity is due to a temporary arrangement between forces in constant mutual conflict, but this arrangement does not guarantee some eternal peace or equal distribution of forces such that the conflicts would cease. The emergence of a dominant drive ensures only a provisional security and order. But the dominating drive must engage in a constant conflict with the dominated forces to maintain this order, since even in the resistance of the dominated forces individual power is by no mean surrendered (KSA 11, 36[22]). It is only through falsification, exaggeration and simplification that we speak of these unities as *pure* "subject," "being," "substance," "reason" and "individuals" (KSA 12, 9[89], KSA 11, 36[23]). The continuous nature of the mutual conflict between forces and their mutual resistances, even those which constitute a relatively stable perspective, reflect the *becoming* character of existence, the "continual transition" of which "forbids us to speak of 'individuals', etc. [since] the 'number' of beings is itself in flux" (KSA 11, 36[23]). This point confirms our argument that Nietzsche's meta-existentialism does not even recognize anything like pure objectivity or pure subjectivity, since such pure concepts would require that these unities are absolute ones. The dynamic nature of the struggle between the forces and the relative unity of perspectives imply a subjectivity already infected by an objectivity and vice versa, and thus a differential framework between the subjective and the objective.

At any rate, a relative unit or "body" is the fundamental concept in the background of which we should understand the interpretative struggle between the subjective and objective terms. Nietzsche makes this methodological point when he writes, "The body and physiology, the starting point" (KSA 11, 40[21]), which is "to be discussed first, methodologically" (KSA 12, 5[56]). Each body or dynamic unity is made up of both subjective and objective tendencies, and once we "start from the *body* and employ it as guide," we can provide an interpretation of these tendencies (KSA 11, 40[15]). First, since there is a continual struggle for dominance, governance and obedience among the various forces that form the relative unity, there is a "fluctuating assessment of the limits of power [as] part of life" (KSA 11, 40[21]). We can take this to mean that the subjective and objective tendencies are basic drives or tendencies of a body, which are involved in continuous mutual evaluations or fluctuating assessments of each other and themselves. The ultimate bid in this mutual struggle is what Nietzsche calls "power." Due to the constant mutual struggle between the drives, the "sphere of a subject [as a 'body' is] constantly growing or decreasing, the center of the system constantly shifting" (KSA 11, 26[137]). In line with its necessary perspectivism, the body "construes all the rest of the world from its own viewpoint, i.e., [it] measures, feels, forms, according to its own force" (KSA 13, 14[186]). Therefore it seeks that which resists it, and *as* a unified "subject" encountering another "object," or vice versa, it "interprets the value of whatever else wants to grow" (KSA 12, 2[148]). At the same time, it also repulses other forces that want to assimilate it, or want to become one with it, for the sake of power. And this repelling force exercised by every atom of force is, for Nietzsche, the common feature, the connection between the inorganic and the organic. In any case, we could say that a body not only thrives on the conflicts of forces and resistances "within" it, but also "outside" of it, since it is only against these resistances that its "will to power" can manifest itself. Hence a center of force can be said to be dependent upon and connected to other forces and centers of force for the sake of a power struggle.

To sum up the foregoing analysis: the realm of existence is made up of multiple, localized concentrations of forces which form relative unities or bodies, and which are involved in a mutual, evolving struggle with other centers of force; also, each center of force is only relatively stable, which is itself involved in constant mutual power struggle with the forces and drives it has already subjugated. Accordingly, "life" is an "enduring form of processes of the establishment of force, in which the different contenders grow unequally" (KSA 11, 36[22]). In this interconnected network, any mutual struggle involves the process of interpretation and evaluation of other forces, because of which orders of rank are set up not only within the domain ruled by a single center of force, but also among all centers of forces. Further, if the basic forces that constitute each body can be described in terms of subjective and objective tendencies, and the whole domain of existence can be seen as a dynamic interconnection of such centers of forces, then existence itself can be interpreted as one "body" with various subjective or objective tendencies in mutual interdependence and differential struggle.[150] Now assuming that power is the ultimate impetus behind all of these struggles, what is the criterion or standard according to which a body evaluates itself and other bodies? What is the basic impulse that compels a body to evaluate other forces and to seek out resistances?

Nietzsche's answer is that a particular body's valuations express its "conditions of preservation and growth [*Erhaltungs- und Wachsthums-Bedingungen*]" (KSA 12, 9[38]). A perspective is an evaluating center, and value is the "standpoint of conditions of preservation and enhancement for complex forms of relative life-duration within the flux of becoming" (KSA 13, 11[73]). So there are two basic impulses behind a life-form's evaluating glance: the impulse for "preservation" and that of "growth" or "enhancement." But the more basic impulse among these two is the impulse to grow or "becoming stronger" (KSA 12, 7[44]). The "truly basic life-instinct" aims at "the *expansion of power*" and in doing so, it may even risk and sacrifice its self-preservation (GS 349). A form of existence "wants above all to *discharge* its force: 'preservation' is only a consequence of this" (KSA 12 2[63]). The instinct to grow, expand and create is the basic instinct of all existence in accordance with will to power as the fundamental principle of evaluation. In this chapter, while discussing the differential interaction between the subjective and the objective tendencies, we will limit our discussion to only the *quantitative* aspect of the will to power, in the expression of which the body seeks to increase or enhance its power. There is also a *qualitative* aspect to the will to power, which is inseparable from the quantitative element, but we will not really focus on the qualitative dimension until the next chapter. As we shall see, the qualitative element, which is associated with growth and creation, becomes crucial when we consider Nietzsche's critique of metaphysics.

---

150 As a body, existence cannot be viewed as a "subject" or "substance" that is firm and durable, but as something that is dynamically and continually in flux.

The basic life-instinct is the instinct to grow and not something else precisely because of the nature of the existential gap, which does not let itself be bridged or directly inhabited, and thereby let existence "settle down" into some sort of finality. The existential gap introduces a certain restlessness and dynamicity to existence, because of which it always aims for something more, inadequate as it is to itself. Self-preservation, on the other hand, aims at adequacy, safety, sufficiency and completion, and this explains why Nietzsche ascribes to it a derivative status.

Now, given life's basic instinct, the body's claim to its own stable horizon may be viewed *simultaneously* from both the subjective and the objective perspectives. On the one hand, it may be viewed as the body's objective towards constancy, making "firm" and "fix[ing] the *real world*," the stability provided by which is essential for asserting its dominion over the subjugated forces (KSA 12, 9[144]). By thus fixating, a particular body first obtains its right to its own *truth*. Nietzsche defines "truth" as a body's "will to be master over the multiplicity of sensations" (KSA 12, 9[89]). It is "a making firm, a making true"; it has fundamentally a creative aspect, and it is something "invented" or posited, not "found or discovered" (KSA 12, 9[91]). The "will to truth" is the will to the "thinkability of all beings" (Z II 12). Nietzsche, at times, also describes the objective tendency to truth as the defining feature of the scientific drive (GS 344; GM III 24, 25; KSA 12, 9[144]).

It is absolutely crucial to note that only in tending towards this fixation and constancy does the body enhance its feeling of power. Hence the objective tendency is an expression of the will to power: "The criterion of truth resides in the enhancement of the feeling of power" (KGW VII/4, 34[264]).[151] Fixation might incidentally also preserve the body, but this is not the main impetus for making firm. The "life" of this body is "founded upon the premise of a belief in enduring and regularly recurring things; the more powerful life is, wider must be the knowable world to which we, as it were, attribute *being*" (KSA 12, 9[91], emphasis added). Even though the stability of the body is only a relative one, the more actively the body "forgets" or "resists" this fact, the better it is for its own immediate feeling of power. Active forgetting allows "above all for the nobler functions and functionaries, for ruling, predicting, predetermining" and also for "happiness, cheerfulness, hope, pride, *immediacy*" which are symptoms of a "*robust* health" (GM II 1).

On the other hand, this very same act of a body claiming its own stable horizon and domain of power may be viewed as the positing of "useful fictions" and "enveloping illusions," and thus the expression of subjective tendency (HL 7). It is a "fundamental *falsification* of all events," since it is a falsification of the very becoming nature of existence from the perspective of which there is no constancy and fixation (KSA 11, 40[13]). Hence Nietzsche calls the body's belief in itself as an "individual" or "subject," a "fiction" (KSA 12, 10[19]). It is a judgment on the very value of life, for

---

151 Also, see Z II 12.

which the body must abstract away or refuse to surrender itself, at least to a certain degree, to the incessant becoming of existence. Nietzsche writes, "every cave" has an "even deeper cave behind it – more extensive, stranger, richer world above the surface, an abyss behind every ground ... There is something arbitrary in [] stopping here" (BGE 289). In positing its domain of truth and thus passing a judgment on the whole of existence, the body has committed something arbitrary, even though this act itself is an expression of the will to power. However, we must recognize that to be able to live at all, this judgment had to be made; it is not "possible to *live* without evaluating, without having aversions and partialities" (with regard to one's own horizon) (HH I 32). But it does not change the fact that these judgments and evaluations are "illogical[] and therefore unjust" (HH I 32). The body's claim to its own truth is but a profound error and illusion that renders only a false reality to a fiction. Hence Nietzsche famously remarks in an unpublished essay that, "Truths are illusions which we have forgotten are illusions" (*On Truth and Lies* 84); and also that, "Truth is the kind of error without which a certain species of life could not live" (KSA 11, 34[253]).

The intention behind pointing out the erroneous nature of truth is not to refute the objective tendency, by opposing the subjective tendency to it. The latter tendency is not the vantage point of a supposed knowledge about the becoming quality of existence, which is more fundamental than the tendency towards being epitomized by objectivity. The objective tendency is not opposed to the becoming quality of existence, like many of Nietzsche's commentators such as Heidegger suppose. The main reason for this is that, for Nietzsche, the objective tendency is not an unfortunate mistake committed by the body, but rather is an equally necessary expression of the will to power, and a drive, which enhances the body's feeling of power. Therefore Nietzsche is not just favoring becoming to being as Heidegger suggests. The subjective tendency is not simply the unconditional recognition of becoming, illusion and error regarding the body's claim to truth from an *external* point of view independent of the body under consideration. For example, with respect to Christian morality, Nietzsche would be the first to acknowledge that at an earlier phase in its history, Christianity's "truths" had a legitimate existence insofar as these truths genuinely held sway in the Western culture, introduced new possibilities to its existence, and produced new types of great human beings, previously unheard of. It is of no use to protest against this stage of Christianity that its truths were simply errors and therefore Christianity should have been discarded straightaway, and Nietzsche does not do this.

The important thing to recognize is that the subjective tendency is a concrete existential tendency that the body itself realizes at some point in its historical development by appropriating the fact that its truths were illusions. This knowledge may not be available to the body at the early phases of its history when it is affirming its objective tendency and its "will to truth" in accordance with its "will to power." Either way, whether it is affirming its objective or subjective tendency, the meaning of the body's act of claiming its own stable horizon is *fundamentally ambiguous*. This act *could* be read as a manifestation of a subjective tendency or an objective one. This means – seen from the viewpoint of the body – the body, when it affirms either tendency, is never affirming a purely objective or a purely subjective tendency. Concretely speaking, for the body, it is always a combination of these two tendencies, and when we say it affirms either one of the two tendencies, it is always by gradations or degrees. When a body affirms the objective side, it affirms more of the tendency towards being and truth, and accordingly from this perspective, it reinterprets its own subjective tendencies as unsuitable for the expression of its will to power. Therefore it does not mean that, when the body affirms its objective side, it has absolutely no drive towards the subjective side, or that it has nothing to do with the latter tendency. At a later stage in its development, it may come to acknowledge its prior truths as falsifications in accordance with its present conditions of growth and power. In doing so, the body is said to have *overcome* itself. The subjective tendency of the body comes into view in the body's current horizon to be affirmed by it through this process of self-overcoming. Now it affirms more of the tendency towards becoming and illusion, and accordingly, reinterprets its objective tendency in a bid to enhance its power. In this subjective affirmation, the body recognizes that its initial act of claiming its own stable horizon was always a falsification, and therefore, it now affirms the subjective tendency that was lurking behind this act. However, this does not change the fact that its earlier tendency to affirm its objective drive was also necessary. Nietzsche sums it up beautifully:

> Something you formerly loved as a truth ... now strikes you as an error... But maybe that error was necessary for you then, when you were still another person ... as are all your presents 'truths', like a skin that concealed and covered many things you weren't allowed to see yet. It is your new life, not your reason, that has killed that opinion for you... We negate and have to negate because something in us *wants* to live and affirm itself, something we might not yet know or see! (GS 307).

"Self-overcoming" is a central notion in Nietzsche's philosophy, but we will not explore it in much detail in this work. What must be noted is that the body is the seat of a great mutual, differential-interpretative struggle between these objective and subjective tendencies. Its act of claiming its own domain of power is an instantiation of *both* the objective tendency towards being and truth *and* the subjective tendency towards becoming and error. These two tendencies are in conflict, vying for the body's affirmation. And the latter affirms either one of these two tendencies in varying degrees, at various stages in its evolution, depending on which tendency it is that is most suitable to realize its instinct to grow, create and enhance its power. Ultimately, the criterion provided by the will to power is decisive. Initially, the body may be compelled to affirm the objective tendency towards truth, if this is the direction in which it can grow and create. It is absolutely crucial to recognize that affirming this tendency is an expression of the will to power itself. The becoming of existence itself creates and necessitates a positing of the truth of being, of individuals and subjects: existence is "a kind of becoming [which] must itself create the deception of beings" (KSA 12, 9[89]). There is a kind of *warp* within existence, which first creates a need to posit objective being as a way to enhance its power, and therefore inaugurate a deep struggle between this objectivity and a subjective tendency. The body is not free to affirm the latter tendency whenever it wants, but it can do so only when such an affirmation would be beneficial to express its will to power, which has now evolved and seeks to grow in a new direction than before. It is the body's "new life" that now wants to "live and affirm itself," which realizes that the only direction in which its power can be enhanced is through the affirmation of the deceptive quality of its previous claims to truths. And from this new creative perspective, the old claims to truths may even appear to be more self-preserving than creative. In affirming the subjective tendency towards error and becoming, the body can be now said to have adopted an artistic tendency, in which the *"will to deception [Wille zur Täuschung]* has a good conscience" (GM III 25). It now affirms the illusory quality of life, instead of its truthful quality: it acknowledges that life aims at "semblance, i.e. error, deception, simulation, blinding, self-blinding" and therefore, it sheds its old truth and revels in the play of lie, semblance and deception (GS 344).

It should not be supposed that in thus acknowledging the illusory quality of its previous truths, the body is now completely in tune with the becoming quality of existence, and that it now possesses some final "truth" as "harmony" with becoming. The becoming of existence cannot be accessed directly, but only indirectly, through the mutual struggle of perspectives between the objective and the subjective tendencies in a particular body. Hence the subjective tendency towards becoming is not the same as the becoming of existence itself. By subjectively acknowledging the illusory quality of its previous truths, the body does not affirm some final truth, but rather it artistically affirms precisely the deceitful, erroneous, illusory quality of life, and that "the conditions of life might include error," without pretending to expose some final truth about existence as the truth about a noumena hiding behind these phenomenal deceptions (GS 121).

Nietzsche's writings affirm both tendencies – the objective as well as the subjective – without really favoring any of them, which is why for many readers his writings appear ambiguous, contradictory or even self-defeating. Whether he is analyzing the Ancient Greeks, Socrates, science, art, culture, nature, Christianity or philosophy, he interprets the relative tensions between these two tendencies at various stages in their evolution, thus providing his genealogical account of these different bodies. He evaluates them by determining the "direction" in which their will to grow or enhance power will be most greatly manifested. In effect, he asks: what should be the differential, mutual interpretations between the subjective and the objective tendencies in a given body such that it expresses its power to the maximum?

It should be obvious from the above analysis that the continuous relative tensions between the two tendencies amounts to an unremitting interplay of differential interpretations between them. Since it is the becoming nature of existence that determines both tendencies of objective being and subjective becoming in a body, these two tendencies are not opposites. Both tendencies are equally demonstrations of the will to power. They compete as conflicting directions in which the body could enhance its power. When the body affirms more of the objective tendency, it interprets the subjective tendency according to this perspective, as something unsuitable for it to realize its power, and so on. And when it affirms the subjective perspective, the objective tendency is reinterpreted accordingly. Moreover, at any point in the history of its evolution, a body exists only by an interpretation and evaluation of both tendencies, irrespective of which tendency it is presently affirming. In other words, these tendencies themselves maybe said to be interpreting each other in the body. And each time a body shifts its perspective from the objective to the subjective or vice versa, it overcomes itself. In this play of affirmations, the body provides an interpretation of the meaning of existence and its becoming character (for example, it acknowledges the unceasing "self-overcoming" nature of life, or the fundamentality of the concepts of power and growth to mere self-preservation) as what is common between these two tendencies. With each switch in the perspective, the body has an opportunity to confront and interpret the warped nature of existence. In this interpretation, the existential distinction, as the gap between the objective and the subjective tendencies, is redrawn and the process of mutual interpretation between the two tendencies begins anew, leading to a new instance of the existential distinction. In the last section of this chapter, I will provide a brief analysis of *Human, All-Too-Human*, the first book of Nietzsche's mature philosophy, in order to offer an example of such a switch in perspective between the objective and the subjective tendencies within Nietzsche's text.

Nietzsche's critique of metaphysics

Nietzsche's meta-existentialism follows this interpretative movement of the body, and the mutual struggle between the two tendencies, and in doing so, it carries out the three main implications of drawing the existential distinction. In accordance with the direct inaccessibility of the existential gap, the basic instinct of life is the instinct to grow and create, which manifests itself simultaneously in two contrary tendencies or drives: the subjective and objective, or the "artistic" and the "scientific." These suggestions that the subjective is the artistic tendency and the objective is the scientific one are, strictly speaking, conditional ones that are open to interpretation. As we shall see, in *Human, All-Too-Human* operating from a particular set of presuppositions, Nietzsche could be seen as equally portraying the artistic tendency as the objective one towards being and truth, and the scientific drive as the subjective one affirming change and becoming. This only confirms the deeply interpretative and perspectival nature of the subjective-objective interaction. Nevertheless, in the differential struggle between these two tendencies, neither tendency is "purely" present for the particular body to affirm, and this brings out the second implication of the existential distinction. The entire struggle may be viewed as that between an "excess" and a "lack," where neither tendency is singly adequate to the body's fundamental will to enhance its power. However, this just means that, for a body, the interpretive struggle is a continuous one, with the possibility of a never-ending series of self-overcomings, through which the body alternatively affirms the objective and the subjective tendencies to varying degrees. Through this process, the existential distinction is redrawn again and again in new ways, which enacts the third implication. In the above analysis, we only discussed the instance of a body overcoming its previous objective tendency to affirm the subjective side. However, it ought to be inferred that this process repeats again from the contrary perspective, with the body discovering a new manifestation of the objective tendency towards constancy and truth in accordance with its will to grow, in the affirmation of which it reinterprets the previous subjective perspective as a means to its present condition. Thus this repetitive process shows how the two tendencies mutually depend upon and implicate each other.[152]

Now, Nietzsche's critique of metaphysics is bound up with the never-ending differential struggle between the objective and subjective tendencies. It coincides with the carrying out of all three methodological implications of the existential distinction not just one or two of them. Ultimately, this implies that his critique of metaphysics is an endless one, with no final, unambiguous outcome to suggest that he clearly overcomes metaphysics or he remains confined within it. To recognize the ambiguity of Nietzsche's critique, I will initially define the objective tendency towards being, truth and constancy as the *metaphysical need* of the body.[153] Nietzsche's own term for what I am calling "metaphysical need" is "will to truth" (GS 344; GM III 24, 27). But since a body does not affirm a purely objective tendency, and since, in its affirmation, there is always an element of the subjective tendency which is interpreted and affirmed, albeit in a lesser degree, we could equally attribute a "metaphysical need" to the body's affirmation of the subjective tendency, where the objective side is also implicitly affirmed. The metaphysical need, therefore, expresses the body's conditions of preservation and growth, which the affirmation of either tendency articu-

---

152 One must not take the above differential struggle to be a sort of "dialectical" exchange in the Hegelian sense. For, unlike the Hegelian dialectic, the differential struggle does not have a progressive bent, where there is neat "synthesis" between the thesis and the antithesis, in which the level of conflict and negation at the previous stage is carefully "preserved" or "sublated" at the next stage. Instead, there is both a kind of excessive expenditure and an irretrievable loss in the switch of perspectives between the subjective and objective tendencies, consistent with the fact that this struggle is reflective of the basic life instinct to grow. In contrast to this, the basic impulse of the Hegelian dialectic would be one of "preservation" and not "growth." A precise comparison between Nietzsche's philosophy and Hegelian dialectic would involve drawing a careful contrast between Nietzsche's "self-overcoming" and Hegel's *Aufhebung*, which is beyond the scope of this work. However, see Gilles Deleuze's *Nietzsche and Philosophy*, trans. Hugh Tomlinson (New York: Columbia University Press, 2006), especially the first and the fifth chapters, where Deleuze argues that Nietzsche is an anti-dialectic (in the Hegelian sense of this term) thinker, by contrasting Nietzschean genealogy with Hegelian dialectic.
153 Our definition of "metaphysical need" is different from Nietzsche's own use of this term in his works. This difference should be borne in mind for the remainder of the study. We will see what Nietzsche's use is in the next section.

lates. However, since the body affirms these tendencies as an expression of its essential life-instinct to enhance its power, one can notice at once that Nietzsche is not simply aiming to overcome metaphysics. This does not mean that he does not have a critical attitude towards it, but that this attitude is nuanced and complex.

Let us consider Nietzsche's own critical characterization of metaphysics. From his very first mature writings to his final works written at the twilight of his sanity, Nietzsche adheres to a conception of metaphysics as the evaluation of existence or life, which sets up an *opposition* between the "apparent" or "sensible" world of becoming and the "true" or "real" or "supersensible" world of "being."[154] Metaphysics sees our world of becoming as full of contradictions, change and sufferings, and therefore, it posits and values a "better" world that is free of these contradictions. It sees the former world as merely apparent and superficial, hiding a true world of being; therefore it "imagine[s] another, more valuable world" of being, truth, permanence and constancy (KSA 12, 8[2]). According to Nietzsche, it is the profound suffering of the sensible world, which inspires these desires and conclusions of metaphysics (KSA 12, 8[2]). But the real world, which is imagined, can never be demonstrated, for this world of being has the "characteristics of non-being, of *nothingness* – the 'real world' has been constructed out of the contradiction of the actual world" with which we are acquainted (TI Reason 6). The only thing metaphysics manages to achieve by this phantom of a real world is not an affirmation, but a *denial* of *this* life of becoming, of sensuality and historical change; metaphysical opposition only results in a "slandering, disparaging and accusing [of] life" (TI Reason 6). Nietzsche sees such a metaphysical basis at the core of philosophy, religions, morality, art and science, and that of almost all the cultural movements in the post-Platonic West.

The vital question one must answer is: at bottom, what makes a particular evaluation metaphysical? Is it the mere *positing* of the so-called illusory "real" world of being and valuing this world more highly that makes it metaphysical *or* is it the very *oppositional structure* between a "real" and an "apparent" world (in which one of them is valued more as the "pure" world) that is the hallmark of a metaphysical evaluation? This is a central question not only for our interpretation, but for all interpretations of Nietzsche's philosophy, since depending on which way one chooses, one attributes to Nietzsche either an *unambiguous* relation to metaphysics and truth (whether by claiming that he firmly remains within the bounds of metaphysics or that he overcomes it) or an *ambiguous* one. Externalists like Heidegger, and naturalists like Cox and Richard Schacht[155] incline towards the former condition, namely the very setting up of the illusory real world of being, as the defining feature of metaphysical evaluation (there are plenty of passages in Nietzsche's writings which, on the surface, seem to endorse this view). Internalist commentators tend to run these two condi-

---

154 See HH I 1, 5, 8, 9, 222; BGE 2; TI Reason 6, TI Real World; and KSA 12, 9[91], KSA 12, 8[2], KSA 12, 9[60], KSA 13, 14[168].

155 See Richard Schacht, *Nietzsche* (London: Routledge & Kegan Paul, 1983).

tions together, as if they implied the same thing. My argument is that the setting up of a "true" world in itself does not necessarily mean the metaphysical will to deny life, but it is the positing of an oppositional structure that implies a denial of existence. Therefore the above two conditions need to be differentiated from one another.

Let us first consider Heidegger. Attributing to Nietzsche the view that metaphysical thought consists in the positing of a real world of being allows Heidegger to substantiate his claim that Nietzsche's philosophy is a form of inverse Platonism. Platonism is understood to exemplify the essential trait of "metaphysics," as an evaluation that posits a supersensible world of being to be more valuable than the sensible world of change and becoming. Thus Platonism sets up an opposition between a real world and an apparent world. According to Heidegger, although Nietzsche rejects the Platonic notion of truth and being, his rejection is only apparent, since he only manages to reverse Platonism. Nietzsche, argues Heidegger, opposes the affirmation of the world of being by metaphysics through an affirmation of the "actual" sensory world of becoming, thus "permanentizing" the latter.[156] (One must note that the claim that Nietzsche's attack against metaphysics consists in an oppositional stance towards the affirmation of the world of being follows from the initial characterization of metaphysics as the thought that posits a true world of being). For Heidegger, Nietzsche still maintains an interpretation of truth and being, where now the being of beings would be the "becoming" of the sensory world, which he claims Nietzsche affirms.[157] Hence Nietzsche's "overcoming" of metaphysics is unsuccessful, and he is very much trapped within its confines, insofar as he still ends up providing a metaphysical interpretation of the being of beings and the truth of beings through his inversion of Platonism. The key to this Heideggerian reading is the attribution to Nietzsche of a purely *conceptual* struggle against metaphysics. What I mean is that – and to use Climacean-existential terms – this reading assumes that for Nietzsche the metaphysical nature of an evaluation consists more in the "what" of the evaluation or in "what" world it sets up and values more (world of "being" instead of "becoming"), not in the "how" of this evaluation. In contrast, I argue that it is precisely the latter aspect of the evaluation, which is crucial from Nietzsche's point of view.

Contemporary naturalist readings are a bit more careful than Heidegger about acknowledging the necessarily illusory and perspectival qualities of Nietzsche's affirmation of the sensible, "natural" world of becoming. For instance, in Cox's characterization of "metaphysics" as any discourse that maintains a "strict division between the natural ... and the extra-natural ... and grants to the latter an ontological and epistemological superiority and priority," he does somewhat recognize the oppositional

---

156 *Nietzsche* III: 156.

157 Heidegger establishes his conclusions through his interpretations of "will to power" and "eternal recurrence of the same." The former is the "essence" of the being of beings and the latter is the "*way in which*" the whole of beings comes into presence. See especially *Nietzsche* III: 193–215.

structure itself as characteristic of metaphysics for Nietzsche.[158] He also stresses the fundamentality of the doctrine of perspectivism in Nietzsche, which sees ourselves enmeshed in a world that is "contingent, conditional, temporal and affective" forbidding any claims to a final truth that only a "God's-eye view" can have.[159] However, given his basic naturalistic commitments, he does not really follow through to exploit the consequences of these insights. Instead, he sets up his own version of an opposition between "naturalism" and "metaphysics."[160] While the former is concerned with affirming the "very world with which we are most intimately acquainted," the latter fabricates another transcendent world "through a *negation of* ... the world we know."[161] But what about this appeal to the "world we know"? It appears that, in such a characterization, there is an appeal to the natural sensory "world we know" as a *self-evident* fact (with which we are "intimately acquainted"), even if it is qualified that this world is "constructed by the many interpretations/perspectives."[162] If we take Nietzsche's perspectivism seriously, the task would be to provide precisely an endless interpretation of "this actual world" and the "other supersensory world." It is hard not to see an inconsistency in Cox's approach, since an appeal to such a basic fact – which is essential to defend naturalism – runs contrary to the supposed fundamentality of perspectivism and interpretation. It attributes an unequivocal concept of "truth" to Nietzsche, after all, to at least claim him as a "naturalist," even if it is said that this naturalism is internally consistent with a sort of perspectivism.[163] It appears that the naturalists are more Heideggerian than they would want to admit.

Internalists such as Michel Haar also grant the basic Heideggerian argument that Nietzsche takes the most popular understanding of metaphysics as granted without prior examination. This understanding is none other than the supposition that metaphysics is the "belief in 'another world', in a world that is ideal and true in itself."[164] Haar holds that Heidegger is right in insisting that Nietzsche holds the doctrine of "two worlds" to be the essence of metaphysics.[165] But he also defines the Nietzschean concept of metaphysics as any thought that "opposes" a true world to the world of appearances, thus equating this latter condition to the previous one (as the belief in another world).[166] Haar goes onto argue against Heidegger that although Nietzsche's philosophy "originates" in the overturning of Platonism, "nothing in

---

158 Cox 71–72.

159 Cox 105.

160 Cox 71.

161 Cox 96.

162 Cox 96.

163 Schacht is also guilty of similar problems, although his arguments unfold in a different way. See his *Nietzsche*, especially chapters II, III and IV.

164 Haar ix.

165 Haar x.

166 Haar x.

his philosophy can be reduced it."[167] The key to Haar's argument is the claim that Nietzsche does not just invert the order of metaphysical binary oppositions, but he provides an "immanent" critique of it.[168] This critique involves a new interpretation of sensibility or the world of appearances that undermines the very possibility of permanence or self-identity, which Haar takes to be also the essential features of any metaphysical thought. Hence Nietzsche's interpretation of sensibility "makes impossible the restoration, pure and simple, of metaphysics or its 'completion', that is to say its absolutization."[169] I suggest that Haar's reading is typical of the internalist position, which does not question the Heideggerian interpretation of the *starting point* of Nietzsche's critique of metaphysics, but diverges from Heidegger in their understanding of where Nietzsche ends given this starting point.[170]

Traditional existentialist accounts such as those of Jaspers, Fink and Kaufmann also see, like Heidegger, the gist of Nietzsche's critique of metaphysics in its oppositional stance to "other-worldly" evaluations that condemns and denies "this" world of suffering and becoming. In contrast to all these approaches, I argue that we need to fundamentally re-orient ourselves with respect to Nietzsche's critique of metaphysics. It is not simply the setting up of a real supersensible world of being *in itself* that is problematic for Nietzsche, but rather the oppositional schema between a real world and an apparent world, which is the hallmark of metaphysical evaluation. The latter insight focuses more on "how" metaphysics comes to evaluate life, and not "what" it evaluates. It is Nietzsche's own remarks in the second section of *Beyond Good and Evil* about the nature of metaphysics – that it believes in "oppositions of values" – that I want to express with this insight. What Nietzsche means here is that, *because an oppositional value schema has been set up*, it has led to the invention of a "pure" realm (which he calls the "real world") that is more highly valued. The former condition is prior and more decisive than the latter. So if metaphysics denies life (we have to still see how this is possible), it is because of its oppositional schema, and not because of the mere setting up of the real world. Nietzsche confirms this reading when he notes that if his philosophy abolishes the "real world," it is not to hold onto the merely sensory, "apparent world": "*with the real world we have also abolished the apparent world*" (TI Real World). This means that his critique of metaphysics aims to abolish the very opposition of values, which posits a real world in opposition to an apparent world.

---

167 Haar xi.

168 Haar x.

169 Haar xi.

170 Müller-Lauter has a similar argument as Haar to undermine Heidegger's interpretation. For him, Nietzsche's critique of metaphysics does not end with a mere inversion of metaphysics but to a self-destruction of it through the depiction of reality as essentially groundless. The "contradiction" and the plurality of impulses that signify reality cannot be reconciled and traced back into a foundational ground or unity. See Müller-Lauter, *Nietzsche*, especially chapter 8.

Therefore a body's affirmation of the objective tendency in itself – by which it posits a world of being and truth – does not imply a metaphysical evaluation that denies life; on the contrary, this affirmation is an expression of the body's will to power. Nietzsche is not simply aiming to overcome the metaphysical need or the will to truth in his critique of metaphysics; so the central task he assigns to himself and to the future philosophers, I suggest, is to call into question not so much the will to truth itself but the "metaphysical faith" in the value of truth or to inquire into the meaning of all *unconditional* will to truth (or "truth at any price"), which leads to a denial of life (GM III 24, 27; GS 344).[171]

Hence we must distinguish the "metaphysical need" from what Nietzsche calls "metaphysics" (which is characterized by an evaluation that denies life). It is the oppositional schema "behind" the body's expression of its metaphysical need that is problematic for Nietzsche, which could potentially make a body's affirmation of its objective (or subjective) tendency an expression of its metaphysical will to deny life. In other words, a body's expression of its metaphysical need – whether through objective or subjective affirmation – does not *necessarily* imply the metaphysical will to deny life, since this need is itself an expression of its will to enhance power. What follows from this is that the mere quantitative aspects of the will to enhance power are not sufficient conditions for us to determine that the evaluating body does not commit the metaphysical evaluation of life-denial. Therefore to fully understand Nietzsche's critique of metaphysics, we need another criterion than the present one we have employed in the analysis of the objective and the subjective tendencies of existence, where we have considered only the quantitative dimension of the will to power – such as the notions of the "amount" of power or growth – as decisive. We need to explore the qualitative aspect of will to power, which will introduce us to a *typology* of wills – "affirmative" or "strong" type of will and "negative" ("denying") or "weak" type of will – and this qualitative dimension will lead us to the problem of origin of the oppositional schema of evaluations which is the essence of metaphysics. We will address these important issues in the following chapters.

---

171 In these passages, Nietzsche critiques and calls into question modern science as well insofar as the latter, too, has the metaphysical faith in an unconditional will to truth. It seems to me that this critique of science applies just as well to all naturalistic interpretations insofar as they too ascribe to Nietzsche, even if unwittingly, something like an unconditional will to truth by appealing to the self-evidence of the natural world with which we are supposedly "intimately acquainted." If naturalists deny that they are indeed ascribing such a position to Nietzsche, then it is hard to see why Nietzsche's philosophy must be seen as methodologically consistent with the best available sciences or why it must read primarily through the naturalistic lens, since it would appear that Nietzsche is more interested in affirming the interplay between the "scientific" and the "artistic" perspectives, which keeps the unconditional will to truth at bay. The naturalists would do well to heed to Nietzsche's own warning: "Whoever ... tries to place philosophy 'on a strictly scientific foundation' [instead of the other way round], first needs to *stand not only philosophy on its head* but truth itself as well: the worst offence against decency ..." (GM III 24).

Human, All-Too-Human: metaphysics and the struggle between science and art

In *Human, All-Too-Human*[172] – the first volume of which was published in 1878 after his decisive break with Wagner and Schopenhauer – Nietzsche begins his all-out confrontation and critique of metaphysics. In this book, more so than in his later works, his criticism of metaphysics seemingly takes on a positivistic-naturalistic tone, where he upholds the methodology and virtues of what he calls "science," and anticipates the future "free spirits" as having championed a scientific rigor that has delivered them from old metaphysical shadows and errors. But I will argue in this section that Nietzsche's argument is better understood in terms of a subjective-objective interpretative interplay, where both science and art are seen to be mutually implicating each other. I will suggest that Nietzsche does not simply overcome metaphysics through his concept of science, but that his ambiguous critique of metaphysics must be sought in this interplay between science and art.

Nietzsche's avowed project in *Human* is to debunk and demystify the metaphysical[173] pretensions of philosophy, religion, morality and art by exposing their all-too-human origins, motivations and errors. For this purpose, he decidedly invents and employs his acute "psychology"[174] to discern what lies behind the surface of metaphysical thought, reading the latter as signs and symptoms of deeper, hidden, but earthly and modest origins that invoke the confusions, dreams, superstitions, fears and hopes of *this* world.[175] In doing so, he reclaims the "virtue of modesty" (HH I 2). This constitutes the first step of his complex argument, where he translates the evaluations of metaphysics back into the sphere of life. To this end, Nietzsche also employs a "historical" method of philosophizing (that seeks out hidden origins) in conjunction with the psychological approach.[176] Nietzsche's translation of metaphysical evaluations back into the sphere of life may be read in either one of the following two ways.

It may be interpreted as a subjective interpretation of a supposed objectivity. Here the "objective" claims of "being" and "truth" made by metaphysics are seen from the perspective of "humanly" sensibilities, becoming and errors, which "science" (as a combination of Nietzsche's peculiar psychology and historical method) aims to unveil. Or it may be equally read as an objective interpretation of a supposed

---

172 Henceforth referred to as *Human*.

173 What exactly makes these pretensions "metaphysical" and how Nietzsche can claim that philosophy, religion, morality and art are guilty of a metaphysical fallacy are the key questions, with which we shall deal below.

174 See HH I Preface 8 and AOM Preface 1.

175 In *Ecce Homo*, Nietzsche later sums up his achievement in *Human* by writing, "where *you* see ideal things, *I* see what is – human, alas, all-too-human!" (EH Human 1).

176 HH I 1, 2, 10, 17.

subjectivity, taking Nietzsche's descriptions about the "superstitious,"[177] mystifying, unclear, falsifying and boastful qualities of metaphysics as aspects of its subjective nature. The latter is now measured up to the rigor of objective-scientific method that estimates "little unpretentious truths," which are closer to life (HH I 3). In the text, Nietzsche's own analysis of science and his critique of metaphysics do in fact display a constant oscillation between the objective and the subjective viewpoints. The fact that Nietzsche's translation of metaphysics into the realm of life could be plausibly read in either one of these two directions, confirms our earlier argument that the subjective and objective tendencies are thoroughly interpretative concepts with fluid meanings. This reveals that Nietzsche's endorsement of science in *Human* has a fundamentally ambiguous meaning, since "science" could be read either as an instantiation of the subjective tendency or an objective one. Either way, what we can say for certain is that Nietzsche immediately undertakes a differential critique rather than beginning with an oppositional one that entertains something like "pure" objectivity or subjectivity.

I want to pause and compare the interpretation offered here to that of Jacques Derrida who reads Nietzsche as a precursor to his philosophy of "deconstruction." According to Derrida's *"general theory of deconstruction,"* deconstruction is a *"double science"* the first stage of which consists of an "overturning" or reversal of the "violent hierarchy" of binary oppositions that make up metaphysical thought.[178] Deconstruction's first stage is comparable to Heidegger's thesis that Nietzsche reverses the evaluations of metaphysics by favoring the other term in the oppositional structure ("body" as opposed to "mind," "error" and "becoming" as opposed to "truth" and "being"). The deconstructive reading implies that, in order to overturn, Nietzsche's critique must, at least temporarily, submit to metaphysical discourse, its standards of truth and its oppositional schema. For Derrida, "the necessity of this stage is structural [since] the hierarchy of dual oppositions always reestablishes itself."[179] Only then can one proceed to the second stage of the deconstruction, which entails a "displacement," a "dislodging" that involves a kind of retraction of the earlier submission in such a way that the very schema of metaphysical opposition is annulled and replaced by a non-conceptual, interpretative play of differences.[180] However, Derrida's starting point (at the first stage of deconstruction), like that of the other internalists, is the same as Heidegger's interpretation of Nietzsche's critique of metaphysics, which requires that Nietzsche succumb to the oppositional discourse of metaphysics.

But this is precisely where the reading I have put forward varies. Nietzsche's meta-existentialism, which radicalizes Climacus' existential approach, takes existence as the ultimate presupposition; straightaway, it interprets the evaluations of metaphys-

---

177 See HH I 20, 110.
178 Derrida, *Positions* 41–42.
179 Derrida, *Positions* 42.
180 Derrida, *Positions* 42–44.

ics as involved in an ongoing differential, interpretative struggle between the subjective and the objective tendencies, without the need to first acknowledge or submit to the oppositional structure of metaphysics. This is evidenced, for example, in the argumentative structure of *Human*. Nietzsche's thought does not feel the impending weight of the "hierarchy of dual oppositions" that threatens to reestablish itself, as Derrida's thought does. The internalists, including Derrida, miss this radical aspect of Nietzsche's existentialism precisely since they do not really pay attention to the existential dimension of Nietzsche's philosophy. Although the second stage of the deconstructive process has numerous commonalities with the differential-interpretative exchange between the subjective and the objective discussed above, the initial stage of the deconstructive argument betrays the meta-existential position of Nietzsche, which bypasses the need to submit to an oppositional discourse.

Let us return to our discussion of *Human*. The aphoristic style of writing, which Nietzsche inaugurates in *Human*, complements his psychological-historical approach and his perspectivism. In their fragmentary, yet meaningful way, these aphorisms demonstrate how terms which are usually held to be opposites by metaphysics actually differ only in terms of degrees, and usually share similar origins, assuming that one of the terms does not actually originate from the other (for example, "vice" from "virtue"). This practice perfectly complements the psychological unraveling of metaphysical concepts, by showing that the latter have all-too-human origins. Nietzsche's fluid movement between these terms, often conflating any exaggerated distinction between them, performs precisely the function of translating the oppositions of metaphysics into gradations of differences involved in a mutual interplay. To take but one example, in *Assorted Opinions and Maxims*, Nietzsche observes that the path to virtue might consist of apparent "vices" or "impure" motives such as "utility, personal comfort, fear, considerations of health, of fame or refutation," but we still embark on such paths provided they incite us to so-called virtues like "renunciation, dutifulness, orderliness, thrift, measure and moderation," since once these virtues are achieved, they "*ennoble[]*" the remoter motives "through the pure air it lets us breathe and the psychical pleasure it communicates" (AOM 91). In this typical short aphorism, Nietzsche unravels the continuity between concepts, here between vices and virtues, which are usually held to be opposites by Christian moralists. Similarly, in another aphorism he remarks that not "every good thing has always had a good conscience," and that good conscience "has a preliminary stage, the bad conscience – the latter is not its opposite: for everything good was once new ... contrary to custom, *immoral*, and gnawed at the heart of its fortunate inventor like a worm" (AOM 90). In this aphorism, Nietzsche's intention is not simply to trace good conscience back to bad conscience (and thereby undertake an overturning or reversal of a traditional hierarchy), since "bad conscience" has the sense it does only in its metaphysical opposition to "good conscience." Instead, in tracing the original manifestation of the good back to something new and contrary to custom, Nietzsche is dissolving straightaway any opposition between good and bad consciences.

Coming back to the more substantial arguments of *Human*, we must note that there is an underlying assessment and evaluation of modernity and its culture that runs parallel to the critique of metaphysics and morality. For Nietzsche, to confront the chaos and the promise of modernity in an honest way, one must first ruthlessly clear its ground, in order to get rid of all mystifying and unclear interpretations, mostly handed down from history, so that the future is ready to adopt a scientific free spirit. To this end, he sets out to attack what he calls the "metaphysical need" – to be distinguished from our use of this term – which he sees not only in the philosophy, religion and art from earlier times, but especially in the latest philosophies and cultural movements of his time, such as Schopenhauer's pessimism and German romanticism (HH I 26). In Nietzsche's sense, the metaphysical need is not associated with that which drives the creators of religions or metaphysical systems, but with that which preserves them (the followers of religions and philosophies) through an unconditionally positive evaluation of truth. Therefore Nietzsche uses this term more in the context of his critique of modern culture, society and philosophies, which are not courageous enough to dispel the need for the shadows of old metaphysical constructs, whose real meaning is, strictly speaking, lost on them.[181] For Nietzsche, this need, so conceived, *must* be overcome for the future growth of modern humanity.[182]

And so in *Human*, Nietzsche laments that, even though Schopenhauer comprehends all the illusions of philosophy and religion, he does not use this comprehension to liberate himself and affirm life. Instead, he gives into the metaphysical need, and devices a pessimistic philosophy, which conceives "willing" itself as the cause of all suffering, and therefore proposes denial of willing as the only means of salvation. For Nietzsche, the negative judgment upon life implied in Schopenhauer's diagnosis of life and his proposed cure is not much different from the metaphysics that Nietzsche reads in the Christian conception of the world; it is, in fact, an honest and extreme consequence of it. The problem, Nietzsche remarks, is that in Schopenhauer, "the scientific spirit is not yet sufficiently strong" (HH I 26). Similarly, Nietzsche finds the Reformation as having undone the advancements made by the youthful science of Renaissance, and likewise, he reads German idealism and romanticism as retrogressive, re-instilling a weak moral-metaphysical-religious tendency back into the intellectual terrain after the achievements of scientific spirits such as Voltaire. In the spirit of Renaissance and French Enlightenment, Nietzsche launches his uncompromising effort to "overcome metaphysics," but also to grasp the "historical" and "psychologi-

---

181 In *The Gay Science*, he associates the "metaphysical need" particularly with a need of his contemporary Europeans who cling to Christianity since it provides a "foothold, support," and therefore belongs to their *"instinct of weakness"* (GS 347).

182 As I have argued in the previous section, Nietzsche does not recommend a simple overcoming of metaphysical need in our sense of the term, since the latter refers to the conditions of growth and preservation of a life-form, and is hence an expression of its will to growth.

cal" justification that resides in metaphysical ideas (HH I 20).[183] Morality and religion were essential for humankind because they provided a sense of security, meaning and direction to people's lives, by offering a mythology of meaning as an "ultimate foundation upon which the whole future of mankind is then invited to establish and construct itself" (HH I 22). Their concern was essentially one of utility. In fact, the first indication that "animal has become man" is when man has made the leap to ask the broader question of utility and "enduring wellbeing," after having overcome the base need of mere "procurement of momentary wellbeing" (HH I 94).[184]

Specifically, religion has served the useful purpose of interpreting humankind's illnesses and weakness by "changing the effect it produces on our sensibilities," for example by "changing our judgment as to the nature of our experiences" or "through awakening the ability to take pleasure in pain" even if this meant investing in a belief that redemption is to be found in an after-life or in another, more perfect, less sinful world, thus robbing the present world of its good conscience and innocence (HH I 108). Religion has given hope for the weary by creating fictions and resorting to erroneous inferences, like that concerning causality ("the supposed cause is inferred from the effect and introduced *after* the effect" (HH I 13)). Art, too, like religion, endeavors "to bring about a change of sensibility" (HH I 108). In fact, art merely "takes over a host of moods and feelings engendered by religion" insofar as it belongs to a later stage in the progression of human history (HH I 150). Even when one has overcome the need for religion and philosophy, one clings to art since it serves the "metaphysical need," even if by "deliberately and playfully embellish[ing] life with lies" (HH I 153, 154). But all of these metaphysical projects were *necessary* at different points of human history, and are historically justified since a belief in these projects served a purpose, and furthered the flourishing and growth of humankind. Whether interpreted objectively or subjectively, they are expressions of a culture's will to enhance its power, and therefore, Nietzsche is insistent upon historically justifying these metaphysical projections. However, he also argues that modernity has no need for these old metaphysical constructs and illusions. Religious superstitions and metaphysical mythologies have lost their hold on modern man, and thus he is ready for a new Enlightenment, if only he can find the courage and the strength to shrug off the need to find comforts in the old ideals.

To bring his modern readers to acknowledge the great task impending on them, Nietzsche provides an account of the "origin of religion, art and morality," without the "postulation of *metaphysical interference*," by tracing them back to drives, needs,

---

183 As we shall see, this effort does not yield a straightforward, unambiguous overcoming of metaphysics. I suggest that in section 20, where Nietzsche is motivating the effort to "overcome metaphysics," he is talking about a "high level of culture's" ability to leave its old superstitions and "metaphysical needs" behind.

184 Nietzsche advances similar arguments regarding the becoming and emergence of humans from their animal past in GM, especially the second essay of this book.

utilities and affects, with the aid of "physiology and history" (HH I 10). His psycho-logical method opposes the host of "psychological error[s] and insensibilit[ies]" that belong to the history of metaphysics, which has always had a certain "blind faith in the goodness of human nature, an innate aversion to the dissection of human actions," essential as these errors are for the "total happiness of the individual" and general humanity (HH I 36). Nietzsche employs his psychology to smoke these errors and confusions out of their hiding places. In thus exposing the errors behind previously held "truths," we may say that Nietzsche is affirming a subjective tendency of modernity by reinterpreting the previous affirmation of an objective tendency accordingly.[185]

In his interpretation of history, Nietzsche sees a continuous progression from religion to art, which inherits the "wealth of feelings" from the former, and he sees another progression from art to what he calls "science" (HH I 222). There is a logical development of "science" from art because what art adds to the evolving metaphysical spirit is also something positive, which is the ability to "look upon life in any of its form with interest and pleasure" and to say, "life, however it may be, is good!" even if it had to create illusions and falsities to do so (HH I 222). The most important contribution of art is that it teaches that human life is a part of nature, a discovery that Nietzsche thinks is a crucial requirement of knowledge in his novel conception of science. Therefore the scientific human being is the further development of the artistic. However, Nietzsche maintains that this "true science" which is the product of "Enlightenment" and is the symbol of the "progressive *masculinization* of man" (HH I 147), is indifferent to religion and metaphysical philosophy (HH I 110). The "needs which religion [and philosophy] have satisfied" can be "*weakened* and *exterminated*" (HH I 27). The new scientific Renaissance, even though, it retains the artistic-cheerful disposition towards life, has extinguished the dramatic, emotional, confounding effects of art and religion, which lead to an over-excitation of the nervous and thinking powers, and has replaced them by objectivity and clarity. The scientific spirit makes one more skeptical and it "cools down the fiery stream of belief in ultimate definitive truths" (HH I 244).

But in exactly what way is the new science anti-metaphysical? In *Human*, Nietzsche defines the "metaphysical outlook" as the "deification of becoming" (HH I 238). Through its deification, metaphysics posits a world of being, truth and constancy. It fabricates a "real" world of being in order to provide a mythology of meaning for people, and also offer them, in a religious-moral form, a hope of redemption in "another" world. However, affirming the tendency towards being and truth and fabricating an illusory "real" world does not necessarily imply a denial of life. It only reveals the metaphysical need (in our sense of the word) or the will to truth of religion and art, and their creators, and is the vehicle for the enhancement of power

---

185 But equally, Nietzsche's argument may be read as the affirmation of an objective tendency, which exposes the truths of previous subjective errors and superstitions.

of a particular life-form. Constructing an illusory world in itself is no objection against religion because, as we shall see, Nietzsche's new "true science" is also in need of illusions insofar as it seeks to grow and enhance power. Nietzsche's science, too, expresses its own metaphysical need (or a will to truth), although it does not express an unconditional will to truth. Hence "deification of becoming," as a criterion, does not by itself capture the life-denying aspect of metaphysics. However, an evaluation that posits a fabricated world of being *could* entail a denial of life, if the evaluation inherently springs from an oppositional schema, and we would need another criterion to determine whether this is the case or not with respect to a particular evaluation.

Nietzsche, for sure, has the conviction that whatever he is attacking meets the metaphysical criterion of life-denial.[186] He argues, for example, that metaphysics wishes that things were otherwise in this world, that this world was not a mere world of appearances and becoming, that there were some secure ground to stand upon, that suffering and contradictions of this world were not necessary, that man's actions and deeds "need *not* have taken place of necessity" (HH I 39). Morality, for instance, rests on the "error of freedom of will," and therefore of the "error of accountability"; it teaches man to regard himself as free, so that "he feels remorse and pangs of conscience" about his sensual drives and lust (HH I 39). But the consequence of such moral and religious evaluation is a negative interpretation of the world: earthly existence itself is viewed as a sin, as if through free will one willed oneself into existence. For Nietzsche, this mythology of free will rests on an error and fable.[187] We are not born guilty, we are neither born nor suffer because we have sinned: "No one is accountable for his deeds, no one for his nature; to judge is the same thing as to be unjust" (HH I 39). Therefore, against metaphysics, the new science acknowledges that we are born innocent, and we are innocent in our actions, whether they are considered good or bad: "everything here is necessary, every motion mathematically calculable. So it is too in the case of human actions" (HH I 106). The "new knowledge" of science sees the necessity in nature, a necessity for which metaphysics had previously, but senselessly, censured nature (HH I 107). It sees that "everything is innocence, and knowledge is the path to insight into this innocence," a path which is itself necessary (HH I 107). In this way, the new knowledge affirms the necessity of the previous metaphysical delusion of free will as well. Initially at least, the new science is not concerned with passing judgment on the entirely of life, but only with comprehension. Thus Nietzsche hopes for a transformation from "*a moral to a knowing mankind*" (HH I 107).

Nietzsche reveals his apparent "naturalism" when he writes that the "philosophical science" (HH I 27) of the future is the "*imitation of nature in concepts*"; like "nature," science "knows no regard for final objectives" (HH I 38). Philosophical science loses the old question of *telos* – "to what end? of what utility?" – pursued

---

186 In HH I 1, he notes that the "metaphysics" he is attacking is characterized by a faith in value oppositions, which in our analysis accounts for the denial of life.
187 We will return to Nietzsche's claim that free will is an error in the next chapter on will to power.

by metaphysics since Plato (HH I 6). It does not read or interpret spiritual things into nature. Nietzsche asserts that the science of the future "could assert nothing at all of the metaphysical world [i.e. the supersensible world of being] except that it was a being-other, an inaccessible, incomprehensible being-other" (HH I 9). Instead of aiming at eternal truths that belie the world of becoming, it would focus on "little unpretentious truths" that are closer at hand, on "viable, enduring knowledge," and also on "simplicity" and clarity instead of "splendid, intoxicating and ... enrapturing" insights (HH I 3). Science is therefore closer to the roots of the world than arts or religions are, which are more like sublimated fruits of the world. Since Nietzsche's new science is not concerned (initially, at least) with the eternal truths and mythologies of meanings that bind cultures and generations, it is well suited to the fragmentary, polyphonic and restless nature of modernity. It captures the spirit of modernity by not conceding that religious phenomena like holiness or asceticism are inexplicable because of their supernatural and miraculous quality; instead, it would venture an explanation of them in terms of individual and complex drives, and thus it would reveal their all-too-human origins (HH I 136). Against the moralizing tendency, science sees that "the world is neither good nor evil," and these concepts "possess meaning only when [unjustifiably] applied to men" (HH I 28). Science must also counter art's belief in "miraculous suddenness," its illusions and falsifications of life, its false conclusions, and its fascination for the "fantastic, mythical, uncertain, extreme, the sense for the symbolical" (HH I 145, 146). It should replace these propensities with its own "cooling ways," which would again be a remedy for modernity (which is the heir of two millennia of cultures, art, religion and philosophy), in which the "the sum of sensations, items of knowledge, experiences, the whole burden of culture... has become so great that an over-excitation of the nervous and thinking power is now a universal danger" (HH I 244).

What really becomes of what I have called the metaphysical need? Is it completely dispelled by the modern free spirit? Is Nietzsche saying that modernity and its future would be content in existing as merely a "scientific" culture, having cast away the illusions of metaphysics, art and morality forever, limiting itself to little unpretentious truths, without ever needing to asking the loftier question about the meaning of its own existence? Does it have some "inhuman" strength to endure life without ever falsifying it? If Nietzsche's answers to the last two questions are affirmative, then he is indeed a positivist-naturalist, who is operating in some fantastic post-metaphysical terrain. But we can anticipate what Nietzsche's response to these questions might be. The new science and future humankind spearheaded by the free spirits are indeed conceived with the condition that they eliminate the "metaphysical need" (in Nietzsche's sense of the word) of current humanity, and there is no conceptual reason for us to doubt that the new scientific culture would not do this. From a methodological viewpoint, the removal of this metaphysical need is not only possible, but also necessary, since with the affirmation of the new science, Nietzsche is envisaging a differential change in perspective of modernity from an objective to a subjective tendency (or vice versa). The "self-overcoming" of modernity through the affirmation of the new science requires that the lingering metaphysical need must vanish, and the old metaphysical ways of thinking be re-interpreted from the current viewpoint as inimical to future existence and growth of modernity. However, this also implies that the affirmation of the new science cannot dispense with the "metaphysical need" in our sense of the term, since it is only through an expression of the latter can modernity express its basic life-instinct to grow. In other words, if future humankind affirms the scientific tendency to discover unpretentious truths, it would also need the aid of its own versions of falsifications and illusions regarding existence in order to express its instinct to enhance power.

And so we must not be surprised to find key passages where Nietzsche concedes the importance of the latter metaphysical need for the future humankind as conditions of the latter's preservation and growth. For example, in the passage, "Error regarding life necessary to life," Nietzsche acknowledges that fundamentally one cannot exist or endure living without a "belief in the value and dignity of life" (HH I 33). But such a belief is gained only by falsifying life, by limiting oneself to a relatively constant perspective of a firm and fixed horizon which fences off others, and therefore, does not participate in the "universal life and suffering of mankind," which would lead one to "despair of the value of life" (HH I 33). However, this belief in life is gained only at the expense of a judgment on the whole of life, as to the "value of life" (HH I 32). Fixation of life is nothing but an "objectification" of life, an evaluation of life. The latter is an expression of the truth-drive, the "will to truth," through which one secures one's own horizon of perspectives in order to further exert one's domain of power. If Nietzsche had detected a drive towards truth in the old religions and moralities – which posit a second world of being – purchased at the price of a falsification of existence, he envisions a similar phenomenon with respect to his projection for a future humanity. Both instances are expressions of what I have termed the metaphysical need. This is the reason why the truly "metaphysical" aspect that Nietzsche attacks in the religions, morality and art cannot consist in the expression of the latter's metaphysical need, or in the fact that the latter set up an illusory world of truth and being, since Nietzsche's future culture is also guilty of similar needs and illusions as expressions of its basic life-instinct to grow.

Elsewhere, Nietzsche calls the "truthful" judgment concerning life an "antinatural tendency" (KSA 13, 11[115]), which is surely a damaging observation for a naturalist interpreter. Such a truthful judgment is essentially illogical and unjust, as "all evaluations are premature and are bound to be," since we cannot gain a perspective outside of life insofar as we judge as living, existing beings (HH I 32). Even though it is not possible to live without evaluating, without having aversions and partialities, our evaluations nonetheless falsify the conditions of life, and are illusory and unjust. Therefore, the judging individual's "will to truth" is unavoidably bound up with a fundamental process of falsification. Nietzsche calls this "the greatest and most irresolvable discords of existence" (HH I 32). The "illogical is a necessity for mankind," and to "recover nature," one must recover the "*illogical original relationship with all things*" (HH I 31).

The necessity of the illogical and illusory for future humankind is furthered concretized by Nietzsche when he ponders about the necessity for a kind of "non-science," a kind of *art* to complement the new science of future (HH I 251). He discusses how the new science would give one who "labors and experiments" and the one who casts "suspicion on the consolations of metaphysics, religion and art" less and less satisfaction, since these consolations are precisely what gave "joy" to humankind for centuries (HH I 251). The joy afforded by the falsifications of religion, art and metaphysics is a "demand of health," on which the possibility of a future "higher culture" depends (HH I 251). Therefore the "cooling" ways of science must still be "heated with illusions, onesidednesses, passions, the evil" which is the domain of "metaphysics" or "art" (HH I 251).[188] So from the perspective of the health and growth of the future culture, Nietzsche argues that "art" should complement the new science; he speaks of a "*many-stringed* culture" (HH I 281), in which science and art co-exist, and are involved in an "audacious dance" (HH I 278). The higher culture "must give to man a double-brain, as it were two brain-ventricles, one for the perceptions of science, the other for those of non-science" (HH I 251). To be sure, these two elements must be separated and not be confused; they must lie "beside one another" (HH I 251).

These arguments do not prove that Nietzsche is inconsistent, but rather they reveal the complexity and ambiguity of his relation to metaphysics. They indicate that he is not simply aiming to "overcome" metaphysics in the name of some pure "science," and much less is he seeking to abolish what I have termed the metaphysical need.[189] Even the new science must be complemented by art. And this necessity

---

188 In HH I 154, he notes that a strong culture of an earlier period – the Homeric one – made use of art in order to soothe their "over-subtle intellect" because of which life appeared "cruel and bitter." Due to the demands of health, the Greeks willfully and actively adopted the "Homeric fantasy," and art in general which provided them "enjoyment" by "deliberately and playfully embellish[ing] life with lies." In many ways, it would appear that Nietzsche's critique of metaphysics from the scientific point of view in *Human* is inspired by his reading of Ancient Greek culture. His contention in his earlier unpublished lectures on the Greeks is that the distinguishing mark of the Homeric people is their noble, scientific spirit, which distinguishes them from their Asiatic origins (which was essentially wrapped in superstitions and false beliefs). Nietzsche sees that the greatest danger for modernity is that it would lack the courage to relinquish the safety net that is provided by religions and philosophies of older times, and continue to nihilistically adopt them, even if it is not capable of producing any new metaphysical inventions of its own. Thus by emulating the Greeks, he seeks to re-install the scientific spirit in modern man. In this way, we can make sense of his overt recommendations for a new "philosophical science" and his "naturalistic" undertones in this work. But this is just *one* side of his solutions for modernity, since even the Greeks needed art and metaphysics.
189 We could speculate from the point of view of his later works whether the positivistic tone in *Human* is a kind of exaggeration that he felt he had to undertake in order to dispel the metaphysical hangovers of his modern readers to make room for his later philosophy, or whether moving over to the scientific side is something he had to do for himself in order to compensate for his earlier "aber-

cannot be grounded from within the nature of science or scientific method, since, as Nietzsche argues, these two things must be held separate. Rather, this necessity expresses the demand of the basic life-instinct to grow (in terms of the growth of the future culture), which is behind the affirmation of the new science. In *Human*, Nietzsche reveals what a perspectival-differential interplay between the affirmations of the subjective and the objective tendencies looks like by showing how science and art mutually implicate and depend upon one another. The new science, in tandem with art, creates relatively stable worlds by championing multiple perspectives with the "greatest circumspection," and thus enacting the play of affirmations between the two tendencies, which do not oppose one another, but differ only in terms of degrees (HH I 635). Therefore the mutual struggle between science and art is better understood from the perspective of a meta-existentialist project, which reveals a series of self-overcomings that alternates between the subjective and the objective tendencies, and in which the existential distinction (conceived as the dynamic gap between science and art) is redrawn again and again. In this play of affirmations, Nietzsche indirectly reveals something about existence and its becoming, warped nature. Even though at the time of writing *Human*, Nietzsche had not yet formulated the idea of the will to power, this work can be read as already anticipating the genealogical and existential themes, which he would explore in his later works. From this viewpoint, his task in his later works remains the same as what he considered to be his project in *The Birth of Tragedy*: namely, to view science through the prism of the artist, but also to look at art through the prism of life.

Nietzsche's critique of metaphysics is caught up in the prismatic struggle between science and art. Right at the outset, he places the evaluations of traditional religion, morality, philosophy and art as part of a differential-interpretative conflict between the objective and the subjective tendencies, in order to overcome these evaluations in modernity and affirm the contrary perspective. For now, we have left open the question of how Nietzsche knows, that the metaphysics he attacks actually denies life, and thus has at its basis an oppositional structure of values, and is not just a kind of falsification of life that once provided goals and directions to culture.

At any rate, Nietzsche's affirmation of the new science, complemented by art, picks up and continues the differential critique of the subjective and the objective tendencies, showing how the previous instance of falsification by the metaphysical need is overcome in the next instance of falsification, and so on. In the series of overcomings the metaphysical need is affirmed, overcome and affirmed again in a different fashion, but not just overcome once and for all. The affirmation of the metaphysical

---

ration of [] instincts" and "idealism" that lead him to place trust in Wagner's art and Schopenhauer's metaphysics (EH Human 3). In the latter case, as Nietzsche himself notes, this "scientific" book had a therapeutic value and it signified a "return" to himself, and a "supreme kind of recovery" by which he cast off what did not belong deeply to him (EH Human 4). The positivistic call to embrace a methodology of "science" would then be mostly an occasion for Nietzsche's own return to himself.

need occurs already *within* the structure of the differential play, as the expression of the conditions of preservation and growth of a life-form. It cannot be relegated simply to the status of some "necessary evil" in the two-step process of deconstructive "textual strategy" by which, as the internalists argue, Nietzsche reverses the hierarchy of oppositions of metaphysics (and thereby temporarily subscribes to this very oppositional structure). Nietzsche's critique of metaphysics endlessly unfolds within the continuous and differential struggle of overcomings. Nietzsche begins with a differential critique of metaphysics and ends with it, and so there is no final step to his critique of metaphysics, after which one could claim that he has overcome or refuted it. In this sense, his meta-existentialist critique goes hand-in-hand with the ambiguity and the elusiveness of the existential distinction.

Our next task is to go beyond the merely quantitative aspect of the will to power, to which we have limited ourselves in this chapter, and examine its qualitative aspect. For this, we must examine what is meant by will to power. In our analysis, we will also be able to shed light on a vital problem left unanswered in this chapter, namely the source of the oppositional schema of evaluations, which is characteristic of metaphysics and its will to deny life.

Chapter Three
Will to power: existence and the qualitative aspect of power

The critique of cause and effect and the will to power

The "will to power" (*Der Wille zur Macht*) is perhaps the most central concept of Nietzsche's mature philosophy. This phrase first appears in his published works in the first part of *Thus Spoke Zarathustra*,[190] where Nietzsche calls the tablet of things held to be good by a people, and which hangs over it, the voice of its will to power, which is also its tablet of "overcomings" (Z I 15). Then in an important section entitled, "On Self-Overcoming," Zarathustra traces back the essence of the living, its basic life-instinct – which aims for growth and expansion for the sake of which it may sacrifice life itself – to the will to power (Z II 12). The claim that the essence of "life" or "world" is the will to power is repeated in numerous places in Nietzsche's subsequent writings.[191] Will to power not only denotes the ultimate principle of organic functions, of human actions and impulses, but also of the inorganic world and the cosmos. In other words, will to power is the essence of existence.

To explain what is meant by will to power, let us discuss Nietzsche's critique of the traditional understanding of cause and effect, which, according to him, governs both usual cosmological theories about the world and also moral understandings of human life and purpose. I have chosen the theme of causality to explain the notion of will to power, because, in Nietzsche's writings (especially his published works), the passages where he carries out a critical assessment of causality usually leads to a critique of "free will" and finally to that of the very concept of the "will" as a simple unity.[192] Through the latter critique, we may transition to an analysis of the will to power. There

---

190 There are quite a few passages in *Human All-Too-Human*, *Daybreak* and *The Gay Science* where Nietzsche analyzes one's actions or motivations by attributing them to one's compulsion to demonstrate "power" without actually using the term "will to power." For example, he notes that for a person of power, the act of gratitude towards his or her benefactor is a form of revenge, since it demonstrates and restores one's powerful status, which had been compromised due to the action of benefaction (HH I 44). In another passage, the origin of "vanity" is connected to the powerful person's strategy to "augment *belief* in his power" and also to his "*need for the feeling of power*" (WS 181; D 189). In *Daybreak*, Nietzsche attributes the source of moral concepts such as "rights" and "duty" to power-relationships (D 112). He also traces back the impetus behind "striving for distinction" (D 113), "cruelty" and "voluntary suffering" (D 18), "self-control" (D 65) and the condemnation of the "guilty" (D 140) to the feeling of power. Also see GS 13 ("On the doctrine of the feeling of power").
191 See GS 349; BGE 36, 186, 259; GM II 12; and also some of the *Nachlaß* notes of the 1880s, especially KSA 12, 2[189–190], KSA 11, 38[12].
192 For example, see HH I 39; GS 127; BGE 16, 19, 21; and the entire chapter, "The Four Great Errors," in TI.

are other trajectories in Nietzsche's texts, which would also serve this function, such as his critique of the origin of "logic" (where logic presupposes the erroneous treatment of what is merely similar as identical), which sets up his attack against the belief in a self-identical subject.[193] However, pursuing the trajectory provided by the critique of cause and effect has an advantage in that it will introduce us directly to the qualitative dimension of the will to power, the main concern of this chapter.

Nietzsche attacks the traditional understanding of causality by arguing that its most common error is to mistake what is an effect for a cause. He finds this misinterpretation to be one of the most persistent and profound errors of philosophy, religion, science and morality (TI Errors 1). To demonstrate an instance of such an error, Nietzsche discusses Luigi Cornaro's work, *Discourses on the Sober Life*, where Cornaro recommends a meager diet as the recipe for a long and happy life. A meager diet is presented as the "cause" of a long life; but in fact, argues Nietzsche, "an extraordinary slow metabolism, a small consumption" are themselves the causes of a paltry diet (TI Errors 1). What we have here is a case of confusing the effect for the cause, but it is not an innocent confusion. Treating the meager diet as a cause is indicative of Cornaro's tacit belief that he was *free* to eat more or less. Specifically, it signifies his belief that his frugality is an act of his "free will," and that his "will" is the "cause" of his decision to eat less (TI Errors 1). But the belief in free will is an illusion as it falsifies the fact that if Cornaro had eaten more he would have become ill given his slow metabolism. It betrays that there is a *necessity* that binds him to his meager diet.

For Nietzsche, Cornaro's example is indicative of how, generally speaking, philosophical, moral, scientific and religious interpretations of phenomena proceed. On the one hand, mistaking the effect for the cause in the moral, religious and scientific domains implies, as in Cornaro's case, the immodesty of falsely believing in the causality of the will and the freedom of the will. On the other hand, the error of confusing cause and effect in the philosophical, moral and scientific domains implies that explanations of phenomena are not really explanations at all, but rather they are modest "descriptions" (GS 112). We will discuss these two implications in detail below. Nietzsche's critique of cause and effect attacks this immodesty and also rectifies the modesty, and in doing so, it introduces us to the notion of will to power.

Taking for cause what is an effect allows for the formulation of imperatives such as "Do this and this, refrain from this and this – and you will attain happiness or salvation" which are at the center of every morality and religion (TI Errors 2). These imperatives presuppose that one's "will" is actually the cause of one's actions, and that one is free not to do this or that. Nietzsche criticizes this presupposition by calling it the "error of a false causality" (TI Errors 3). He argues that the error of false causality is itself grounded in the supposition, which is common to both morality and religion, that our "inner world" is accessible to us as a basic fact. In particular, it is believed

---

193 See, for instance, GS 111 and BGE 17.

that we can view ourselves as causal agents in the act of willing. The tracing back of actions to "consciousness" or "motives" or "intentions" as their causes (and thus the moralistic ascribing of the value of actions to these causes) is itself based on taking the causality of the will as a basic fact (TI Errors 3).[194] It is apparent that the error of the causality of the will goes hand-in-hand with the error of free will (TI Errors 7).

Furthermore, Nietzsche argues that the belief in the freedom of the will is complemented by the belief in laws, whether these laws are moral or religious. Laws imply that there is a lawgiver (God or one's own conscience), who is absolutely free to command, prescribe and regulate human actions and thoughts, such that human beings can take the righteous path towards salvation or proper moral conduct. Since it is assumed that human beings are also free, such laws are required, since without them, humans would act in whatever way they pleased, thereby committing sins and evil deeds. Both willing a command (as a law) and obeying this command presuppose that the two parties possess free will. Nietzsche argues that the positing of laws and lawgivers is not limited to the religious and moral domains, but it extends also to the scientific domain. When a physicist speaks of "conformity of nature to law," he or she exhibits residual moralistic or religious tendencies of a belief in the causality of intentions or of free will (BGE 22).[195] In effect, by speaking of the laws of nature, one claims that if a thing always acts or happens in particular way, it is a "result of obedience to a law or a lawgiver, while it would be free to act otherwise were it not for the 'law'" (KSA 12, 2[142]). Hence, on the other side of the error of free will, is the belief in the *necessity* of the effect: "Since it is almost always the case that there is will only where the effect of command, and therefore obedience, and therefore action, may be *expected*, the *appearance* translates into the feeling, as if there were a *necessity of effect*" (BGE 19). Nietzsche therefore writes, "Causality is created only by thinking compulsion into the process" (KSA 10, 24[9]). If freedom is placed on the side of the cause, necessity is placed on the side of the effect.

Ascribing our actions to an antecedent cause serves two main purposes. First, it satisfies a deep need in us to look for a *reason* why certain events occur, why we feel the way we do, or why we suffer (TI Errors 4). We have a hard time simply ascertaining the fact *that* something has occurred or *that* we feel the way we do without further "explaining" it, since we need to have a grip on the occurred event. Explaining an event allows us to grasp it by making it appear familiar, recognizable and reasonable. This is when our "cause-creative drive" becomes active and posits "imaginary" causes (like "will") for events (TI Errors 4). For instance, a person may rationalize that the reason why she currently suffers a huge loss in her private life is because of her previous sins (for example, she made somebody else suffer when she had the opportunity to do so). Thus she "trace[s] something unknown back to something known" as a way

---

194 Thus Nietzsche argues that the common belief that there is "no effect without a cause" is a generalization of a narrower proposition that there is "no effecting without willing" (GS 127).
195 Also see KSA 12, 7[14], KSA 11, 36[18].

of explaining the unknown (TI Errors 5). Her present state is God's way of punishing her for her prior sins, and so, in the future, she must be nicer to other people. Such reasoning soothes and alleviates her, by giving her the belief that she "understands" why she suffers. It also allows her to have the illusory conviction that she has some control over her present situation. It increases her "feeling of power" and mastery over her current state.

As discussed in the previous chapter, for Nietzsche, this falsification and fixation in itself, through the invention of imaginary causes, is not something that should be or could be avoided. And whether understood as the instantiation of an objective or subjective tendency, the will to truth as the positing of illusory causes enhances one's feeling of power (for instance, by making things "thinkable"), and thus could be seen as the expression of the will to power (Z II 12). Nevertheless, Nietzsche criticizes the error of false causality insofar as, only by doing so, he can clarify his concept of will to power.

The attribution of events to a prior cause serves a second purpose: it allows one to hold something or someone *responsible* for an action or a condition. Morality and religions typically reason that, if one is happy or if one is sorrowful, it is because one did this or that, presupposing that one was free to do otherwise. Through the error of the freedom of will, humankind was made "accountable" (HH I 39); the punishing and judging instincts of theological and moral interpretations sought accountability everywhere. Hence the whole history of punishment, guilt and bad conscience that Nietzsche's genealogy unearths may be ascribed to the history of these errors of the causality of will and of the free will.

In his critique of these latter errors: (1) Nietzsche argues that there is no such thing as a "will" regarded as a simple unity, and instead conceives of the "will" as a multifaceted, pluralistic phenomenon; (2) he counters the thesis of the (false) freedom of the will with a different notion of "necessity" derived from his concept of will to power; (3) and he counters the belief in the necessity of the effect following from the causality of the will with his idea about the relative independence of the "effect." Let us consider his arguments in detail.

Nietzsche questions the conviction that the "inner world" can be accessed simply and directly, and that the will can be isolated as a basic fact. He argues that the so-called "inner world is full of phantoms and false lights" (TI Errors 3). It is not a text that can be simply read off, but a "*complicated*" phenomenon that must be interpreted (BGE 19). What the philosophers, moralists and theologians call "will" is not something that causes an action, but rather is itself an offshoot, a late product of complex phenomena, which, if anything, only "accompanies" the action (TI Errors 3). The same holds true for "motives" and "intentions" that are "surface phenomen[a] of consciousness," which "conceal[] rather than expose[] the *antecedentia* of the act" (TI Errors 3).

Nietzsche argues that the tendency to conceive the will as a simple unit that causes action is reflective of the belief in the "subject" or "ego" as a "unity," as a substratum underlying various impulses (KSA 12, 10[19]). This belief is indicative of that in a clear-cut demarcation between the subject and the world of events.[196] To every deed, we add a doer who causes the deed, to every thought, a something, which thinks. Thus we see the world as a "multiplicity of agents [or subjects]," an agent "foisted itself upon every event" (TI Errors 3). Attributing actions and deeds to a unitary, constant, self-identical source (subject, will or ego) humanizes the world. It allows us get a grasp on the continuous flux of events in the world, and so, enhances our feeling of power. But this does not change the fact that the single unit, the subject as a fixed entity, is a "fiction" and a falsification inserted by us (KSA 12, 10[19]). The ego is a "fable, a fiction, a play on words" (TI Errors 3). The fictitious insertion of the subject signifies that the limits of our knowledge and interpretation have been reached and that beyond this point our ignorance begins. But the invention of the subject covers up this ignorance – even if it facilitates a limited comprehension of the world – in the immodest claim that we have reached a foundational truth. It is through our belief in ego that we arrive at the concept of "being" as fixation and constancy, which is "not affected by becoming and development" (KSA 12, 9[89]). In other words, it is through our "will to truth" that we arrive at the concept of being. Notions like "substance," "beings," "things," "God" and also the physicists' conception of "atoms" reflect nothing but the belief in an enduring subject as a unity that "causes" the world in its own image and regulates the continuous becoming of all things.[197]

But what are these "complicated" phenomena, of which Nietzsche's speaks, and of which the traditional notions of "will," "ego," "motives," etc. are gross simplifications and falsifications? In providing his answer, Nietzsche retains the word "will" to designate the complex set of phenomena. In any act of willing, in Nietzsche's sense, there is a "plurality of feelings," namely: "the feeling of the state *away from which*, the feeling of the state *towards which*, and the feeling of this 'away from' and 'towards' themselves" (BGE 19). There is also a feeling of bodily reactions, of the muscles that accompanies these other feelings. Further, in addition to feelings, there is a "commandeering thought" in every act of will (BGE 19). But above all, the "will" is fundamentally an "affect," specifically the "affect of the command" (BGE 19). Willing is not primarily wanting, striving, desiring or demanding something, whether this thing is power, life or truth. It is primarily an affect of commanding. Willing is always willing *something*: something is commanded in willing. Willing implies relationality and directionality. However, it does not imply a one-way relation, since willing involves both the state "away from which" and the state "toward which." Therefore willing does not emanate from an independent, self-sufficient and absolutely free unit called

---

196 As we have seen in the previous chapters, Climacus' initial distinction between subjectivity and objectivity, too, is a somewhat strict one, which does not allow for a mutually interdependent interaction between these two terms.

197 See TI Errors 3, KSA 12, 10[19], KSA 12, 9[98], KSA 12, 6[11], KSA 12, 9[89], KSA 12, 2[91], KSA 12, 7[55], KSA 13, 11[73].

"subject" (call it God or ego), which, in principle, is exempt from being commanded. Hence one must not identify willing as an isolated act, and thus "remove the aim from the total condition" (KSA 13, 11[114]).

Instead of unity, Nietzsche portrays the "subject" as "multiplicity" (KSA 11, 40[42]). The will is a plurality rather than a singular entity. The Nietzschean concepts of will and the subject resemble what we have described in the previous chapter as the "body" and its political structure. That is, the "feelings" and "thoughts" that constitute the will may themselves be traced back to a multiplicity of forces, impulses, instincts or drives that are involved in a *power* struggle, the basic forms of which are commanding and obeying. In this struggle, there is subjugation, mastering, exploitation, assimilation and disintegration as basic modes of interpretation, due to which "the sphere of a subject [is] constantly growing or decreasing, the center of the system [is] constantly shifting" (KSA 12, 9[98]). We cannot speak of a durable unity or being, but, at best, only of relatively stable perspectives or dominating centers that have secured a temporary domain of influence through subjugation, alliance and avoidance. Strictly speaking, there is never "a" will but only "treaty drafts of will that are constantly increasing or losing their power" (KSA 13, 11[73]). In any case, these treaty drafts that have attained a relative stability are not "causes" but are themselves products of an underworld of power-struggles, which do not necessarily come to the surface (and therefore, mostly unknown to our consciousness). Intentions and motives are "innocent of any of the essential processes of our preservations and our growth" (KSA 11, 36[29]). As terminal phenomena of consciousness, they merely serve to orient us towards events, "even as symptom of events," but are not their causes (KSA 12, 7[1]).

We should further observe that power is not the *object* of this continuous struggle between impulses and forces. The will is not the subject that is "seeking" power. The notions of seeking and desiring go together with that of subject as a unity. With command being the basic affect, the struggle between the forces fundamentally involves, not the seeking, but the demonstration of power. This is the reason why Nietzsche uses the term "will *to* power." This term indicates a dynamic, active and creative process as the essence of interaction between "wills." The will to power is defined as the insatiable tendency to "manifest power" or as the "employment and the exercise of power, as a creative drive" (KSA 11, 36[31]). Nietzsche also expresses the basic tendency of will to power as the drive to "grow" or the need to "discharge" force (KSA 12, 2[148], KSA 12, 2[63]). But to manifest power, resistances are required, which would provide the occasion for the possible enhancement of power through appropriation, assimilation, "forming, shaping [and] reshaping" (KSA 11, 36[21]). Even in submitting itself to a greater command, a force does not relinquish all its power, but finds in this submission an opportunity to increase its feeling of power. So understood, will to power is not just the essence of all processes in the organic world, but also the inorganic world. Since the bond that links these two worlds are the "drive to approach" and the "drive to thrust something back" – given the struggle to demonstrate power – there is "will to power in ever combination of forces" (KSA 11, 36[21]).[198] Therefore "life is merely a special case of will to power" (KSA 13, 14[121]); the latter applies to the entire domain of existence.

The concept of will to power not only undermines the immodest belief in the causality of a simple being called will, but it also attacks the idea of (causal) "explanation," especially scientific-mechanistic explanations of phenomena. Nietzsche argues that the progress of modern science lies in the fact that it has become better at "describing" phenomena, but "we explain just as little as our predecessors" (GS 112). Modern science has "perfected the picture of becoming, but [it has not] got over, got behind the picture" (GS 112). Thus he criticizes science for its apparent modesty when it comes to its ability to explain phenomena. We can surmise why Nietzsche makes this charge. The inability to really explain phenomena is only the other side of the immodest belief in the causality of the will and of the humanizing tendency to see everywhere atomic units or subjects underlying the events of the world. For example, science subscribes to things like "atoms," "lines" and "surfaces" which are invented, metaphorical fictions just like the subject is a fiction; and so when science attempts to explain things in the world, it discovers the very same fictional concepts that it had projected on to the world (TI Errors 3). Therefore, at best, these explanations are descriptions in a language, which contain terms like atoms, our own idealized concepts. To express it differently, typical causal explanations of phenomena (including scientific ones) inadvertently subscribe to the belief that the will, the ego or the atom causes events in the world. But as Nietzsche's arguments reveal, these supposed causal agents are themselves ephiphenomena or late offshoots of complex processes, and which, if anything, only accompany events in the world, directing our orientation towards these events. However, one must not suppose that the complex processes are, consequently, the "causes" of the ego or the atom. This is so precisely because these processes are not rigidified units that simply cause the ego. And hence, the latter do not just "follow" from the processes as a separate entity. On the contrary, the ego and the processes are involved in a mutual struggle (rather than in a cause-effect interaction), and they together form a complicated phenomenon, which is constantly shifting and growing.

In any case, Nietzsche's point is that the ego, the will and the atom, usually portrayed as causal agents, are themselves simplifications since there are an infinite number of processes that elude us. When we resort to these fictional causal entities to explain phenomena in the world, the best we can do is to describe them: "The concept of 'causa' is only a means of expression" (KSA 11, 36[28]). These descriptions are themselves symptoms that need to be interpreted, rather than pure explanations, which would result if one could somehow take a step back from the world and comprehend the phenomena. The same can be said of explanations of moral phenomena that resort

---

198 In KSA 11, 36[22], Nietzsche defines the "repelling force" or resistances as determining the connection between the organic and the inorganic worlds.

to the causality of "intentions" or "purposes" to explain actions. As Nietzsche argues, our ideas of means, ends and purposes do not completely understand a given action; these ideas are *selective* as they focus on and emphasize only certain aspects of an action (which might be insignificant from alternate points of view), and suppress the majority of others. So they only provide an "indescribably imprecise description" of an action, even if they claim to explain its meaning (KSA 12, 7[1]).

According to Nietzsche, a scientific explanation of an event is a symbolization of the event by means of sensation and thought that *succeed* the event, whereas a moral explanation is given through aims, purposes and intentions which *precede* the event (KSA 10, 24[13]). Scientific explanations cannot explain the origin of events; they leave reason and purpose out of their account as much as possible. Scientific explanations are given only in terms of pure "quantities": "knowledge ... refers to the domain of reckoning, weighing, measuring, to the domain of quantity" (KSA 12, 6[14]). Hence Nietzsche calls these accounts, "mechanistic" (KSA 11, 36[34]). In contrast, moral explanations in terms of values resort to "qualities," but they lack the objectivity that science has. Qualities are nothing more than "perspective truths" for human beings, not an "in-itself"; it is *our* way of evaluating, judging and falsifying events in accordance with our conditions of growth and preservation. We feel that "quantitative differences are something fundamentally distinct from quantity, namely they are *qualities*" (KSA 12, 6[14]). Nietzsche, therefore, counters scientific-mechanistic explanations for their lack of qualitative and evaluative power, which would explain the origins of events, and he attacks moral explanations for their purely qualitative prejudices that lack objectivity. But both these kinds of explanations receive their fire from the same source, i.e. their basic belief in atomistic subjects and the causality of the will. So these kinds of explanations manage only to give descriptions.

The concept of will to power is meant to rectify this deficiency. With this concept, Nietzsche wants to go "behind the picture" and beyond mere description, but not by re-installing a foundational ground which would "truly explain" phenomena. Neither does he want to reduce all qualities to quantities (KSA 12, 2[157]). In a sense, with the will to power, Nietzsche wants to make evaluative judgments more "quantitative" and physical explanations more "qualitative." He views "force" itself as a *qualitative* notion by ascribing an "inner will" to the physicists' concept of force (KSA 11, 36[31]). This inner will is the will to power as the insatiable tendency to manifest power. Willing has a fundamental directionality, given that commanding is the essence of willing. Hence we could say that the will to power as the inner will is a vector quality that *orients* the forces, gives them their direction, their trajectory, their "meaning" and their "purpose." But we should be careful in describing what kind of purpose is involved here. Nietzsche repeatedly emphasizes that it is not a foundational meaning or an absolute purpose or finality. Will to power, writes Nietzsche, is "not a being, not a becoming, but a *pathos*" (KSA 13, 14[79]). As an affect, it has essentially a process-like quality: it is a "dynamic quanta" (KSA 13, 14[79]). The will to power does not yield a fixed essence, a constancy of meaning, a central subjectivity that is the origin of all purpose. Rather, it is the element out of which "being" or "beings" – as localized, temporarily and relatively stable centers of meaning – emerge as an offshoot of an ongoing underworld of power-struggles. It is also the element out of which "becoming and effecting first emerge" (KSA 13, 14[79]). And therefore, Nietzsche argues that the "will to power [itself] cannot have become" (KSA 13, 11[29]). This is the reason why we have distinguished between "becoming" as a subjective tendency (as a transformation undergone by existence) from the "becoming" of existence itself. In the above quotations, Nietzsche is suggesting that the will to power, as the essence of existence, is the origin of becoming as a subjective tendency. In connection with existence and will to power, if the term "becoming" can be used at all (which Nietzsche does use at times (see KSA 12, 2[149–152], KSA 11, 38[12])), it should be taken to imply the elemental affect of commanding.

Nevertheless, we must still evaluate the *metaphysical* status of the will to power as an affect and a pathos that defines the becoming character of existence. Does claiming that the will to power is the origin of both being and becoming (as the objective and the subjective tendencies) commit Nietzsche to a metaphysical position of his own? Is the Heideggerian interpretation correct after all in holding that with the will to power Nietzsche inverts the metaphysical tradition (affirming existential becoming instead of being), but nevertheless confirms it just as much?[199] We will return to these questions below. But as a way of setting up the discussion to follow, we must complete our foregoing exposition by analyzing how it is that, as dynamic quanta, the will to power ascribes orientation and a non-final purpose to the forces.

The inner will qualifies the forces and directs them. Nietzsche writes that this qualification involves defining "limits, determin[ing] degrees, variations of power" (KSA 12, 2[148]). Mere quantitative variations of power could not "feel themselves to be as such," and so there must be something that qualifies these variations by comparing them and determining their mutual values (KSA 12, 2[148]). In other words, there cannot be anything like a "pure" quantity of force that stands absolutely on its own, unrelated to other quantities of force. The concept of an absolute quantity unconnected to other quantities is a frivolous hypothesis, and for Nietzsche, it is nothing but a contradiction in terms just like the idea of "*causa sui*" (BGE 21). The notion of quantity makes sense only with respect to and only in *relation* to other quantities. Quantity itself has a differential aspect. But since quality refers to the difference in quantity, the concept of quantity inevitably implies that of quality.

Now, defining the will to power as the basic tendency to command and manifest power already indicates a qualitative aspect, and hence provides the criterion according to which this comparison and evaluation take place. In what way? Commanding involves that which commands and also that which obeys this command;

---

199 Heidegger, *Nietzsche* III: 212.

it presupposes inequality or differences in power quanta. So in commanding, a relatively stable force not only refers to itself, but also to that which resists it; that is, commanding presupposes that there is both an evaluation of one's own power in comparison to that of another force that resists one, and vice versa. The will to power necessitates that this which "wants to grow" also "interpret[] the value of whatever else wants to grow" (KSA 12, 2[148]). Commanding implies a comparison and relativization of power quanta. Therefore it yields the qualitative dimension. Accordingly, we can introduce two of the most fundamental concepts in all of Nietzsche's philosophy: the *active* force or the *strong* will (that which commands) and the *reactive* force or the *weak* will (that which is commanded). It is important to recognize that both active and reactive forces are essentially defined by their will to power. The forces that obey do not relinquish their power – "resistance is present even in obedience" – in the same way that, in commanding, is implicit an admission that the "power of the opponent has not been vanquished, incorporated, disintegrated" (KSA 11, 36[22]). Further, we must also note that since quantity necessarily implies quality, "strong" and "weak" wills do not refer to purely quantitative notions (that is, it is not just a question of the "amount" of power). The designations "strong" and "weak" wills already imply both quality and quantity. We shall return to the topic of strong and weak wills later as they become crucial to our analysis of Nietzsche's relation to metaphysics.

If we apply this model of interaction of forces (as commanding, evaluating and obeying) to the entire domain of forces, we arrive at the Nietzschean picture of existence or world. The application to the whole field of forces is not arbitrary, since the differential nature of the quantity of force (or the inseparability of quantity and quality) implies the interconnection of a force with all other forces. Accordingly, existence may be viewed as an interconnected web of forces in continuous, mutual and dynamic interaction, the essence of which is will to power. The nature of this interaction is such that each force or each localized center of power affects, and is in turn affected by, all other forces. All we have are "dynamic quanta, in a relation to all other dynamic quanta: their essence lies in their relation to all other quanta" (KSA 13, 14[79]). "Every atom affects the whole being" (KSA 13, 14[79]). Nietzsche describes existence or world as "a play of forces and waves of forces, at the same time one and many, increasing here and at the same time decreasing there; a sea of forces flowing and rushing together, eternally changing ..." (KSA 11, 38[12]). Commanding, obeying, growing, receding, and all the other forms of interpretation such as assimilation, overpowering and exploitation, belong to the essence of this dynamic interaction. The continuous mutual exchange between the "individual self" and the "world," which forbids any strict boundary between them, and the whole interpretative and perspectival interplay between "subjectivity" and "objectivity" (discussed in the previous two chapters) are rooted in the will to power as the essence of existence: "*This world is the will to power – and nothing besides! And you yourselves are also this will to power – and nothing besides!*" (KSA 11, 38[12]).

In this Nietzschean world, there is no cause and no effect, but rather what we confront is a "continuum" of moving and dynamically interacting forces (GS 112). According to Nietzsche, "cause" and "effect" are two overly disjointed concepts; instead, he argues for a dynamic mutual interaction between complex processes and their offshoots. Instead of succession, there is interpenetration of forces. What matters in this continuum is not the freedom and causality of the will and the necessity of the effect that follows, but rather the degree of superior power and the degree of resistance in any event: "it is only a matter of *strong* and *weak* wills" (BGE 21). But the degrees of power and resistance of a dynamic quantum, at any given moment, are themselves constrained by those of every other quantum, given the interconnected nature of the interaction. As Nietzsche puts it: "every power draws its final consequences at every moment" (BGE 22). Therefore, at any precise moment, each force has a definite polarity, "purpose" and orientation, given that it is in mutual struggle and evaluation of all other forces and itself. However, a definite orientation means that there is a certain *necessity* to every event in the world, but "*not* because laws are dominant in it, but rather because laws are totally *absent*" (BGE 22). Laws presuppose the freedom of a subject unit or will that can unconditionally begin a course of events. Implicitly, laws presuppose a strict boundary between the subject (an individual or an atom) and the world. The former is assumed to be free or independent of the latter, even though it can have an effect on the latter. But given the thoroughgoing dynamic interaction of forces, there cannot be a fixed demarcation or an unconditional beginning, and consequently also no "free will." Thus in opposition to the freedom of the will, Nietzsche proposes the necessity of events in a world defined by continuous, mutual struggle. Therefore a thing is "neither free nor unfree but simply thus and thus" (KSA 12, 2[142]); "calculability exists precisely because things are unable to be other than they are" (KSA 13, 14[79]). If a sequence of events repeats itself in the same manner again and again it does not reveal the presence of a "law," but a certain kind of power relationship between multiple forces.

At the same time, if every power draws its ultimate consequence at every moment, then it would appear that each event, although necessary, is also relatively *independent* or novel. That is, an event is not absolutely dependent upon a prior one to be "caused," even if it matters what the exchange of power quanta between forces at a previous interaction was, for the course of the current event. In other words, since it is not a question of two successive states (cause and effect), but rather a struggle between elements of unequal power which, after the interaction, emerge with different quanta of power, a new arrangement of forces is achieved according to the measure of power of each of them (KSA 13, 14[95]). This novel arrangement means that the current event is "something fundamentally different" from the previous configuration of forces, and not its "effect" (KSA 13, 14[95]). In this way, Nietzsche counters the supposed necessity of an event ensuing from its cause, with the idea of the relative independence of each event.

Thus with the will to power, which introduces the qualitative aspect of forces through a radicalization of the notion of quantity, Nietzsche is able to go beyond a mere description of phenomena to an "explanation" of them. But it is a peculiar sort of explanation, since, with the theory of will to power, Nietzsche does not stand "external" to or "beyond" existence in order to disinterestedly gaze at its phenomena, or to establish the final truth about existence. In other words, the will to power as the essence of existence is not a metaphysical theory in the Heideggerian sense. Heidegger's reading implies that to "permanentize" the continuous becoming of existence, Nietzsche must go above and beyond the "instability" implied by the latter.[200] Precisely in order to secure the flow of becoming, Nietzsche must affirm being as permanence. Heidegger acknowledges that, for Nietzsche, there is a sense in which being as fixity and stability is a possibility within existence. But he insists there is another sense in which "being nonetheless pertains to will to power, which must secure stability for itself by means of permanence, solely in order to be able to surpass itself; that is, in order to *become*."[201]

However, for Nietzsche, the will to power is no such externalist theory. As he insists, "The world seen from *inside*, the world *determined* and *described* with respect to its 'intelligible character' – would be just this 'will to power' and nothing else" (BGE 36, emphases added). The will to power is a theory about the essence of existence, but it is pronounced from *within* the realm of existence. With this theory, Nietzsche does not abandon existence as the ultimate presupposition of his philosophy to give a direct reading of it, as if it was a text. Rather, the will to power affirms precisely the indirection of existence. It does this by not just describing but also "determining" existence. It can do this only by itself being an *interpretation* from within existence: "Granted, this is only an interpretation too – and you will be eager enough to make this objection? – well then, so much the better" (BGE 22). With will to power, Nietzsche risks an interpretation and he exposes himself to all the struggle and uncertainty to which a philosophical theory is exposed, if indeed the will to power is the essence of all interactions within existence. The theory of will to power is itself *not* exempt from subjection to the very interpretative conditions that this theory engenders.

The issue here is one of finality: a theory which purports to give the final truth about the world believes itself to be, at some level, independent of the becoming conditions of the world, and its multiple apparent truths. However, for Nietzsche, the interpretative conditions that are determined by the will to power are not those of a fixed and final meaning, but of multiplicity of meanings that are essentially incomplete and perspectival. These meanings reflect the continuously transforming nature of the eternal struggle, the ebb and flow of strong and weak forces. The development of a thing or an organ, for example, is not its progression towards a fixed meaning but a series of

---

200 Heidegger, *Nietzsche* III: 212–213.
201 Heidegger, *Nietzsche* III: 212.

more or less mutually independent processes of subjugation exacted on the thing, added to this the resistances encountered every time, the attempted transformations for the purpose of defense and reaction, and the results, too, of successful countermeasures. The form is fluid, the "meaning" even more so (GM II 12).

Therefore Nietzsche talks not about *a* truth, but about many truths: "There are many kinds of eyes. Even the sphinx has eyes – and consequently there are many kinds of 'truths', and consequently there is no truth" (KSA 11, 34[230]). Although any relatively stable center of force may be said to have a more or less definite orientation or essence, this orientation is not final since the center of force is always engaged in a power struggle between other perspectives and modes of interpretation. Hence "essence ... is something perspectiv[al] and already presupposes a multiplicity" (KSA 12, 2[149]). This applies even to the concept of the will to power as the essence of existence.

Will to power and metaphysics

What, then, is the relation of the theory of will to power (and hence Nietzsche's philosophy) to metaphysics?

As I have argued in the second chapter, we must differentiate between the oppositional schema between a real and an apparent world and the mere positing of a real world. The former condition is what Nietzsche equates with metaphysics as it leads to a denial of life, while the latter condition may or may not lead to this denial. In itself, the mere positing of a true world of constancy is an expression of a particular force's or a body's metaphysical need and, therefore, a demonstration of its will to power. But most commentators tend to consider this latter condition as definitive of metaphysics for Nietzsche, which allows them to claim either that Nietzsche's philosophy is a mere reversal of the Platonic-metaphysical tradition (Heidegger), or that Nietzsche sidesteps or does not busy himself with metaphysical questions about the "other world," but that he is instead concerned with providing a naturalistic interpretation of our "actual" world (Cox).

The internalists, on the other hand, do recognize that metaphysics for Nietzsche refers to the oppositional structure itself between a real and an apparent world. But they equate this condition with that of positing (believing) in another world or the true world. Equating these two conditions allows them to make their essential arguments against Heidegger that Nietzsche moves entirely within immanence, and that he does not set up "becoming" and "will to power as the truth of being"[202] (and therefore, he does not just invert metaphysics by setting up his own version of a "true" world). Rather, internalist commentators, such as Haar, argue that, with the theory

---

202 Heidegger, *Nietzsche* IV: 52.

of will to power, Nietzsche puts forward a new interpretation of the becoming of the sensible world that exposes us to a play of differences, a "plurality of meanings [which undermines] any logic based on the [metaphysical] principle of identity."[203] Thus Nietzsche's philosophy, which moves entirely within the realm of immanence, manages to overcome metaphysics.[204] Müller-Lauter, too, adopts a similar strategy against Heidegger when he writes that in Nietzsche's interpretation of the sensible world, the will to power does not refer back to "*one* willing entity, a single will, but rather merely to the *complex* of willing that interrogates itself concerning its ultimate actual givenness and withdraws into the undeterminable."[205] Thus he remarks, "metaphysics collapses under [Nietzsche's] incessant questioning."[206] The will to power implies a non-foundationalism; it is not a foundationalist theory that appeals to a thing-in-itself hiding behind the sensible world. For Müller-Lauter and Haar, the Heideggearian interpretation presupposes that Nietzsche's philosophy subscribes to the principle of identity and also to the unquestionable and determinable "givenness" of the will as a self-identical unit. Only through such a presupposition can Heidegger argue that the will to power is Nietzsche's term for the being of beings. The internalists question this assumption, but they do not really challenge the common supposition that metaphysics, for Nietzsche, is the doctrine of two worlds or the belief in another world.

In contrast, my strategy has been to interpret the positing of a true world as signifying primarily a metaphysical need corresponding to the quantitative dimension of will to power, by denying this mere act of positing an *evaluative* power to affirm or deny life. By doing this, I have re-interpreted all concerns about Nietzsche's apparent inversion of affirmation from being to becoming – which is central to the interpretative efforts of the above-mentioned commentators – to his alternative affirmations of being and becoming as instantiations of objective or subjective tendencies of existence, where neither being nor becoming is unequivocally preferred. This frees up the question of what metaphysics is, for Nietzsche, from the dialectic of being and becoming, and makes it a purely *existential* question, corresponding to the qualitative aspect of the will to power. Thus, in my interpretation, the problem of metaphysics shifts from the doctrine of two worlds, to the evaluative schema that would oppose a real to an apparent world. Consistent with a meta-existential approach, Nietzsche defines metaphysics by "how" it evaluates life rather than "what" it evaluates. In other words, the metaphysical nature of an evaluation does not consist in "what" world it posits and values higher (the real world of being as opposed to the sensible world of becoming). But rather, metaphysics pertains to the very oppositional schema between a real and an apparent world (which brings out the "how"), which is at the

---

203 Haar 3.
204 Haar ix–xiii, 1–5. Also, see Kofman 120–121 and Blondel 5.
205 Müller-Lauter 122.
206 Müller-Lauter 122.

root of all evaluations that deny life. Accordingly, Nietzsche's critique of metaphysics does not begin by first acknowledging an opposition between the real and the apparent world, but rather it immediately targets the source of all oppositional schema. Now, given what will to power means as the essence of existence, we must tackle the vital issue of the source of the oppositional structure of evaluation.

Perhaps the clue to determining the source of metaphysical oppositions lies precisely in the procedure by which Nietzsche explicates will to power. As we saw in the last section, this procedure involves a critique of the concept of causality, and also of the traditional notions of will, freedom and subjectivity. Nietzsche questions the belief in subject units seen as free to cause or "will" the events in the world. For Nietzsche, this belief involves a gross falsification of underlying complicated phenomena – that point to a multiplicity or plurality of forces that are involved in a never-ending power struggle – which absolutely forbid the possibility of a self-identical or unitary will. Given this, one could perhaps venture the thesis that the origin of the metaphysical oppositions lies in the gross falsifications carried out by the will to truth that posits a self-identical unity of the will. Nietzsche's will to power would then be an anti-metaphysical philosophical theory that opposes this falsification by affirming the non-foundational plurality of wills and their interpretative struggles. Whereas the will to truth of metaphysics affirms unity and stagnation, which is the origin of the concept of being, the will to power affirms plurality, multiplicity, chance and becoming.

There are some key passages in which Nietzsche seems to endorse the view that it is the will to truth, which determines the essence of metaphysics. For example, explaining his task and that of the future philosophers, he writes, "The will to truth needs a critique … the value of truth is tentatively to be *called into question*" (GM III 24). For Nietzsche, the "will to truth" needs a "justification," and the "value of truth" has itself become a "problem" (GM III 24, 27; BGE 1). And elsewhere, he comments that "those who are truthful in that audacious and ultimate sense … *affirm another world* than that of life, nature and history; and insofar as they affirm this 'other world', must they not by the same token deny its counterpart [*Gegenstück* (opposite)] this world, *our* world?" (GS 344). However, as I suggested in the previous chapter, a careful reading of these passages indicates that Nietzsche is operating with an important distinction in the background between *unconditional* will to truth and (mere) will to truth, which a glib reading might overlook. Nietzsche intends to problematize the will to truth, not to overcome it and set it aside, but so that he can question the metaphysical value of truth, which, for him, is expressed only in the "unconditional will to truth" (GM III 24). Thus what he is targeting is the "unconditional" variant of will to truth, the truth in an "audacious and ultimate sense," truth "at any price," which expresses a "*metaphysical faith*" (GS 344), and not mere will to truth, which in itself is the expression of a metaphysical need, and thus is nothing more than an expression of a life-form's conditions of growth and preservation.

If one disagrees with the assessment offered here, then one must contend with Nietzsche's insistence that the will to truth is a "word for the 'will to power'" (KSA 12,

9[91]). In my view, there is no choice but to acknowledge that will to truth and will to power are not opposites, but rather the former is a kind of expression of the latter. The internalists and the naturalists, who want to claim, contra Heidegger, that Nietzsche has already overcome metaphysics with his theory of the will to power do make this acknowledgment. In the next few paragraphs, I will analyze the strategy they adopt. I will show that these interpreters bring out important facets of Nietzsche's philosophy, which are suppressed by the Heideggerian reading. Nevertheless, at some point in their interpretations, they subscribe to a kind of oppositional schema precisely in order to gain that critical purchase necessary to portray Nietzsche as a post-metaphysical thinker. Insofar as they do this, ironically, their Nietzsche interpretations turn out to be just as metaphysical as Heidegger's, assuming that the quintessential aspect of the latter's reading is to ascribe to Nietzsche an oppositional structure in order to claim him as a metaphysician.[207] Thus my strategy is to use Heidegger against the other groups of interpreters, not to side with the former, but to isolate the precise way in which the will to power can be seen to provide a critique of metaphysical oppositions without thereby setting up its own set of oppositions. Such a critique, as we shall see, will be necessarily an open-ended one, befitting the radical indirection of a meta-existential approach.

First, I consider Cox's naturalistic interpretation, since in recognizing that the will to truth and the will to power are not opposites, he, too, distinguishes between mere will to truth and the unconditional will to truth. While the former belongs to will to power, and is necessary for life, the latter brings out the essence of metaphysics, as it leads to an affirmation of another world and a denial of life.[208] In Cox's view, the unconditional will to truth which values truth absolutely leads to a "dogmatism" since it does not recognize that the conditions of life might include error and perspectivism, and therefore, "against the requirements of 'this world' ... 'the world of life, nature and history,'" it receives its justification solely from the otherworldly domain.[209] On the other hand, the will to truth which belongs to the will to power acknowledges the necessity of falsity, and its own "conditionality and contingency," and thus the "actual" conditions of our existence.[210] Thus Cox's naturalist argument relies on the opposition between the non-dogmatism of the will to truth and the dogmatism of metaphysics corresponding to the unconditional will to truth.

Although Cox's reading is promising, it does not go far enough to inquire into the source of the unconditional nature of the will to truth, which would makes its evaluation metaphysical, given that metaphysics is characterized by oppositional

---

207 As we know, the central opposition that Heidegger attributes to Nietzsche is the one between becoming and being. Other commentators, as we shall see, avoid this opposition, but unwittingly posit other ones.

208 Cox 22–26.

209 Cox 22–26.

210 Cox 45.

schema of evaluations. What is exactly metaphysical about the unconditional will to truth? It is insufficient, and even misleading, to describe that the latter implies a form of "dogmatism," which does not recognize the necessity of error and perspectivism, since it would beg the question about why dogmatism should be avoided. If one responds to this last question, as Cox in effect does, by claiming that non-dogmatism is desirable since it affirms the requirements of "this world" of life, nature and history, while dogmatism does not do this, then it appears as if one is already working within an opposition between a kind dogmatism and non-dogmatism, which one takes for granted. Consequently, we find that Cox treats the "actual" or "natural" world, which is *what* the non-dogmatic will to truth supposedly affirms, just as self-evidently as he treats the affirmation of the "other" world. But we should able to guess that treating the "actual" world as if it is a basic fact is indeed essential for naturalistic theories precisely in order to get their explanatory machinery running. In the end, Cox only manages to posit his own dogmatic opposition between "metaphysics" (unconditional will to truth) and "naturalism" ("non-dogmatic" will to truth)[211] – the very opposition he presupposed to offer his interpretation – accepting at face-value Nietzsche's remarks that metaphysics denies life, nature and history through its extra-natural commitments. He does not really investigate, and therefore, begs the question about, what denying life, nature and history means, or how this denial is possible. And from a Heideggerian point of view, this "dogmatic" reading of Nietzsche is just as metaphysical as Heidegger's own interpretation of Nietzsche – if not more – however much Cox is determined to distance himself from the latter.

There is also a further set of issues associated with presupposing and subscribing to a set of oppositional concepts, which Cox does not really address. If the essence of world is will to power, how does the metaphysical and unconditional will to truth which is opposed to the non-metaphysical will to power, relate to the latter? Does it arise out of the will to power in defiance of it, or in spite of it? Can it arise at all? Does it have the same origin as mere will to truth?

A more productive approach to the problem of will to power and its relation to metaphysics is the one taken by the internalists. They readily acknowledge that the will to truth and the will to power are not opposites, and therefore the former – even in its "unconditional" form – cannot *explain* the source of metaphysical oppositions. They recognize the ubiquity of will to power for Nietzsche, which entails, among other things, a radical interpretation of immanent "reality," something which Heidegger does not acknowledge. This interpretation implies an irreducible multiplicity of forces in mutual, evolving and non-final power struggle. The symptomatic (or "metaphorical") nature of this perspectival struggle forbids any fixed meaning. Given this, the will to truth is not primarily to be understood as a life-denying force. But if the will to truth does appear, at times, to be bound up with the will to denial of life,

---

211 Cox 71–75.

as in the case of unconditional will to truth, it is because the will to truth itself is a symptom of a *prior* interpretative process or condition which would reveal the source of the oppositions of values.

What is this prior interpretative process? For the internalists, the answer to this question does not lie in some substance or cause that is external or opposite to will to power, but rather in the qualitative dimension of will to power. And this is indeed a step in the right direction. Specifically, the internalists argue that the origin of metaphysics must be traced back to the distinction between "active" and "reactive" forces, between "strong" and "weak" wills. The latter distinction is a fundamental one that resides at the very heart of will to power, reflecting the inequality of power quantities, and determining the differential and evaluative power struggle between forces. For the internalists, all the power struggles between the forces may be interpreted as those between these two basic types of wills: the strong and the weak. Hence, according to Haar, the will to power's internal imperative – "to be more" – yields "*right at the origin* ... of the will to power, two types of force, two types of life":[212] the active force, or ascending life, and the reactive force, or descending life. The "initial bipolarity of the will to power" forms the basis of Nietzsche's genealogical method, which traces "any given value to the originary direction of volition" (ascending or descending life).[213] Similarly, Deleuze also observes that Nietzsche's genealogy implies a "nobility and baseness ... nobility and decadence in the origin."[214] He writes that, "at the origin, there is the difference between active and reactive forces. Action and reaction are not in a relation of succession but in one of coexistence in the origin itself."[215] For Deleuze, this implies a "typology of forces."[216]

Let us examine the claim that at the origin there are two basic types of forces or wills. As we have noted, the active and reactive forces do not refer to mere quantities or amount of power. The will with "more" power is not necessarily the "strong" will and vice versa. Active and reactive forces refer to both quantity and quality of power given that commanding is the basic affect of the will to power. In every power struggle, each faction involved emerges with different quanta of power, which in turn affects the resultant quality of power of each faction. There is either a growth in power or a decline in power.[217] Of course, there could also be interactions where the factions emerge with the same quantity of power as before, in which case they appear to have only "preserved" themselves. However, Nietzsche insists that the consequence of "self-preservation" is only an offshoot, which may or may not happen. The basic

---

212 Haar 8.
213 Haar 9.
214 Deleuze 2.
215 Deleuze 55.
216 Deleuze 110.
217 Here growth (and decline) refers both to the quantity and quality of the will to power. In the previous chapter, we considered only the quantitative aspect of the will to grow.

impulse in every interaction is "growth," "mastery," "becoming strong" and the "discharging" of force (KSA 12, 7[44], KSA 12, 2[63], KSA 13, 11[121], KSA 13, 14[174]). Hence the aim can never be to remain the "same," or to be "safe." In commanding, there is risk: a unit of force evaluates itself relative to whatever else wants to grow, and vice versa; it wagers itself in a bid to grow. If it does not grow, it risks decline and degeneration. But what do the terms, growth and decline, signify? They cannot mean mere accumulation and reduction of power.

Nietzsche uses the term "self-overcoming" to signify the basic thrust of life as will to power (Z II 12). This term signifies simultaneously both quantitative and qualitative growth. Ridiculing Schopenhauer's "will to life," Nietzsche argues that for the sake of power, life itself is risked in the act of self-overcoming: life is something "*which must always overcome itself*" (Z II 12). Given this, we may define "growth" as the enhancement of power in such a *way* that self-overcoming is achieved, leaving aside the issue of what self-overcoming exactly involves. And "decline" or "degeneration" is still a demonstration of power, but in such a way that self-overcoming is denied. It is a question of which direction the force takes, and hence of the quality of the will to power. Decline still involves a progression of power, but in an inverted direction. The crucial point, the fundamental criterion, on which this inversion hinges, is whether the basic impulse of life as self-overcoming is affirmed or denied, and consequently whether life itself is affirmed or denied. So "affirmation" or "denial" of life defines the ultimate quality of will to power, which provides a definite standard according to which we can differentiate between a strong and a weak will. A strong will affirms life's basic conditions, and it affirms the will to power as the essence of all life. A weak will denies life by denying the will to power.

Nietzsche corroborates this reading when he writes that there are "fundamental prerequisites [or conditions] of life," which the strong will affirms and against which the weak will "rebels" or has an "aversion" (GM III 28). The difficult, but critical, thing to grasp is that the possibility of the denial of life is given by will to power itself. If all willing is willing to grow and to demonstrate power, then there is possible a type of willing which denies the very principle of will to power, precisely because in this denial it finds an occasion to enhance its feeling of power. From an internalist point of view, the denial reflects an *internal contortion* of the will to power, because of which "the direction of the will is reversed: growth becomes *advance in decadence*."[218] The contortion is internal to the will to power since the denying will does not relinquish its power, but demonstrates it in such a way that the principle of growth is denied.[219] The will to power is still operative in the weak will, but in such a manner that the basic principle of operation is rebelled against. The denying will does not operate

---

218 Haar 8–9.
219 As we shall see later, the weak, life-denying will does this by adherence to a principle of self-preservation rather than to the one of growth.

from outside or external to the domain of will to power to deny the latter: the "negative" has an internal origin.

Nietzsche expresses this point in the following way: "a condemnation of life by the living is after all no more than the symptom of a certain kind of life" (TI Morality 5). The extreme denial of life epitomized by the "*will to nothingness* ... is and remains a *will*," the essence of which is will to power (GM, III 28). Haar calls this a "paradox."[220] But we should not be too surprised that there is a paradox here, since we know that the will to power as the principle of existence is not a foundational principle or a final truth that determines an absolute or univocal essence for all forces, interactions and interpretations. On the contrary, for Nietzsche, the will to power means that no interpretation of the world, not even "will to power," is in principle undeniable or indisputable.[221] This follows from the claim that all willing is willing to grow, since it implies that there is a multiplicity of non-finalized meanings all subject to re-interpretations. And Nietzsche does present the will to power as one of the possible interpretations of the world, particularly a "strong" one, and not as a foundational meaning exempted from the conditions of the world.

For the internalists, the above account of the origin of the negative in the internal contortion of the will to power makes Nietzsche a profoundly anti-Hegelian philosopher. In Nietzsche, the negative has a "real" status that it does not have in Hegelianism. The will to power is not a purely "positive" essence but it contains an original negation. To put it in other terms, the activity of forces is not derived through an opposition to a prior negation; on the contrary, as Deleuze argues, the negative "is a result of activity ... [it is] a product of existence itself."[222] The denying will is only possible due to the active principle of the will to power as will to growth. The reality of the negative, of the denying force, warrants the postulation of two fundamental types of wills. Hence Deleuze talks about the "origin and inverted image" alluding to the "coexistence" of both active and reactive forces at the origin.[223] Like Haar, Deleuze, too, finds Nietzsche's "typological method" crucial for establishing him as an anti-metaphysical thinker, especially as an anti-Hegelian one.[224] The typological method consists in maintaining that there is a basic clear-cut distinction between two types of wills: one that affirms life's will to power, and the one that denies it. Once this typology is established, then the internalist argument that, Nietzsche is a "philosopher of differences" who overcomes metaphysics, readily follows. As noted earlier, the inter-

---

220 Haar 8.
221 The deniability of the will to power must not be taken in a merely epistemological sense. Here we are dealing with the basic evaluation of life through the affirmation or denial of will to power. And as we know, for Nietzsche, evaluation has more of an existential meaning, in the sense that a life-form lives only by evaluating. The affirmation and denial of the will to power primarily correspond to two different forms of life, and not (or, only derivatively) to modes of knowledge.
222 Deleuze 9.
223 Deleuze 55.
224 Delezue 163.

nalists take metaphysics to imply a belief in the other world (a condition, which they equate to the setting up of an opposition between the other and this world). The belief in the other world is then understood as the defining characteristic of the life-denying, weak will. The other world is invented through an opposition, by saying "no," on principle, to "this" world, and this "no" is the weak will's active and creative deed (GM I 10). Hence it is an expression of its warped will to power indicating a "reversal of the evaluating glance" (GM I 10). The weak will's "action is a basically a reaction," which is the origin of metaphysics (GM I 10). The will to truth *could* also be an expression of the invention of the real world through opposition, but it does not necessarily have to be so. Not all expressions of the will to truth indicate the positing of an oppositional structure. Life-denial is prior to the truth drive. The latter is symptomatic (in our terms, it is an expression of a metaphysical need, and hence, of an objective or subjective tendency), but not the origin of life-denial.

In contrast to the weak will, the strong will says "yes" to life by saying "yes" to itself (GM I 10). It says "yes" not only to joy, but to "*all* woe as well" (Z IV 19:10). This self-affirmation is its primary, creative deed, which indicates its will to growth. Again, the will to truth could be complicit with the yes-saying, but there is no necessity that it must be. Further, Deleuze points out that the self-affirmation of the strong will is an "affirmation of its difference."[225] That is, in affirming itself, it affirms the uniqueness of its own being, its own pride and happiness. It does not define itself, like the weak will does, by first opposing other wills: "it drives others away" (KSA 11, 36[21]). If it seeks resisting wills at all, it is only so that it can affirm its own difference from the other wills more pointedly. Given this, the Nietzschean differential critique would involve a process of displacement of the oppositions of metaphysics and its concepts into a dynamic play of differences, where there are "only degrees and multiple, subtle shades of gradation" (BGE 24). In other words, Nietzsche's critique achieves a displacement of the "weak and reactive" oppositions into the "strong and active" differences.[226] The key to Nietzsche's critique is his genealogical method, which asks, "*from where an ideal comes*."[227] Genealogy relates any given value to the "original" direction of willing. In doing so, it provides an interpretation of the will to power as underlying not only the strong values, but also the weak metaphysical ones. By thus showing the common origin of both strong and weak wills in the will to power, Nietzsche provides an immanent critique of metaphysics. He shows how truth can arise out of error, good out of evil (and vice versa), and thus concludes with a differential discourse. This latter discourse provides a new, radical interpretation of sensibility or of the "body" that does not recognize either self-identical unities or foundational grounds.

---

225 Deleuze 9.
226 The two-step process of the deconstructive critique, which we considered in the previous chapter, provides one prominent way in which the displacement of oppositions to differences could happen.
227 Blondel 190.

Rather, as an instantiation of the will to power, it affirms a multiplicity and plurality of dynamic interpretations that have no final purpose.

Among all the groups of interpreters, the internalists' stance is closest to the position I am arguing for in this book. I agree with the internalists that the origin of metaphysics has something to do with the typology of wills. However, I contend that the internalist position does not quite escape the Heideggerian reading of Nietzsche insofar as this position resorts to a *strict* typology of wills, as the fundamental distinction of Nietzsche's philosophy, to guide their interpretation. Specifically, I argue that the internalists' interpretation of the typology of wills implies a *clear-cut* distinction between a strong and a weak will. This becomes apparent when they attempt to analyze *what* characteristic feature it is about the strong (or weak) will which allows this type to affirm (or deny) existence. The assumption that the typological distinction is unambiguous is indispensible for the internalists to generate the critical machinery necessary to substantiate the claims that Nietzsche overcomes metaphysics by providing an internal critique of it. Again, my tactic will be to use the Heideggerian reading against the internalist one, in order to bring out my critique of the latter, and also to open up the direction in which I want to proceed at the next stage of my argument.

In particular, I argue that even the distinction between the strong and weak wills is not an unambiguous, unquestionable distinction for Nietzsche, although, I concede that if there is any distinction that comes close to a basic presupposition of his philosophy, it is this one. To put it in other terms, I do not deny that there is indeed a typology of wills for Nietzsche, reflected in the fundamental claim that the strong type affirms life and will to power, while the weak type denies life. But when we attempt to substantiate this claim by detailing the peculiar *quality* or characteristic of the strong or weak type that allows for the affirmation or denial, what we observe is that a pure typology fails, and that things are more complicated than what the internalists acknowledge. In fact, what we see is a *continuum* between the two types, which forbids any strict or clear-cut distinction between them. Ultimately, therefore, I show that the qualitative difference between the strong and the weak will – pertaining to the directionality of willing – depends on the elusive "how" of the willing. This will complete my argument about the thoroughly ambiguous nature of Nietzsche's critique of metaphysics, which complements his meta-existential philosophy. The specifics of my argument will be taken up in the last two chapters.

With the distinction between the two types of wills, we have reached the fundamental idea of Nietzsche's philosophy, especially with respect to the question of the origin of metaphysical oppositions and of life-denying evaluations. And to this extent, I agree with the internalists' analysis. The question is whether our search for the source of the oppositional schema in the quality of the will to power necessarily implies an unambiguous distinction between the two types of wills. Could we not instead understand the two types themselves as variable notions with meanings that are unfixed and open to interpretation? Could the two types have overlapping boundaries, leading into one another in such a way that the distinction between them reveals different levels of ambiguity? This issue is a complex one in Nietzsche. He tends to treat these two types as if they were fixed types, providing us with various typological differences to unequivocally differentiate between them. But as we shall see in the following chapters, Nietzsche *also* tends to treat the two types as if there existed a continuity between them, which would undermine strict demarcation. Specifying their status as non-absolute, variable notions, he underlines that the "strong" and "weak" are themselves "relative concepts" (GS 118). The internalists fail to pay attention to this "relational" aspect between the two types.[228] The implication of this failure is the tendency to posit some characteristic or the other as belonging solely and purely to the weak type, which would serve as the reason why the latter type denies life.

Consider, for instance, Eric Blondel's argument. After clarifying the irreducibly interpretative nature of the world as will to power – in which there is no closed system or the "true" text, but in which perspectivism implies the "infinite possible interpretative plurality" – Blondel insists that we should no longer distinguish between "true interpretation and false interpretation."[229] Instead, he argues that we must make a distinction between "plural" and "dogmatic" interpretations, between "strong" and "weak" interpretations, between "genealogical" and "superficial" interpretations.[230] The unique feature of the dogmatic (weak) interpretation – which is not present in the plural (strong) interpretation – is that this type "does not recognize itself to be an interpretation made against the background of plurality, but presents itself as the unique and absolute truth of the text."[231] Therefore the dogmatic interpretation is a metaphysical one. For this reason, Blondel maintains that the plural interpretations are "preferable" to the dogmatic ones.[232] Now, even if we grant that Blondel does not mean the above distinction to be a strictly categorical one, it is obvious that he is insisting on a clear-cut, unambiguous distinction between the two types that remains "constant" in some sense. That is, the criterion for distinction ("recognition" of itself to be an "interpretation") is set once and for all in an unequivocal manner: if an interpretation passes this criterion, then it is a life-affirming strong type; otherwise, the interpretation is a weak type which denies life. This criterion, therefore, serves to typologically distinguish the two types. It sets up a kind of opposition between them.

Blondel's reading betrays Nietzsche's own complex analyses of the various characteristics of the two types. To take an example, Nietzsche often mentions willful

---

228 One exception is Deleuze, who comes closer to the interpretation put forward here, since he also suggests the idea of continuity between the two types of wills through his discussion of the "becoming reactive" of the active forces. We will return to Deleuze in the next chapter.
229 Blondel 145–146.
230 Blondel 146.
231 Blondel 146.
232 Blondel 147.

ignorance or self-forgetting as a necessary condition for the "happiness" and "pride" of the strong, noble type (GM II 1). Accordingly, Nietzsche recommends, "Whenever you reach a decision, close your ears to even the best objections" as a sign of "a strong character" (BGE 107). Such a willful ignorance would seem to imply a "dogmatism" that affirms its own perspective as unique and true, precisely as a necessary require-ment for its activity and its noble expression of power. Hence, Blondel's interpretation does not necessarily turn out to be incorrect, but too simplistic. Moreover, his crite-rion that the strong type "recognizes" its own interpretation *as* just an interpretation appears to revert to a notion of "truth" as "correspondence" or "correctness" (which, in this case, "self-recognition"). This criterion resembles the metaphysical criterion for truth as harmony with the actual, which Heidegger attributes to Nietzsche. So if Blondel's interpretation is correct, ironically, it would make Nietzsche's philosophy continuous with the long line of "metaphysical" thought from Plato to Hegel, as Hei-degger insisted.

Similar objections are in order against the efforts of Sarah Kofman, who like Blondel insists on a clear-cut qualitative criterion that establishes a strict typology of wills. For instance, Kofman writes that the strong can "reflect their perspective *as* a perspective" and they "recogni[ze] ... interpretation *as* the primary fact," whereas the weak are unable to "recognize the legitimacy of other evaluations."[233] The strong "recognize the mask as mask thanks to a superabundance of life" whereas the weak are incapable of doing this.[234] But to say that the strong is strong because it has a "superabundance of life" is to say the strong is strong because it is strong. It is circu-lar and question-begging. Kofman's argument, too, does not really escape the reach of the Heideggerian reading, however much she insists, against Heidegger, that the strong type's "recognition" does not yield the "essence of being" but only "a new perspective."[235]

Kofman's insistence reflects the typical internalist thesis that Nietzsche's replace-ment of truth with the fundamentality of interpretation and perspectivism, or his replacement of self-identical unities with the non-foundationalism, pluralism and multiplicities of the will to power (thereby providing an internal critique of metaphys-ics) is *enough* to free him from Heidegger's metaphysical interpretation. For the inter-nalists, these replacements ensure that the will to power is neither a "thing-in-itself" nor another term for the "being of beings," and they take this result to be sufficient for refuting Heidegger. But I have argued that although these replacements are necessary they are not sufficient to escape the Heideggerian reading. Insofar as the internalists subscribe to a pure typology, which reflects a clear-cut distinction between the two types of wills, as the guiding thread of their interpretation, their argument fails to completely counter Heidegger's reading.

---

233 Kofman 133, emphases added.
234 Kofman 74–75.
235 Kofman 133.

The postulation of an unequivocal distinction between the two wills suggests an opposition between them, and, in the end, it is equivalent to positing an opposition between the real and the apparent worlds, and thus to a kind of externalist account of the "being of beings." In Heideggerian terms, this postulation implies a clear-cut way of showing what is in being (the strong type) and what is not in being (the weak type). Therefore, from the Heideggerian perspective, these poststructuralist readings do subscribe to a metaphysical interpretation of truth. In effect, Heidegger's account precisely parallels those of the internalists, notwithstanding the immense differences in their respective interpretations of the will to power. This is so since Heidegger, too, in his Nietzsche lectures acknowledges that there is a new interpretation of sensuousness in Nietzsche, which conflates the distinction between truth and falsity. Nevertheless, he argues that Nietzsche retains a metaphysical conception of truth as harmony with the actual insofar as he seeks to affirm the actual as the realm of becoming and semblance instead of denying it. This distinction between affirmation and denial exactly parallels that made by the poststructuralists between the strong and the weak types. Hence, at bottom, it would appear that both Heidegger and the internalists see metaphysics as setting up a real world in itself, whether this real world is interpreted as the world of being as Heidegger does, or as the interpretative perspective of a dogmatic or a weak will as Blondel and Kofman do. In either case, they lose sight of Nietzsche's basic understanding of a metaphysical evaluation, which focuses on the very oppositional structure between the real and the apparent world.

Nietzsche himself provides the most effective resistance against Heidegger. Although the concept of typology of wills is a fundamental notion of Nietzsche's thought, his complicated analysis of the two types shows that they are not "fixed" or "given" types. Rather these two types themselves "become" (they either undergo decadence or ascension), where at times they may even share some overlapping qualities. Their typical traits undergo transformation, at times leading into one another, implying not only a continuity, a "topology,"[236] between the two types, but also a gray area of transition between them, in which the very distinction between the strong and the weak types appears indiscernible. By suggesting this, I do not argue that Nietzsche finally escapes the Heideggerian interpretation, if to do this means to "overcome" metaphysics. On the contrary, my analysis reveals that Nietzsche neither simply overcomes metaphysics nor is he stuck within its confines, but rather he provides a thoroughly ambiguous, open-ended critique of metaphysics.

The ambiguity of Nietzsche's critique is apparent in the fact that he does not set up oppositions to counteract metaphysics, since he sees precisely the schema of oppositions to be symptomatic of metaphysics. He does not begin his radical criticism by conceding first that there is a metaphysical opposition (for instance, between the

---

236 I borrow the term "topology" from Deleuze's *Nietzsche and Philosophy*. I take this term to refer to a displacement that makes possible a continuity of terrain between two types. We will consider this notion in detail in the next two chapters.

real and the apparent world) – even if to invert or overturn this opposition – since to do so would be tantamount to setting up one's own set of oppositions. Even at the very summit (or the depths) of his philosophy – to which the discussion of the two types of wills takes us – Nietzsche is consistently vigilant to avoid positing oppositional schemas. Instead, his analysis moves between a topology and a typology of wills without settling on a singular criterion of distinction to ultimately qualify the wills. With this movement, Nietzsche consistently affirms his "indirect" meta-existential approach,[237] thereby providing a radically ambiguous criticism of metaphysics. And only through this movement is the becoming of existence revealed, which is something other than the becoming of the subjective tendency of existence.

The internalists fail to see the above as they strive to provide unique, distinguishing, qualitative criteria that would clearly distinguish the strong and the weak type, in their quest to portray Nietzsche as the thinker who has overcome metaphysics. But in doing so, they unwittingly posit an opposition schema, which I maintain, is not present in Nietzsche. Therefore, their account is more "external," more Heideggerian, than they would have liked, as the examples of Blondel and Kofman reveal. In other words, I am suggesting that one can be a thorough internalist only if one is also an existentialist, specifically a meta-existentialist. Since, only then can one provide an account of Nietzsche's critique of metaphysics, from the point of view of Nietzsche's own philosophy, without positing one's own oppositional structures. Therefore the reading I am presenting in this study may be viewed as an internalist-existentialist one.

The internalists intend to claim that Nietzsche's notion of "becoming" is not the same as what Heidegger calls "becoming" as the counterpart of "being." However, insofar as they seek to provide a clear-cut qualitative distinction between the two types, the kind of "becoming" they unveil, corresponding to the play of differences, is not quite exempt from the Heideggerian critique. From a certain perspective, Nietzsche could be still seen as carrying out a reversal of metaphysics through an affirmation of the "being" of "becoming." The only way to set the concept of becoming free from the Heideggerian reading is to release it from the constraints of all oppositional schemas. Nietzsche does this through his complex discussion of both the typology and topology of wills, without resorting to an unequivocal qualitative distinction between the two wills. Only in this way, does Nietzsche's notion of the becoming of existence turn out to be something different from Heidegger's understanding of becoming.

I am sympathetic towards the internalists' interpretation insofar as they, too, seek the source of metaphysical evaluations in the quality of will to power, and not "outside" of the will to power. For them, this establishes the fact that the life-denying evaluation is a "real" negation, which has its source in the world of will to power,

---

237 That is, this movement is consistent with the carrying out of the three implications of making the existential distinction, especially the third one, which entails the repetitive process of re-drawing the existential distinction again and again.

and not in an "other" world opposing will to power. And I concur that establishing the reality of the negative is an essential aspect of any serious attempt at a radical critique of metaphysics. However, a real negation does not mean that there must be two fixed types, where one of the types clearly represents that quality of the will to power corresponding to the denial of life. On the contrary, the reality of the negative precisely means that the two types are not "there" as fixed types, but that these types themselves are subject to becoming and interpretation. We can still maintain the initial qualitative distinction between the strong and the weak types, which is that the former affirms life, and the latter denies it. So there *is* a typological difference between the two types, as Nietzsche's various distinctions regarding them reveal. But when we set about defining *what* quality it is about a type that makes it affirm or deny life, things get more complicated and ambiguous, since one cannot say what this quality is without setting up one's own set of oppositions.

In other words, Nietzsche's analyses of the two types reveal that the precise quality of will to power "behind" the affirmation or denial of life cannot be "directly communicated" or clearly delineated. Rather, it can be interpreted only in terms of a movement between a differential continuity and a typology of wills that resists a definitive qualitative demarcation.[238] Every demarcation that one supposes will capture this qualitative distinction is revealed to be just an element belonging to Nietzsche's movement between a topology and a typology of wills. Therefore, for Nietzsche, the quality of will to power as the source of metaphysical oppositions is always up for interpretation; it is never settled in a final, definitive way. Hence we end up with an essentially ambiguous critique of metaphysics. The quality of the will to power indicates the ultimate "how" of Nietzsche's philosophy, which is ever-elusive. And so corresponding to his radically indirect meta-existential approach, he interprets the quality of the will to power through his complex analysis of the two types of wills.

In the next chapter, we will consider Nietzsche's analysis of the strong and weak wills by investigating the problem of decadence. In particular, we will examine the phenomenon of the decadence of the strong type, since this phenomenon not only provides us the occasion to discuss the typological characteristics of the two types, but also the topological variations undergone by the strong type as it decays and tends towards the weak.

---

238 This movement is analogous to that between the subjective and the objective tendencies of existence discussed in the previous chapter, but they are not the same. The reason is that the latter movement deals only with the quantitative aspect of will to power, while the typological-topological interaction has to do with the quantity as well as the quality of will to power.

Chapter Four
Nobility and decadence: the vulnerabilities of Nietzsche's strong type

The decadence of the strong type

> Nothing has preoccupied me more profoundly than the problem of decadence – I had reasons.
> (CW Preface)

I have argued thus far that the essence of a metaphysical evaluation lies in the positing of an oppositional schema (which leads to a denial of life), whether the opposition is between a real and an apparent world, or between the strong and the weak types of wills. Hence Nietzsche's critique of metaphysics does not set up its own set of oppositions. Nietzsche does not begin his critique by first acknowledging that metaphysics opposes the real world to the apparent world, or the weak will to the strong will, in order to either reverse this opposition or to displace it into a play of differences. Instead, he operates radically indirectly and thoroughly differentially, thus developing a meta-existential critique of metaphysics. In doing so, he carries out a critical investigation into the source of the oppositional schema, the source of life-denial, in the qualitative element of the will to power.

However, Nietzsche's investigation does not provide an unequivocal answer by submitting to a pure typology of wills that would provide a clear-cut criterion to distinguish between the strong and the weak wills. We can still define the strong will as the affirmative will and the weak will as the denying will. But we cannot say, unambiguously, which quality it is about the strong or the weak type that allows them to affirm or deny life. Ultimately, the source of the oppositional schema remains ever-elusive and open for interpretation. To the question, "How does Nietzsche know that a particular evaluation is of the strong type (hence, affirmative) or of the weak type (hence, negative)?" there is no definite answer. Nietzsche's argument progresses *as if* he can distinguish the one type from the other. And therefore, we find various analyses of the typical traits of the two types in Nietzsche's works, which point to a typological distinction between them. At the same time, as we shall see below, there are various other remarks in his writings that point to a *topological* continuity between the two types, which would imply that there is no strict distinction between them. Therefore Nietzsche's critique of metaphysics will be ultimately revealed as ambiguous and open-ended.

To demonstrate both the typological and the topological nature of the wills, I turn to the problem of decadence. Nietzsche explicitly discusses the latter problem more frequently in his final works such as the *Twilight of the Idols*, *The Case of Wagner* and *Ecce Homo* than in his earlier ones. Some discussion about the meaning and nature of decadence is also to be found in his notebook entries from around the same period. However, I suggest that the problem of decadence, especially in the particular form to be highlighted in this chapter, occupied and determined the course of Nietzsche's thought for almost the entirety of his philosophical career. He never ceased to think and write about how it is that a Socratic-dialectical moral philosophy arose out of the strong, noble, Dionysian Greek soil. Either by looking at science through the prism of the artist in *The Birth of Tragedy*, or by confronting the "problem of Socrates" in the *Twilight of the Idols*, Nietzsche endlessly grappled with the issue of the decadence of the Ancient Greek culture. This issue, of course, is a particular historical instance of the general concern central to Nietzsche's genealogical project, namely, the problem of how a strong type loses its battle against the weak, and in what way the weak re-evaluate and impose its value-systems on the strong. Nietzsche recognized that coming to terms with the latter two issues is absolutely crucial for the positive and creative aspirations of his philosophy: to effect a re-evaluation of the prevalent weak values of modern humanity. I argue that the problem of decadence takes on a particular sense and form in this *transitional* stage – when the strong type loses its struggle against the weak – which I want to investigate, both in the present chapter and in the final one. In examining the problem of the decadence of the strong type, we will not only encounter the various typological distinctions between the two types, but, given the transitional aspect of the problem, we will also see what is entailed by a topological continuity between the two types.

Nietzsche describes the issue of decadence in various other contexts, and therefore attributes different meanings and senses to it. For example, in one of his final works, in depicting the sickness of modernity, Nietzsche describes modern decadence as a case of instinctive contradiction, and that "modern man represents a *contradiction of values*" (CW Epilogue). The meaning of the decadence of modern morality is elaborated elsewhere as the propensity to instinctively choose "what is harmful to *oneself*" (TI Expeditions 35). Nietzsche comes to see modernity as caught up inextricably in a kind of "passive nihilism," which indefinitely prolongs its impending demise by lingering in the space of its own meaninglessness. Passive nihilism represents a "decline and recession of the power of the spirit," where the goals and values of previous times do not have a hold on the current conditions of culture, but also where there is not enough strength for the creation of new values and directions (KSA 12, 9[35]). But Nietzsche reads the nihilistic condition as a "pathological transitional stage" (KSA 12, 9[35]), and therefore, as fundamentally "*ambiguous*," since it gives rise not only to a passive nihilism, but also to an "active nihilism" which is "a sign of increased power of the spirit" (KSA 12, 9[35]). Modern decadence is such that, contained within it, there are also the conditions for the possibility of a future strong culture. These conditions are those of active nihilism, which enacts a violent destruction and a complete devaluation of the highest values hitherto, such that modern culture would not find any refuge for its indifferent attitude towards the creation of values (KSA 12, 9[35]). Hence Nietzsche proclaims a great disgust for the "last human," and promotes the perishing of the latter in order to make way for the birth of the over-human [*Übermensch*] (Z Prologue 5). The theme of active nihilism is explored in detail through various angles in almost all of his works starting from *The Gay Science* to the *Nachlaß* of the late 1880s. And finally, in the *Ecce Homo*, Nietzsche emphasizes the ambiguity of the problem of decadence, when he identifies himself as a philosopher who is both a "*decadent* and a *beginning*" (EH Wise 1). He describes himself as having gone through periods of profound sicknesses, and also having recovered from these sicknesses time and again by using them as energetic stimuli for life. He could do this because he is "*summa summarum*" a "healthy" soul (EH Wise 2). But "as an angle, as a specialty" he is a decadent (EH Wise 2).[239]

In his works, Nietzsche employs different German terms to describe the process of decadence: *Niedergang, Verfall* (decline), *Entartung* (degeneration), *Pessimismus* and *Nihilismus*.[240] I will also include here *Verderbniss* (spoiling or rotting (my translation))[241] and *Zugrundegehen* (destruction or ruination). Both of these terms are used by Nietzsche in connection with the destruction of the strong type or the "higher people" in section 269 of *Beyond Good and Evil*. Typically scholars writing on this topic fail to mention the usage of the latter two terms, and also the context of their usage. Usually, decadence is discussed in the context of modernity, with regard to the devalued Platonic-Christian values, and also to an interpretation of modern culture as the heir to these devalued value-systems. The important question here is: how can weak modernity enact its active nihilism and renew its strength to establish a future strong culture? Accordingly, commentators focus on Nietzsche's role as a "cultural physician," who attempts to provide a possible cure to the modern malaise.[242]

But there is another dimension to the decadence problem, which is as significant to Nietzsche's thought as the problem of decadence of modernity. Here, the emphasis is not on how weak modernity could perhaps restore a higher culture, but on how the strong type lost its battle against the weak in the first place, leading to a predominance of the weak values. I suggest that an inquiry into this latter problem is presupposed by Nietzsche's account of the devaluation of the Platonic-Christian values, and

---

239 For a detailed treatment of Nietzsche's critique of the decadence of modernity, and Nietzsche's complicity in this decadence, see Daniel Conway, *Nietzsche's Dangerous Game* (Cambridge: Cambridge University Press, 1997).

240 Conway notes that Nietzsche first uses the term *Entartung* in *Thus Spoke Zarathustra*, and *Niedergang* and *Verfall* were employed only in the 1886 prefaces to his earlier works. Nietzsche appropriates the French term *décadence* only in his published writings of the year 1888. See Conway, *Nietzsche's Dangerous Game* 23.

241 Judith Norman translates *Verderbniss* as "ruin," but it can also be translated as "spoiling" or "rotting." I prefer the latter terms, as they are more appropriate for the arguments I will be making in this chapter.

242 See Daniel Conway, "The Politics of Decadence," *Southern Journal of Philosophy* 37 (1999): 19–33. Also, see Daniel Ahern, *Nietzsche as Cultural Physician* (University Park: The Pennsylvania State University Press, 1995).

also by his positive project of the re-evaluation of all values. In our investigation into this problem, we must address the following questions: does the decadence of the strong type involve both *Verderbniss* and *Zugrundegehen*? Does the latter rest on the former? We need to understand how these two terms are related to each other, even though Nietzsche himself uses them indiscriminately to refer to the phenomenon of the decadence of the strong in general.

Decadence has various dimensions and meanings because it is not some fixed state for Nietzsche, but one, which essentially indicates the process of the becoming of Western history. It is the process in which the strong type of human being undergoes a certain kind of degeneration and, ultimately, loses its struggle against the weak type. It is also the process in which the highest values of Platonic-Christian morality devaluate themselves, and through which (Nietzsche hopes) a new noble type will be born, one which has surpassed the opposition between good and evil in order to see the whole of humanity hitherto beneath it. Both these processes have peculiar ambiguities, as they refer to transitional stages of history, where there is shift in dominance from one type to another. The ambiguities consist in the fact that, during these transitional stages, there are possibilities for the "strong" type to assume characteristics that are typically considered to be "weak" (and vice versa). In this sense, these types themselves can be seen to be becoming or undergoing topological transformations. These transitional stages not only reveal how one type leads into the other, but also a gray area, in which it becomes seemingly impossible to unequivocally distinguish between the two types.

Hence the problem of decadence in Nietzsche, especially given its transitional aspects, is anything but a simple problem with a straightforward solution. We should resist the temptation to portray it as if it was a self-evident or a "natural" problem. For instance, Conway argues that Nietzsche "locates decadence in the natural, inevitable failure of the invisible body to sustain an efficient propagation through itself of will to power."[243] For Conway, there is a "law of inevitable decay," which he justifies "economically."[244] To be sure, making the claim that, for a body, the process of decadence is inevitable is not incorrect. Nietzsche himself makes this point when he writes that "waste, decay, elimination ... are necessary consequences of life, of the growth of life" (KSA 13, 14[75]). However, noting the inevitability or the naturalness of decadence should not deter us from inquiring into the ambiguity of this phenomenon, which speaks of one of the most questionable and tragic aspects of human existence, and upon which Nietzsche meditated without respite.

Moreover, there is something *unnatural* about the phenomenon of the decadence of the strong type, which would explain why this topic has received so little atten-

---

243 *Nietzsche's Dangerous Game* 48.
244 *Nietzsche's Dangerous Game* 71.

tion in recent literature.[245] Usually, commentators operate with the presupposition – whether directly acknowledged or not – that there are two pure and fixed types of human beings for Nietzsche, namely the life-affirming strong type and the life-denying weak type, and at some point in history the weak somehow came to dominate the strong, effecting an inversion of the old values. Since decadence is usually taken to have a life-denying connotation, it is assumed that only the weak or sick type is susceptible to decadence. Therefore, decadence is not associated with the opposite, strong or healthy type. The guiding thread behind this interpretation is the crucial assumption that Nietzsche provides unequivocal criteria to differentiate between the strong and the weak types – an assumption I believe to be problematic.

This mode of interpretation has its root in Heidegger's influential Nietzsche lectures. As we know, according to Heidegger, Nietzsche's project of the re-evaluation of all values is stuck at an oppositional level, effecting only a metaphysical overturning of the Platonic-Christian system of values. Heidegger considers the problem of decadence, but only in the context of Nietzsche's discussion of the history of nihilism in the weak post-Platonic culture of the west.[246] He considers Nietzsche's starting point to be his interpretation of the Platonic metaphysics of (supersensible) "Ideas." Heidegger argues that, for Nietzsche, all philosophy since Plato is the "metaphysics of values."[247] Even though Platonic metaphysics denies life, it inaugurates a new course in Western history by establishing its own highest values. Nietzsche's account of the history of nihilism is the key to his interpretation of the history of metaphysics, since this account shows how the prior truths and the highest values of Platonism and Christianity have devalued themselves. For Heidegger, the entire concern of Nietzsche's philosophy is to confront the history of this nihilism, to complete it, and carry out a re-evaluation of all values.[248]

But in this Heideggerian interpretation, the claim that Nietzsche is a metaphysician of values goes hand-in-hand with Heidegger's decision to treat the problem of decadence only in the context of post-Platonic nihilism. Heidegger is oblivious to a prior history of decadence, that of the pre-Platonic Greeks, which would show how the strong Hellenic type decays and makes possible something like the Platonic mode of evaluation (Nietzsche has plenty to say about this issue, as we shall see in the next chapter). Because Heidegger fails to consider this prior history, I suggest, he never questions his supposition that the strong and the weak are opposite types for Nietzsche. His argument involves showing that Nietzsche's rejection of truth is

---

245 Deleuze's *Nietzsche and Philosophy* is a notable exception. Although Deleuze does not pose the problem in the terms in which I am posing it here, he is nevertheless concerned in his work with providing a sense and interpretation of the "becoming reactive" of the active forces, and the central role this phenomenon plays for Nietzsche's account of the genealogy of values.
246 See *Nietzsche* III: 201–208.
247 *Nietzsche* III: 201.
248 *Nietzsche* III: 203–204.

only apparent, since he still undertakes a critique of all those weak evaluations that deny life by denying the becoming of the sensible world. Nietzsche's re-evaluation of all values, then, would involve affirming the strength of becoming as opposed to the weakness of being. Thus this Heideggerian reading implies that Nietzsche only transfers the question of truth and falsity to that of strength and weakness; and therefore one must locate Nietzsche's ultimate concern with truth (which in the end takes the metaphysical form of truth as correspondence to strong-becoming, instead of weak-being) within the latter realm of concepts. It is apparent to see that Heidegger's reading essentially relies on the presence of unambiguous criteria to distinguish what constitutes the strong from the weak type. But if there were no such clear distinction between these two types, the entire question of Nietzsche's commitment to truth would be confounded, and Heidegger's reading of Nietzsche as a metaphysical thinker would become questionable.

Contemporary interpreters have mostly rejected Heidegger's historical-metaphysical interpretation. However, in most cases, one can always detect a move in them to locate unequivocal criteria to differentiate between strong and weak wills. We saw this with respect to commentators like Cox, Blondel and Kofman in the previous chapter. Christopher Janaway seems to provide a more promising account. He acknowledges that, ultimately, slave morality has the same origin as the noble mode of evaluation, and thereby points out the complexity and ambiguity of Nietzsche's genealogical critique.[249] Yet he insists that Nietzsche is unequivocally seeking "truth" in giving a critique of slave morality, in order to claim him as a naturalist thinker.[250] It is hard to see how one can ascribe this unequivocal notion of truth to Nietzsche if one seriously considers the ambiguity of his genealogical project. It appears, then, that Janaway too, at bottom, believes that Nietzsche provides a clear way of distinguishing between the strong and the weak types.

It is understandable that these interpreters assume that there is pure typological distinction between the two wills. In many passages, Nietzsche criticizes any evaluation as "declining, debilitated [and] weary" if it denies or falsifies the basic conditions of life and its becoming (TI Morality 5). The decadent will negates life, and in doing so, it posits a world of being as the supersensible world. For Nietzsche, there *are* some "fundamental prerequisites of life" that need to be affirmed (GM III 28). So it would seem that Nietzsche's overcoming of nihilism inverts the negation of life in order affirm life. Even if Nietzsche confounds the distinction between truth and falsity, by arguing that truth itself is a kind of error, he still maintains a proper distinction between affirmation and negation, and therefore between a life-affirming (noble or healthy or strong) will and a life-denying (base or sick or weak) will.

---

249 Christopher Janaway, *Beyond Selflessness: Reading Nietzsche's Genealogy* (Oxford: Oxford University Press, 2007) 101, 209, 252.
250 *Beyond Selflessness* 3, 239.

Indeed, Nietzsche gives elaborate descriptions of the two kinds of wills: the different perspectives out of which they view the world, their respective principles of evaluation, and so on, which seem to clearly mark the boundary between them. For instance, he writes that there are "two basic types" of moralities and that he is pointing to a "fundamental distinction" (BGE 260). He argues that value distinctions arise within either a "dominating type that, with a feeling of well-being, was conscious of the difference between itself and those who are dominated – or alternatively, these distinctions arose among the dominated people themselves, the slaves and the dependents of every rank" (BGE 260). And in *On the Genealogy of Morality*, Nietzsche clearly states that he intends to sketch "*typical character trait[s]*" of the strong type (GM I 5). His character analyses of both the strong and weak types unravel in sections 9–13 in the first essay of the same book.[251] Here, Nietzsche apparently isolates those particular characteristic features of the strong (or weak) type, which would show why they affirm (or deny) existence, thus clearly distinguishing between the two types. Let us consider section 10. In this section, he remarks that the strong type is "*necessarily active,*" and that it does not separate happiness from action. The strong persons *feel* immediately that they are the happy ones; they do not need first of all to construct their happiness artificially by looking at their enemies or by lying to themselves. The strong human being is somebody who is "confident and frank with himself." These traits reflect the fact that all noble morality grows out of a triumphant saying "yes" to itself. This affirmative "yes" is the noble type's basic *creative* deed.

In contrast, Nietzsche argues that the slave morality is principally based on saying "no" to "everything that is 'outside', 'other', 'non-self.'" This "no" is its creative deed. Accordingly, the weak person of *ressentiment* is "neither upright nor naïve, nor honest and straight with himself... his mind loves dark corners, secret paths and back-doors." Everything appeals to him as "*his* world, *his* security, *his* comfort." A weak person does not know how to actively forget, but he waits for an opportunity to exploit the other, "temporarily humbling and abasing himself." He is inevitably cleverer than the noble person, and his cleverness is his "condition of existence of the first rank." Accordingly, Nietzsche draws a fundamental distinction between the two types: while the strong type is dominated by the *creative* instinct, the weak type is governed by the instinct of *self-preservation* (GM I 13).[252]

If one takes these typological differentiations as the sole assumptions guiding Nietzsche's genealogical project, one ends up with an interpretation similar to Hei-

---

251 Nietzsche's characterizations of Goethe, Schopenhauer, Socrates, Plato, Jesus, the pre-Socratics, the Ancient Greeks, Homer, Napoleon, Caesar, and the Roman and Scandinavian nobility, depicting typical traits of the strong and weak, are found throughout his works. Distinctive characteristics of the strong and weak types are also discussed in the chapters, "The free spirit" and "What is noble?" of BGE. Also, see GS 3, 349 and the chapter, "Expeditions of an Untimely Man" in TI. More examination of the typological character traits are also scattered throughout Z and in the *Nachlaß* material of the 1880s.

252 Also, see GS 349.

degger's. For instance, Daniel Ahern maintains that Nietzsche has an unambiguous way of showing how or why a culture, an individual or an epoch is "healthy" or "sick."[253] He argues that Nietzsche only rejects the "truths" of metaphysics, but by drawing out a clear distinction between the healthy and the sick, he wanted to establish "fictional" truths, which, although like metaphysics, is contingent upon the will to power, is nevertheless different in that it falls within an "understanding" of health and strength.[254] Ahern clearly reveals his Heideggerian commitments when he asserts that Nietzsche "sought new foundations, new standards... In this, he remained within the spirit of metaphysics he sought to destroy and was as concerned with the question of values as Plato."[255]

In contrast to these Heideggerian interpretations, I propose that for Nietzsche the distinction between the healthy and the sick is complicated and equivocal. The different descriptions of the healthy and the sick that Nietzsche gives are useful only if one has *already* somehow spotted the strong from the weak or vice versa. The descriptions of strength and weakness, which he provides are symptoms that need to be interpreted rather than some final truths. Because of the symptomatic character of Nietzsche's descriptions, the attentive reader often finds him using, what appears to be, the same characterizations to describe the strong type that he elsewhere used to describe the weak type. To take one example, he writes in a passage that the morality of the strong is characterized by a "profound reverence for age and origins... a faith and a prejudice in favor of forefathers and against future generations" (BGE 260). But elsewhere, raving against a slave morality that uncritically borrows and adheres to traditional and universal values, Nietzsche calls for a "purification of our opinions and value judgments," and for the noble person to "create" for herself her own "ideal," an ideal which is not somebody else's (GS 335). There are plenty of such apparent contradictions in Nietzsche's works, which instead of showing his inconsistency, urge the reader to stay true to the context of Nietzsche's utterances and also to the profound ambiguities they entail. Such reading demands that one should not take his descriptions of the strong and weak types at face value, lest one wants to present a naïve interpretation.[256]

In line with this argumentation, I contend that, at bottom, there is an irreducible equivocation in Nietzsche's analysis of the two types of wills. As Nietzsche himself observes:

---

253 Ahern 2–5.
254 Ahern 5, footnote 9.
255 Ahern 5.
256 For example, Janaway understands the above-quoted passage in GS 335 (without really considering the "contradictory" passage in BGE 260) to mean that Nietzsche is recommending a sort of autonomy and "selfishness" to the one who aspires to be a creator of values (*Beyond Selflessness* 120). I am not suggesting that this reading is wrong, but rather that this naïve assessment hides the immense complexity behind most of Nietzsche's utterances (which demands that one looks at both sides of the coin and may forbid a simple straightforward interpretation).

[T]here is no health as such, and all attempts to define such a thing have failed miserably. Decid-
ing what is health even for your *body* depends on your goal, your horizon, your powers, your
impulses, your mistakes, and above all on the ideals and phantasms of your soul. Thus there are
innumerable healths of the body (GS 120).

Indeed, for Nietzsche, the strong and weak are relative concepts (GS 118). He even
claims that one can, at times, find the master and slave moralities "sharply juxtaposed – inside the same person even, within a single soul" (BGE 260). If we take this
ambiguity seriously, we arrive at the Nietzschean problem of genealogical interpretation. Conway seems to acknowledge this ambiguity when he writes, "The interpretation of entire peoples and ages is a tricky business, however, for any single policy or
practice might signify either strength or weakness, health or decay."[257] But he contends
that Nietzsche solves the interpretative problem by restricting "his focus to those representative exemplars who 'stand for' an age as a whole."[258] However, Conway's solution
is circular, since it begs the question regarding how Nietzsche actually "spots" the great
exemplar of an age, if it is not unambiguously clear whether an instance of practice of
entire peoples signifies either strength or weakness. Why is this ambiguity cleared up
when we instead consider an exemplary individual or the few exceptional ones? How
does Nietzsche know the exceptional to be the exceptional one?

There is no precise way out of this interpretative dilemma, which does not end up
positing some kind of circularity or the other. It is more productive to read Nietzsche's
equivocation as pointing towards a topological continuity between the two types
of wills. I borrow the term "topology" from Deleuze, who in his influential book on
Nietzsche defines the "topology of reactive forces" as their "change of place, their
displacement."[259] I use this term in a similar way to mean a change of place or displacement, which makes possible a continuity between the two types. In our sense
of the term, the topological continuity implies a gray area of transition between the
two wills where the very distinction between a strong and a weak will becomes seemingly non-existent or indiscernible. To understand what this gray area of continuity
implies, I will consider the problem of decadence of the strong type.

As we shall see, there are a plenty of arguments in Nietzsche's works, in which he
suggests that the strong will, which affirms life in all its creative capacities, nevertheless falls into decadence. At times, he even claims that the strong will is not only more
vulnerable to decadence than the weak will, which denies life and seeks solace in a
world of being, but also that its decadence is inevitable. For instance, in the passage
in *Beyond Good Evil* referred to above, he writes, "The ruin [the German word *Verderbniss*, which Kaufmann translates as "corruption," but which could be more usefully
translated as "rotting" or "spoiling"], the destruction [the German word *Zugrundege-*

---

257 *Nietzsche's Dangerous Game* 79.
258 *Nietzsche's Dangerous Game* 79.
259 Deleuze 114.

hen, which Kaufmann translates as "ruination"] of higher people ... is the rule" (BGE 269). This suggests that the distinction between strong and weak wills cannot just be an absolute or a pure typological distinction of two types, which do not intersect or overlap with one another. There must also be a topological aspect to the relation between these two types. If we take up this neglected dimension seriously we will see that Nietzsche has a much more complex and ambiguous relation to metaphysics than is usually acknowledged.

One can perhaps try to avoid this conclusion by arguing that there are actually two kinds of decadences, one corresponding to the strong, and the other corresponding to the weak will, and further that the distinction between these two kinds of decadences is not equivocal. After all, Nietzsche does remark that the strong "suffer differently" from the weak (GS 251).[260] Nietzsche argues in a passage entitled, "What is Romanticism?" that "there are two types of sufferers: first, those who suffer from a *superabundance of life* – they want a Dionysian art as well as a tragic outlook and insight into life; then, those who suffer from an *impoverishment of life* and seek quiet, stillness..." (GS 370). Presumably this implies that the decadence of the first type is also different from that of the second type, and we can discern a purely qualitative, unambiguous distinction between these two kinds of decadences. The decadent strong will, unlike the decadent weak will, still promotes life because the strong will is healthy at bottom (EH Wise 2). Bruce Ellis Benson employs this strategy to clearly differentiate the two kinds of decadences. He argues that the point behind Nietzsche's criticism is to denounce the kind of asceticism symptomatic of the morality, which denies life. Nietzsche promotes his own brand of (strong) asceticism that says to "yes" to life.[261] Nietzsche's asceticism as opposed to Socrates' (which was that of a weak decadent) sought a "'right' ordering of the soul" and the "'true order of life.'"[262] The Heideggerian aspect of Benson's argument is clearly evident here.

In any case, I do not think that insisting on a strict distinction between the strong and the weak varieties of decadence bails us out of the complexity of issue at hand. For Nietzsche, the ambiguity of the typological difference goes deeper than even a differentiation between the two kinds of decadences. As he continues in GS 370, he makes the following decisive observation:

> [T]he question of whether the creation was caused by a desire for fixing, for immortalizing, for *being*, or rather by a desire for destruction, for change, for novelty, for future, for *becoming*. However, both types of desires prove ambiguous upon closer approximation... The desire for *destruction*, for change and for becoming can be the expression of an overflowing energy pregnant with the future... but it can also be the hatred of the ill-constituted, deprived and the underprivileged (GS 370).

---

260 Also, see BGE 270.

261 Bruce Ellis Benson, *Pious Nietzsche: Decadence and Dionysian Faith* (Bloomington: Indiana University Press, 2008) 67.

262 Benson 87.

Indeed, I agree with Deleuze that "interpretation is [] a difficult art – we must judge whether the forces which prevail are inferior or superior, reactive or active; whether they prevail as *dominated* or *dominant*. In this area there are no facts, only interpretations."[263]

Moreover, without the idea of a gray area of transition, it is not possible to completely come to terms with Nietzsche's interpretation of history. The topological transition implies that the two types have become; they change dynamically, undergoing constant metamorphosis, assuming different internal traits, and thereby determining the course of history. Only when we understand that the meanings or the essences of the two types alter over the course of history, can we comprehend, for instance, Nietzsche's claim that with the invention of the "bad conscience" in slave morality, humankind as a whole becomes sick as it turns against itself: "man's sickness of *man*, of *himself*" (GM II 16). The slavish, *ressentiment* type could not turn inward and invert values if there was no gray area of transition between this type and the strong. The definitive moments of human history (and also the definitive moments of the future of humanity as Nietzsche hopes them to be) are precisely those in which the struggle between the two types reach a critical or threshold point, and decisive results are made: either the strong asserts its creative will over the weak, thereby taking humanity into higher and more glorious heights, or they lose this battle, thus inaugurating an era of decadent humanity. But these decisive moments of struggle indeed reveal that there is a gray area on the continuum where the strong can potentially taper away, so to speak, and give birth to the weak type.

Nietzsche's genealogical critique, which inquires into the "*descent* of our moral prejudices" (GM Preface 2), asks the question: "under what conditions did man invent the value judgments good and evil? *and what value do they themselves have?*" (GM Preface 3). Nietzsche apparently presents an "either/or" here by asking further: "Are they [the values] a sign of distress, poverty and the degeneration of life? Or, on the contrary, do they reveal the fullness, vitality and will of life, its courage, its confidence, its future?" (GM Preface 3). However, if in addition to the either/or of evaluations that are typologically differentiated, there is also a topological continuity signified by the degeneration of the healthy type, then there is an essential ambiguity underlying Nietzsche's genealogical project. We could say that there is an "interaction" between the topological and typological aspects, which constitutes the very motor of history. Nietzsche's genealogy investigates this process, through the examination of the descent of moral prejudices. Thus genealogical inquiry presupposes both the topological and typological aspects and the interaction between them.

---

263 Deleuze 58.

Typology and topology

Nietzsche's account of the history of the west unfolds in the following way: Ancient Greek culture grew in power, realizing its golden age (which Nietzsche, in his early writings, determines to be sixth and fifth century B.C.), in which the master race dominates the weak, base or "bad" type as reflected in its "master morality," art and philosophy (BGE 260). The Socratic dialectical-moral philosophy announced the death of tragedy, an inversion of the old Greek values. Nietzsche describes Socratism as "a sign of decline, of exhaustion, of sickness, of the anarchic dissolution of the instincts" (BT Attempt 1). Already in *The Birth of Tragedy* he sees Socrates as the most "questionable phenomenon in Antiquity" who dared to "negate the nature of the Greeks" (BT 13). Socrates was the genuine opponent of tragic art: "the Dionysian versus the Socratic" (BT 12). Nietzsche characterizes the reversal evident in the Socratic turn in the following way:

> Whereas in the case of all productive people instinct is precisely the creative-affirmative force and consciousness makes critical and warning gestures, in the case of Socrates, by contrast, instinct becomes the critic and consciousness the creator – a true monstrosity *per defectum!* (BT 13).

With this inversion Socrates emerges as a new type of sick individual – who is "the forerunner of a completely different culture, art and morality" – in contrast to the healthy Hellenic type (BT 13). But how exactly is this inversion brought about? Did the Socratic weak type always exist as a distinct type lurking behind the healthy Greek culture?

To answer these questions, one may turn to the later Nietzsche, who, at the end of his career, considers the problem of Socrates again. Nietzsche notes that the historic moment when Socrates came onto the scene was unique in the sense that Greek society had already been degenerating and the "old Athens was coming to an end" (TI Socrates 9). Socrates' arrival was timely and he understood that "all the world had need of him – his expedient, his cure, his personal art of self-preservation" (TI Socrates 9). The Socratic cure was welcomed by Athenians whose instincts had become mutually antagonistic. Socrates took advantage of this situation. But this does not mean that the Socratic-rational type always existed as an abstract possibility, lurking somewhere in the background of the Dionysian type. Rather, the Socratic type had become. This type came into being, took form, shape and reality in the Greek soil itself. But it is not the same as the base, bad type, which was dominated by healthy type during the golden period of the Ancient Greeks. Rather, there was a process of decadence internal to the Ancient Greek aristocracy itself, which dynamically gives birth to the rational-dialectic instinct. At a certain point in history, the rational-dialectic instinct crystallized into an autonomous type that turns against aristocratic values. Viewed this way, the mode of being Socrates expresses is not the cause, but the effect or the symptom par excellence of an ongoing decaying process (TI Socrates 2).[264] In other words, it is only because the strong type undergoes decadence that the weak type is able to dominate and impose its mode of evaluation on history. The weak would not have triumphed if the strong had not degenerated on its own terms. But how does this degeneration happen? How does the new Socratic type come to be? How does the Dionysian Greek culture undergo decadence and give birth to the dialectician?[265]

Deleuze developed perhaps the most useful conceptual tools to date to come to terms with this central genealogical problem in Nietzsche's thought. In his 1962 book *Nietzsche and Philosophy*, Deleuze introduces the notion of a "topology of reactive forces" which refers to their "change of place, their displacement."[266] For Deleuze, the topological displacement of reactive forces allows for the emergence of a new weak type that is characterized by *ressentiment*. This type – the dominance of which, for Nietzsche, effects an inversion of the earlier strong values to inaugurate a "slave morality" – is different from the previous weak types that were dominated by the noble type under the rule of "master morality."[267] However, even though Deleuze discusses the "becoming reactive" of active forces, he considers the topology of reactive forces to be more primary. He suggests that the "becoming reactive" of active forces is a consequence of the topological displacement of reactive forces. For him, the topological displacement of reactive forces results in the "separat[ion] of active force from what it can do," which in turn leads to the becoming reactive of active forces.[268] And Deleuze traces back the topological displacement of reactive forces itself to a struggle in the reactive system. I will argue that this interpretation runs contrary to Deleuze's overall reading of active and reactive forces, and also to his thesis that for Nietzsche

---

264 As the leaders of the "herd," the "ascetic priests" (like Socrates) would play an important and decisive role in the re-interpretation of the old weak type and their power structures, and therefore in the inversion of values. This is a vast and complex topic, and we will consider some of its aspects in the next chapter in our study of Greek decadence. But generally, the reader should keep in mind that the topological transition between the two types, involved in the decadence of the strong, is a dynamic process in which both types are mutually re-interpreted and re-defined.

265 It is unproductive at this juncture to say that there is a "natural inevitability" to the decadence of the noble type ("What goes up comes down"). Conway, for instance, writes that "declining ages inevitably succeed healthy ages; strong peoples naturally degenerate into weak peoples," and that Nietzsche views western history in terms of a "renewable cycle of inexorable growth and decay," which is governed by a "natural" immutable law (*Nietzsche's Dangerous Game* 72). Even if this "natural law" of history were true (and I am not sure it is true for Nietzsche, especially with respect to the view that modern culture will be inevitably succeeded by a healthy age), it does not make the process of the decadence of the strong any less problematic and question-worthy. The issue of the decadence of the strong is one of those terrible and tragic processes, upon which Nietzsche ceaselessly meditated. The question "why did life, physiological well-constitutedness everywhere succumb?" triggers and defines the very trajectory of his genealogical thought (KSA 13, 14[137]).

266 Deleuze 114.

267 Nietzsche characterizes "master morality" and "slave morality" in BGE 260.

268 Deleuze 64.

negation and denial are consequences of activity. I will maintain that the topology of reactive forces presupposes a prior displacement of active forces. For example, with respect to Ancient Greek culture we could say that the emergence of an independent, weak, Socratic type presupposes a topological displacement of the Greek noble type.

But what does topological displacement of a type really mean? What does it involve? To explain this, let us briefly consider Deleuze's text on Nietzsche. Until now, we have tended to use the term active/reactive forces as synonymous with strong (affirmative)/ weak (denying) will, and there was no need for us to differentiate these terms. But following Deleuze, we must make an important terminological distinction between "forces" and "wills" to explain the process of topological transformation while at the same time allowing for the fact that there are two types of wills. Deleuze uses this strategy to discuss the "becoming reactive" of the active forces.[269] With the decadence of the strong type, the strong will does not become the weak will, although the strong will does decay. There remain two types of will, and neither type is reduced to the other. Topological displacement refers to active forces, not wills, becoming reactive. "Active" and "reactive" are not purely quantitative terms, but they still refer to the quality of forces, where quality refers to quantitative differences.

The starting point of our discussion is again the Nietzschean concept of "body" as a tremendous multiplicity with a plurality of dominating and dominated forces in continuous mutual struggle. The body is a political structure of organized power in which the "higher type [is] possible only through the subjugation of the lower, so that it becomes a function" (KSA 12, 2[76]). The relative unity of a body is secured through this subjugation, which involves assimilation, appropriation, overpowering, forming, re-shaping, rumination, digestion, nutrition and elimination as various forms of interpretation. Thus the body is a "great reason, a manifold with one sense, a war and a peace, a herd and a herdsman" (Z I 4). It reveals a hierarchy of forces consisting of dominated and dominating forces. With the will to power as the principle of interaction between all the forces, we have a field of interconnected forces governed by the elemental affect of commanding. The will to power's qualitative dimension implies that this which wants to grow must evaluate whatever else wants to grow. Accordingly, at the level of forces, commanding and obeying as basic forms of struggle, yield active and reactive forces. At the level of wills, these same forms of struggle yield the strong or affirmative will and the weak or denying will. Although there is a deep affinity between the two levels, we may still differentiate them as Deleuze does. Deleuze writes, "action and reaction are more like means ... of the will to power which affirm and denies."[270] He further remarks that affirmation is the "power of becoming active, *becoming active* personified," while negation is not simple reaction, but a "*becoming reactive*."[271]

---

269 Deleuze 63–72.
270 Deleuze 54.
271 Deleuze 54.

What Deleuze means by this may be clarified by a simple example. If we consider the Ancient Greek culture as a particular body, Nietzsche's term "strong" or "affirmative" would be used to refer to the culture as a whole. But the means employed by this culture to affirm existence are both the active (i.e., the noble or the "good") type of human being *and* the reactive (i.e., the base or "bad") type of human being (BGE 260). Both these types perform different functions within the culture that corresponds to a master morality that affirms existence. One may make similar distinctions with respect to a "weak," "denying," Platonic-Christian culture and its components. Analogous distinctions may be applied to other "bodies," such as an individual person, a nation, or a time-period in history.

Given this, we can observe that an affirming or denying will uses both action and reaction for the sake of its ends. Affirmation consists of active and reactive forces, since both kinds of forces must be in mutual struggle for the becoming of action. What differentiates an affirmative (healthy, strong) will from the negative (sick, weak) will is the *type of relation* that exists between the active and the reactive forces. I will analyze this issue below. The topological transition from the strong to the weak type consists of a transition from the type of relation between active and reactive forces characteristic of the strong will to that of weak will. For Deleuze, this transition consists in active forces becoming reactive. Further, although the active force becomes reactive, the strong will does not become a weak will. Rather, the strong will decays and can give birth to a new type of weak will (in which active forces have become reactive) which comes to dominate the former will. This ensures that the typological distinction between the strong and weak wills is still maintained, while there is a topological transition at the level of forces.

According to Nietzsche, the strong type is characterized by its active faculty of forgetting. He writes, "Forgetfulness is not just a *vis inertiae*, as superficial people believe, but is rather an active ability to suppress, positive in the strongest sense of the word" (GM II 1). The faculty of forgetting is a form of selective filtering that does not allow everything from the thousand fold processes of strife and mutual struggle that goes on in the underworld of drives, affects, and serviceable organs to enter the realm of consciousness. It filters the content of this complicated process in order to maintain a relative unity, "a little peace, a little *tabula rasa*" at the level of consciousness, so that we can simply live through our experience without having to bother about how our variegated experiences are taken in, processed, assimilated and digested (GM I 1). It sustains a relative stability and health, providing a unity to the bodily system. Specifically, the faculty of forgetting maintains the health of the system in three ways. First, it is responsible for a sort of quick recovery from bad experiences. It helps dispense with the traces of an experience that might potentially induce one to pass a slanderous moral judgment on life. "To be unable to take his enemies, his misfortunes and even his *misdeeds* seriously for long – that is the sign of strong, rounded natures" (GM I 10). Second, it makes room for something new, some new experiences, "above all for nobler functions and functionaries, for ruling, predicting, predetermining"

(GM II 1). Nietzsche describes this faculty as the "doorkeeper or guardian of mental order, rest and etiquette" without which there could be no happiness, cheerfulness, hope and pride (GM II 1). And thirdly, it is this faculty which makes it possible for one to be "done with" any particular experience, not just the bad ones; it enables one to "cope" with experience in general (GM II 1). The faculty of forgetting ensures that one is not overcome by victories, defeats, or spoils. Forgetting helps one to "move on."

This ability to move on is what makes it possible for one to be active, in that one can proactively welcome new experiences. The body in which the faculty of forgetting is damaged is a decadent one since it cannot cope with experience. Nietzsche repeats this characterization of decadence in KSA 13, 14[155] where he maintains that "to be unable to have done with an experience" is the sign of decadence, and he explicitly associates this inability with the Christian type. It is not that the body in which the faculty of forgetting is impaired cannot perform any actions, but rather that the impaired body, unlike the healthy body, can perform only *internalized* actions. Internalized actions can be seen as a consequence of what Nietzsche calls the "internalization" of instincts, the result of the instincts being unable to discharge themselves outwardly (GM II 16). Such actions are not "active" in the genuine sense of the word since, as Nietzsche observes, they are characterized by the "inability *not* to react to a stimulus" (TI Morality 2). Decadence as the inability to cope with or to be done with an experience brings into play the entire analysis of the faculty of forgetting, the body and consciousness, and so is crucial for assessing Deleuze's account of the becoming reactive of the active forces.[272]

How is consciousness related to the body? According to Nietzsche, consciousness is a superficial or surface phenomenon, which only passively reflects that the relative unity of the body has already been achieved. Consciousness is a symptom or a sign to be interpreted which hides rather than reveals the complex struggle of forces "beneath" it. The forces constituting the body engage in a long process of mutual struggle, in which each force imposes its own one-sided perspective on the whole. A kind of truce is reached between the different one-sided perspectives when a single will emerges as the commander which has subjugated resistances, and is now able to marshal the other forces as troops or instruments to accomplish the task it has set for itself. Nietzsche refers to the truce as "a kind of justice and contract" (GS 333). Only when this contract is achieved, do "the ultimate reconciliation scenes and final accounts of the long process rise to consciousness" (GS 333). Therefore consciousness means nothing but "*a certain behavior of the drives towards one another*" (GS 333).

---

272 Nietzsche provides various other definitions of decadence, which are not directly relevant to our analysis here. For example, in KSA 12, 10[96], Nietzsche defines decadence as the "inability to guard against any infection." Elsewhere, he claims that the anarchy of instincts is symptom of decadence (TI Socrates 4), and also that the need to combat one's instincts is the formula for decadence (TI Socrates 11). And further, he suggests that the "inability *not* to react to a stimulus" is a form of degeneration (TI Morality 2).

The greatest part of the activity of the forces remains hidden to consciousness, which represents the mildest and calmest type of thought.

Now, let us consider how the active and reactive forces are related to each other in the strong type. The strong type is strong because the active forces in it dominate the reactive forces, such that the latter obey the former. For Nietzsche, there is a "proper response," or (as Kaufmann translates it, a "true reaction") which is that of action (GM I 10).[273] Deleuze interprets this to mean that in a healthy type it is essential that the reactive forces are "themselves acted."[274] Translated into Nietzsche's language of morality, this means that the noble method of evaluation begins by evaluating itself first, that is, by saying "yes" first to itself. The masters spontaneously act and declare, "We the noble, the good, the beautiful and the happy!" (GM I 10). This affirmative "yes" is the noble type's basic creative deed. Only derivatively do the masters define the base, the rabble as the "bad" ones. What is bad is something that is not good. Thus the "good" sets the "bad" against itself as its own limit point, and it needs this limit to differentiate its elite nobility from the undistinguished. Retranslating back into the parlance of forces, we say that the active force provokes reaction; or action "precipitates reaction," as Deleuze puts it.[275]

When a strong type (e.g., the Ancient Greek culture) dominates, the above relation between the active and the reactive forces has been established and is the prevailing order. At that stage in history, there is yet no *ressentiment* type corresponding to Platonic-Christian slave morality, but there is the subjugated bad type of Greek culture. The *ressentiment* type first emerges or comes into being as a consequence of the disintegration of the strong type. The decadence of the strong type involves precisely a disturbance or malfunctioning of this relation between the active and the reactive forces, resulting in a topological displacement. As this decadence reaches a critical or threshold point on the topological scale, a weak type, typified by *ressentiment*, is born. According to Nietzsche, this new type is essentially characterized by the inversion or the "reversal of the evaluating glance" that characterized the strong type (GM I 10). In contrast to the evaluating stance of the strong, the slave morality begins with a "no" as its creative deed. It says "no" to the previous ideals of the master, thereby branding them as "evil," and only derivatively does it say "yes" to itself as "good," in opposition to the evil. Hence slave morality depends on there being "an opposing, external world... external stimuli in order to act at all" (GM I 10). It defines itself as good, not unconditionally, but in opposition to the evil master. It is good because it is not evil. Unlike the strong type for which the true reaction is that of action, for the weak type, "its action is basically a reaction" (GM I 10). Accordingly, the weak person of *ressentiment* is neither upright nor naïve, nor honest with himself. His mind loves dark corners and secret paths. Everything appeals to him as "*his* world, *his* security,

---

273 Nietzsche's original reads: "...die eigentliche Reaktion, die der That..." (KSA 5, 270).
274 Deleuze 111.
275 Deleuze 111.

his comfort" (GM I 10). Therefore Nietzsche emphasizes the fundamental distinction between the two types: while the strong type is ruled by the creative instinct, the weak type is dominated by the instinct of self-preservation (GM I 13). The problem now is to comprehend how the decadence of the strong type comes about. What exactly happens in the topological process of the decadence of the strong, which gives birth to the new weak type of *ressentiment*? What is involved in the inversion of the evaluative gaze?

We should note, as Deleuze does, that there are two kinds of reactive devices in the body: one corresponding to the unconscious level, and the other to the surface level of consciousness.[276] For Nietzsche, the reactive unconscious refers to the battleground in which the various forces fight for supremacy; it constitutes the "greatest part of our mind's activity" which is unfelt by the conscious body for the most part (GS 333). He describes the greatest part of mind's activity as "spiritual ingestion," invoking a digestive metaphor. It involves endless rumination (something not reducible to indigestion), since this unconscious apparatus is a passive faculty, which cannot get rid of or cope with an impression once it has made its impact. It is the permanent site where "our underworld of serviceable organs work with and against each other" (GM II 1). It resembles the faculty of "memory," of lasting imprints (GM II 1). Hence Deleuze defines the reactive unconscious as the "digestive, vegetative and ruminative system," which is characterized by "mnemonic traces, by lasting imprints."[277]

The unconscious reactive device is indispensable for the healthy body. It is true that this device is like the faculty of memory, which holds on to impressions and experiences and never completely digests them. But this is where the active faculty of forgetting plays a vital part. As a doorkeeper and a guardian, the faculty of forgetting actively suppresses the underworld of ruminative, thousand-fold struggles, precisely in order to ensure that most of what takes places in the unconscious background does not get up to the surface level of consciousness. It suppresses the background so that consciousness – the second of the two kinds of reactive devices in the body – reflects the achieved relative unity of the body. In this sense, in a healthy body there is a unity established by a dominating active force, which transforms the other forces to be its own function. It acts upon the reactive apparatuses, and when the action is successful, it is reflected as a unity at the reactive level of consciousness. The active faculty of forgetting and the two systems of reactive apparatus – spiritual ingestion and consciousness – thus work together in maintaining the health and strength of the body.

Functionally speaking, active forgetting makes it possible for the body's unity to be reflected at the surface of consciousness by keeping the unconscious mnemonic traces at bay. The faculty of forgetting must be seen as the active apparatus that bridges the gap between the two reactive devices, precisely by holding them apart. Suppressing the unconscious impressions not only enables consciousness to reflect

---

276 Deleuze 112–113.
277 Deleuze 112.

the healthy unity of the body, but it also makes it possible for a kind of freshness to be maintained at the level of consciousness, so that it is able to welcome new experiences. If consciousness is fresh, present excitation is not confused with uncountable and conflicting mnemonic traces. Thus it is the active faculty of forgetting – as the doorkeeper or guardian of order – that acts the reactive forces – i.e., that enables conscious excitation and the healthy performance of action by the marshaling of available tools.

What happens during the process of decadence? Deleuze's answer is that the reactive forces *"cease[] to be acted"* because of which there is a change in place, a displacement, of these forces.[278] In other words, when the reactive forces cease to be acted, unconscious mnemonic impressions invade consciousness. The mnemonic traces take the place of present excitation, both indicating the onset of decadence, and constituting a disturbance in the relation between the active and reactive forces. Nietzsche writes, "The person in whom this apparatus of suppression [the faculty of forgetting] is damaged, so that it stops working, can be compared (and not just compared) to a dyspeptic; he cannot 'cope' with anything..." (GM II 1). It is only through damage to the faculty of forgetting that the traces of memory infiltrate consciousness. Because of the invasion, there is an "active *desire* not to let go, a desire to keep on desiring what has been" (GM II 1). A human being who suffers from this is caught up in the spirit of revenge, which is "the will's ill-will toward time and its 'It was'" (Z II 20).

But how does this displacement of reactive forces come about? Where do we locate the functional error – in the reactive devices or in the active faculty of forgetting? Or perhaps in both? Deleuze interprets Nietzsche's statements to mean that there must be "a lapse in the faculty of forgetting" for the mnemonic traces to invade consciousness.[279] The consequence of this invasion is that the active forces lose the immediacy peculiar to perform their function; they are "deprived of the material conditions of their functioning... *they are separated from what they can do*."[280] In this sense, active forces become reactive. Deleuze writes that when the mnemonic traces take the place of excitation, it results in "reaction itself tak[ing] the place of action, reaction prevail[ing] over action."[281] However, he makes a perplexing argument when he traces back the faulty operation of the faculty of forgetting as the effect of a prior decay in one of the reactive apparatus. Specifically, Deleuze argues that for the faculty of forgetting to renew consciousness and keep it fresh for new experiences, "it constantly has to borrow the energy" from the conscious device itself, and then make this energy its own to give it back to consciousness.[282] The decay in the faculty of forgetting, Deleuze maintains, results from the fact that it "no longer

---

278 Deleuze 114.
279 Deleuze 114.
280 Deleuze 114.
281 Deleuze 114.
282 Deleuze 113.

finds in one kind of reactive forces the energy necessary to repress the other kind and to renew consciousness."[283] The reactive forces get the better of active forces and dominate them, but not by becoming superior forces. Deleuze insists that "*Everything takes place between reactive forces*," and that there is a "strange subterranean struggle which takes place entirely inside the reactive apparatus."[284] Hence the lapse in the faculty of forgetting – which results in the topological displacement of reactive forces (i.e., the invasion of mnemonic impressions into consciousness), which in turn results in the becoming reactive of active forces – is itself traced back to a struggle that belongs entirely to the reactive apparatus.

It is difficult to follow this segment of Deleuze's argument, for if the active faculty of forgetting is indeed dependent upon the reactive consciousness to furnish it with the required "energy," it is difficult to conceptualize forgetting as an "active" faculty or consciousness as a "reactive" faculty. If it is up to the faculty of forgetting to act its reactions by holding the two systems of reactions apart, how can the reactive consciousness in the end emerge as the unit, which is responsible for supplying energy to the faculty of forgetting? Is not consciousness a passive device? Moreover, I do not believe that Nietzsche himself indicates anything that directly supports Deleuze's thesis.[285]

Deleuze's argument is perplexing given his own insistence that the negative "is a result of activity" – it is a "product of existence."[286] He insists on this to establish his anti-Hegelian thesis that the negative "is not present in the essence as that from which force draws its activity."[287] In the Hegelian dialectic, although activity could be conceived of as primary, the force which makes itself obeyed does so only by denying that which it is not. Such a conception of activity implies a metaphysics of pure act or pure thinking, but it thrives essentially on the denial of or opposition to the other. In contrast, Deleuze argues that for Nietzsche the force which commands and says "yes" first to itself "affirms its own difference and enjoys this difference."[288] The negative is a result of activity, not an essential determination of it. The will to power is not a purely positive essence, but the denying will is possible only due to the active principle of the will to power as will to growth. However, Deleuze's proposal that "everything takes places between reactive forces" and that the active faculty depends on the reactive apparatus for its energy seems to suggest that the negative (as decadence) does not result from activity. Instead, it results from a prior negative activity "that takes place entirely inside the reactive apparatus." Hence it appears that Deleuze's

---

283 Deleuze 114.

284 Deleuze 114.

285 Perhaps, Deleuze's argument is partly inspired by Freud's view of the relation between consciousness and the unconscious. In the passages where he presents his argument, Deleuze compares his account to that of Freud's "topical hypothesis" (Deleuze 112).

286 Deleuze 9.

287 Deleuze 9.

288 Deleuze 9.

account of the origin of decadence is inconsistent with his (internalist) thesis about the origin of the negative. Deleuze's interpretation implies a strict typology of forces, even though he emphasizes the topological dimension.

To set right this inconsistency, I argue that the origin of the disturbance to the active faculty of forgetting lies in the active apparatus itself. This would indeed establish Nietzsche as the anti-Hegelian philosopher par excellence as Deleuze wanted to do. Decadence does not have its source in a prior reactive process. The becoming reactive of the active forces is a possibility that belongs to the active forces, to their very activity. Hence there is an irreducible ambiguity in the decadence of the strong type. The active forces are not only "delegated by activity to work with reactive forces" and their activity is not merely "functional," as Deleuze maintains.[289] The active forces have the freedom to exceed this functionality precisely as an affirmation of the strength of the body. And it is this excessive quality that makes the active apparatus *vulnerable* to decadence. As I shall demonstrate below, the tendency to exceed mere functionality is grounded in the very fundamental instinct of the strong type, which is the creative instinct governed by the will to power. In other words, the very basic traits which make the strong type what it is, also make it susceptible to decadence.

It still holds true that the emergence of a new weak type – the sick type of *ressentiment* – is connected to the topological displacement of the reactive forces. And to this extent, my argument is similar to Deleuze's. However, I differ from Deleuze in that I locate the source of the topology of reactive forces in a prior topological displacement of active forces, which is a result of their very activity. The interaction between the topological and the typological aspects during the process of decadence follows the same basic structure as outlined above. Topologically, at the level of forces, there is a gray area of continuity between the active and the reactive forces in which the former becomes the latter. The becoming reactive of the active forces refers to the dynamic movement of history, in which a new weak type comes to be and takes its own shape to dominate the course of history. However, at the level of wills there are still two distinct types of wills (affirmative and negative). So the topological ambiguity at the level of forces remains even if the strong and the weak are typologically distinct.

I must note a final point about Deleuze's analysis. Even if we were to assume with Deleuze that it is the reactive apparatus that is ultimately responsible for decadence, he has no account of why there is a lapse of forgetting or how this lapse of forgetting itself happens (or, in other words, why or how the reactive conscious apparatus cannot provide the necessary energy to the faculty of forgetting). Deleuze does not indicate how those decisive moments in history – that trigger the topological process of transition of active forces – are themselves brought about. At crucial points in his

---

289 Deleuze 113.

text, he passes over this issue: "Let us suppose that there is a lapse in the faculty of forgetting,"[290] or "let us suppose that, with the help of favorable external or internal circumstances, reactive forces get the better of and neutralize active force."[291] But what are these "favorable external or internal circumstances"? I suggest that Deleuze does not really consider this issue precisely because he locates the cause of the faulty operation of the active faculty in the reactive apparatus. With such an account, if one tries to indicate what these favorable circumstances are one is able to come up only with a still prior reason, which is located in another reactive feature of the body. To avoid this regress, we must locate the circumstances conducive for the lapse in forgetting precisely in the activity of the forces themselves. In doing so, we would show how the nature of activity itself leads, at a certain point, to a condition which makes the strong vulnerable to a lapse in the forgetting function.

In what follows, relying on Nietzsche's later texts (from *The Gay Science* onward), I isolate four typical characteristics of the strong type that not only make the strong type what it is, but also make it vulnerable to decadence.[292] I refer to the four distinctive traits as the "virtues" of the strong (the final trait, "corruption," is more of a consequence of possessing virtues such as the other three). With respect to each of these four characteristics, I show that there is the real possibility of a conflict between the strong type's "will to create" and its "will to self-preservation."[293] This conflict signifies a point of vulnerability to decadence insofar as it leads to a lapse in forgetting. The active force of forgetting may exceed itself. If too much is forgotten, the drive to create will exceed the limits of self-preservation, imperiling creativity itself. Such risk is always present, but not always excessive, in the strong type. When it becomes excessive the domination of the strong type declines. In the four sketches that follow I suggest that Nietzsche understood the strong type as vulnerable to such decline. Thus the sketches begin to make the case for the thesis that the decline of the strong type originates in excessive active force.

Further, the four traits to be discussed below bring out the different ways in which the strong could be vulnerable to decadence by showing the different ways that the strong type could undergo spoiling or rotting (*Verderbniss*). My claim is that the actual decadence of a particular strong culture or individual, its destruction or

---

290 Deleuze 114.

291 Deleuze 56.

292 To be sure, the four character traits to be discussed below are not meant to be exhaustive of the strong type. One may discern other traits by studying Nietzsche's rich descriptions of the strong. But I believe that the characteristics isolated below are sufficient to show thoroughly the different ways in which this type can be seen to be susceptible to decadence. They will also suffice for my analysis in the next chapter where I take up the issue of how mere vulnerability to decadence might turn into a case of *actual* decadence, when I discuss the "death of tragedy" in Ancient Greek culture.

293 Although the dominant drive in the strong type is the will to create, it also has a secondary drive towards self-preservation. This should not surprise us since the strong type is not only constituted by active forces, but also reactive forces.

ruination (*Zugrundegehen*), occurs when these different ways of *Verderbniss* come together in a specific way unique to that culture or individual. In the next chapter, where I will carry out a case study of the decadence of the Greek culture, I will show the particular way in which mere susceptibility to decadence is converted to the actual, historical decadence of a noble culture. This analysis would then show the way in which the *Zugrundegehen* of a particular culture would depend upon or rest on its *Verderbniss*.

The "weak" sides of the strong type

(a) *Solitude*

The strong type is essentially creative, and the strong person creates her own values. Strong morality is based on an awareness of the distance between the strong and the weak. This situation is in contrast to that of weak morality, especially the slave morality of *ressentiment*. Pity for others' suffering, equality, mediocrity and justice for all are some of the ideals which weak morality preaches, even though this preaching betrays the underlying quality of the will to power that takes pleasure in conspiring against and defeating the strong. However, there is strength in this morality of numbers: the strength of self-preservation. In its dealings, the weak never loses sight of its advantages, and the "thought of purpose and advantage is even stronger than its strongest drives" (GS 3). It is this very conserving principle that is not dominant in the strong, which "succumb[s] to its drives" (GS 3). The greatness of the strong type lies in its "being different, in incommunicability, in distance of rank" (KSA 13, 16[39]). The noble soul is typically reluctant to admit of equals to itself. It takes pride in the duties it sees as its destiny, and is neither eager to share these duties with other people, nor perform them for the sake of others. But it is exactly this quality of the strong which constitutes its solitude and isolation. Nietzsche describes "solitude" as the strong person's "virtue" (BGE 284). And as a virtue, it is something that is possessed in "common with no one else" (Z I 5). He associates such lofty notions as the destiny of humankind with the fate and responsibility of the stronger, higher nature. The heavy responsibility creates a solitude that is inaccessible to praise or blame, and a sense of justice that is beyond appeal. The strong person is rare and must live alone, away from the "market-place," the petty and the wretched (Z I 12). Only individuals able to endure and love themselves sufficiently, uninterested in comfort, are able to breathe the icy breath of solitude.

There are dangers and challenges inherent in the solitude of the strong type that point to a conflict between its essential to will to create and its will to self-preservation. This conflict reflects the greatest challenge for the strong type, which is to exercise its creative instinct while, at the same time, preserving or maintaining itself. There is a very thin margin of error at the height of the conflict. The strong type often risks self-preservation in order to create and grow (GS 3).[294] We must note that the weak type does not have to contend with the conflict between creation and self-preservation because it is dominated by the will to self-preservation. From this point of view, the weak has an advantage over the strong. The "spoiling" or "rotting" (*Verderbniss*) and the "destruction" (*Zugrundegehen*) of the strong type is the rule rather than the exception.

The person who carries out tasks in solitude risks being misunderstood. There is also the tendency for noble souls to misunderstand one another because of the unique meanings of each of their tasks. At times they remain hidden and even misunderstand themselves (KSA 11, 25[348]). They "suffer too deeply from the smallest wounds" (Z I 12).[295] The strong soul shivers in the "frost of solitude" and there is a danger it "might become insolent, scornful and an annihilator," and that it might lose its "highest hopes" (Z I 8). Living alone also means a noble person is prone to accidents and rarely propagates. Because of the diversity of the noble type's conditions of life the "likelihood that it will get into an accident and be destroyed [*zu Grunde geht*] is truly enormous" (BGE 276).

Most importantly, there is a pride associated with solitude which demands that the solitary keeps his distance from the common and the wretched.[296] The solitary one preserves and conserves himself by avoiding mingling with the common.[297] However, because of its proud solitude and reticence, the noble soul can "misjudge[] the sphere [of the base] it despises" (GM I 10). For instance, one cause of misjudgment is the incorrect self-estimation by means of which alone the strong may continue to endure the weak type, albeit from a certain distance (Z III 9). But this just means that the strong misjudges the worth of, and is gentle toward, the weak, even though the latter may not deserve it. The weak repays the strong type's generosity by taking advantage of the erroneous self-estimation in a cruel manner; it makes the noble type pay dearly for the mistake in its judgment by subjecting it to slander, suspicion and conspiracy. It punishes the strong for its virtues, and thus subjects it to its "poisonous injustice,"

---

294 Also see GS 349, where Nietzsche remarks, "To wish to preserve oneself is a sign of distress, of a limitation of the truly basic life-instinct, which aims at *the expansion of power* and in doing so often enough risks and sacrifices self-preservation."

295 One should note that this characteristic of the strong type is ambiguous because Nietzsche also often describes the weak type as suffering from small wounds (since the latter type has an inability to forget or "digest" its bad experiences).

296 In this section, the "common," the "wretched," the "base," the "weak," and the "sick" are not terms for the unique character of *ressentiment* which comes to define the dominant slave morality after the strong has been defeated. Rather, these terms refer to the weak type under the rule of the master morality. Of course, this does not mean that the two weak types do not share common features. On the contrary, they share a large number of common traits, since self-preservation is the dominant drive in both weak types.

297 See GS 293. Here, Nietzsche notes that the higher nature must take precautions to ensure that "large amounts of [its] strength are not sapped uselessly!"

which may in the end be responsible for the strong type's "undoing" (Z I 12).[298] To make matters worse, the strong natures then take "revenge" on themselves for misjudging themselves and for being gentle towards the ignoble many (Z III 9).

This series of events culminates in the spoiling or rotting of the strong and has at its origin the pride associated with solitude. The misjudgment of the common, which results from proud reticence, must not be seen merely as a "fault" of the strong, but more crucially as a consequence of its overabundance of strength. This overabundance compels the noble type to maintain its distance from the common, as is essential to exercise its creativity, but it also may lead to various misjudgments and deeply reactive repercussions, signaling the beginning of the strong type's degeneration. Due to an excess of activity, the strong type forgets its place, missteps, and misjudges the place and worth of the weak. Thus solitude reveals one possible way in which there could be a lapse in the forgetting function, making the strong type vulnerable to decadence.

Finally, at times, Nietzsche describes the solitude of the strong type in the same vein as he describes the solitude of the "hermit" or "saint" or the "priest." He associates the noble tendency for the "strangest and most dangerous solitude, in the form of a holy saint" with the "highest instinct for cleanliness," and defines holiness itself as the highest spiritualization of the latter instinct (BGE 271). Such passages, which point to an asceticism of solitude shared by both the strong type and the priest, indicate the essential ambiguity in the character of the strong. Zarathustra describes the priests as his "enemies," although he is also their blood relative (Z II 4). One should also recall Nietzsche's famous analysis of the ascetic priest in the third essay of *Genealogy of Morality*, which highlights the ambiguous role played by the priest – who is both a decadent and a strong type – in the overturning of the previously healthy ways of evaluation. My suggestion is not that the strong type is actually the ascetic priest in disguise or vice versa. But rather, notwithstanding the many qualitative differences between the two, which Nietzsche discusses in length, the analysis of solitude suggests a topological continuity between the strong type and the ascetic priest. My interest is in the gray area where the strong type disintegrates, giving birth to other weaker types.

(b) *The bestowing virtue*

Out of solitude comes the great need to bestow. Zarathustra expresses this thought at the beginning of the second part of *Thus Spoke Zarathustra*, when he finds himself drawn towards the very human beings from whom he had previously withdrawn: "Indeed a

---

298 In a discarded note originally intended to be included in a passage in the *Ecce Homo*, Nietzsche writes, "If there are any means at all for destroying me who *are destinies*, the instinct of poisonous flies discerns these means. For one who has greatness there is no fight with the small: hence the small become masters" (EH Zarathustra 5, footnote 3).

lake is within me, solitary and self-contained; but the river of my love draws it off – down to the sea!" (Z II 1). Unlike the theoretician or the hermit who abstracts away from the world in which he exists, the joyful wisdom of the convalescent draws him towards the very world which he must now, with necessity, create and shape out of his will. "And what you have called world, that shall be created only by you: your reason, your image, your will, your love it shall become!" (Z II 2). But what kind of necessity it is that draws the noble person to the world? It is the necessity born out of "love." For Zarathustra, love has the quality of superabundance or excess; love, essentially has the quality of "flowing-over" to the other. Zarathustra says, "My impatient love overflows in torrents, downwards, toward rising and setting" (Z II 1). We must understand bestowing as the highest virtue, involving the surging of heart with overflowing love and the compulsion to give. The one who bestows has the thirst to pile up all riches in his soul, and therefore, like a star, he compels everything towards him, not in order to devour them, but rather so that these things flow back out of his "wells as gifts of [his] love" (Z I 22:1). There is a happiness associated with the power that wants to overflow, that is conscious "of a wealth that wants to make gifts and give away" (BGE 260).

But what does the bestowing virtue give? And what effect does this virtue have on the individual who bestows? Nietzsche's answer is that only through bestowing does one create values. Bestowing is the highest virtue of the strong creator-soul. The necessity with which the giver gives pertains to the necessity of the one who wills with one will (Z I 22). And when the strong individual wills in this way, she is liberated (Z II 2). The lover experiences freedom. And out of this experience, she attempts to create the world in her own image, by tempting and seducing the world through the virtuous strength of her will. Bestowing and creating are thus the great redeemer of the strong and healthy person who has suffered too much under the "spirit of gravity," carrying the responsibility of world on her shoulders. Bestowing redeems by making the creator "lighter," and thus may be seen to perform an active "forgetting" function (Z II 2). Nietzsche often uses the metaphor of "pregnancy" to describe the plight and redemption of the creator. The "wild wisdom" of the creator becomes "pregnant on lonely mountains," and she reaches a point where her wisdom wants to overflow (Z II 1). The solitary's "great love of oneself" is the true sign of her pregnancy (Z III 3). She has suffered enough in bearing the questionable burden of humankind, and in being assigned the task of its future course. As the creator becomes ripe with her pregnancy, she begins her "going-under" (*untergehen*) and going beyond herself. The burden the creator bears can be lightened only if she finds her "children," that is, the values she can call her own. She realizes that she cannot discover her children and her values already present in the world. Rather she must invent them first. She gives birth to her values, and through this creative deed, she redeems and unburdens herself. In thus overcoming herself, she determines the course of future humanity and redeems the past (Z III 12:12).

But these very great virtues of love and bestowal can also make the strong type vulnerable to weakness. The strong type tends to be naïve precisely because of its bestowing power. Because the compulsion to bestow is blind, the strong soul can often suffer "attacks of [] love" and it can be indiscriminate about the kind of persons towards which it extends its giving hand (Z I 17). For instance, the strong person may irrationally waste his gifts on the common people, who only hate and vilify the former for inventing virtues (Z I 17). This irrationality and blindness imply an inability to see the "commonplace people as what they are" (GS 3). The exceptional natures "do not themselves feel like exceptions" and therefore, they fail to "understand the common natures and arrive at a proper estimate of the rule" (GS 3). As a result, the higher natures are sometimes not able to keep that essential "distance" from such people, and thus may not be able to preserve themselves and their energies for worthier tasks. Nietzsche calls this the "eternal injustice of the noble" (GS 3). The misjudgment of the base type and the inability to maintain the essential distance from them may be interpreted as involving excessive forgetting on the part of the strong natures. Bestowing as forgetting is required to relieve the noble type of the questionable burden of humankind. However, loving and bestowing indiscriminately, as extreme manifestations of the creative drive, result in the active force of forgetting exceeding itself, because of which the strong fails to keep its distance from the weak. Paradoxically, this excessive forgetting appears precisely as the failure to forget, as the strong soul, which naively loves even those unworthy of its love, ends up "carr[ying] on its shoulders too much that is alien" (Z III 11:2). Thus "*love* is the danger of the loneliest, love of anything *if only it is alive*!" (Z III 1). We see here a necessary conflict between the will to create, which at times compels it to bestow its love upon others indiscriminately, and the will to preserve oneself that demands that the strong type use its bestowing virtue prudently.

However, the strong type pays a huge price for exceeding its creative drive beyond the limits of self-preservation. As it carries too much burden on its shoulders, at its more vulnerable moments the strong soul may *expect* something (perhaps, a kind of recognition or mutual understanding) from the weak upon whom she bestows. Such expectation may lead to a chain of repercussions that ultimately leads to the disintegration of the noble type. In bestowing gifts upon humankind, the strong natures can naively assume that their "own passion [is] something that is present in everyone" (GS 3). They expect and hope that there is someone who "approaches them with as much as a thousandth part of their suffering and passion" (KSA 13, 11[25]). When this hope is upset, the strong person thinks to himself, "They take from me: but do I yet touch their souls?" (Z II 9). However, he soon realizes that there is an infinite chasm between giving and taking, which perhaps cannot be bridged, and that he cannot know about the happiness of those who take. This discovery might lead to frustration due to which there is a danger that the noble natures lose "their sense of shame," and their "hands and heart[s] [may get] calloused from sheer distributing" (Z II 9). A spite may grow up from the depth of solitude, which desires to "cause pain to those [they] illumine" and to "rob those upon whom [they] have bestowed" (Z II 9). Thus the frustrated strong type hungers after wickedness and revenge. This is another manner in which spoiling or rotting may arise from excess of strength. Zarathustra says: "Withdrawing the hand when another hand reaches out for it; hesitating like the waterfall, which hesitates even in plunging – thus do I hunger after wickedness" (Z II 9). Hence the strong type may feel that bestowing itself is a curse. Just like a star, which can neither expect the planets and other bodies revolving around it to illuminate, nor other stars to do the same for its sake, the strong type is left to contend with the wretchedness of its bestowing power. As a consequence, there is a danger that the strong individual's "joy in bestowing die[s] away through bestowing," and the bestowing "virtue gr[ows] weary of itself in its overflow!" (Z II 9). The greatest task for the bestowing nature, therefore, is to "preserve [its] modesty as a bestower" (Z II 1). And this task is incredibly difficult to achieve consistently. Thus the bestowing virtue, which essentially characterizes the activity of the strong type, also makes this type vulnerable to frustration, weariness, disillusionment, and to decadence.

(c) Need for challenges

In accordance with its will to demonstrate over-abundance of power, the prodigal will desires challenges. The greater the challenge, the grander is the platform on which such a will can put its power and magnanimity to test. This is why the strong person has a "certain need to have enemies" (BGE 260). A strong individual honors and respects her enemies, since the greater enemy would push her to examine the extent and limit of her own strength and courage. She seeks challenges to overcome. We must acknowledge that the need to have challenges is not just an empty show of egoism. Rather, it belongs essentially to the creative impulse of the noble type. Nietzsche writes: "That one stakes one's life, one's health, one's honor, is the consequence of high spirits and an overflowing prodigal will" (KSA 13, 11[44]). The strong type, who commands, has a deep necessity to be adventurous and experimental. But this life-affirming necessity also makes the type vulnerable to dangers and destructions, a vulnerability about which the weak knows little. Commanding is much more difficult than obeying, and often the one who commands puts his whole life at risk. This is so since the "commander bears the burden of all who obey, and this burden can easily crush him" (Z II 12). Just as the smaller person yields and makes way for the greater, such that the latter exercises power over the former, "so does even the greatest yield, and risks for the sake of power – life itself" (Z II 12). In this dice-playing with life and death in the balance the strong type becomes its own sacrificial victim. For the sake of power, life is sacrificed, since life is something "*which must always overcome itself*" (Z II 12). In other words, since the principle of life is will to power, the preservation of life in the strong type takes a backseat to its creative and life-affirming impulse: "the tremendous squandering of all defensive energies [] is a presupposition of every *creative* deed ... Our *small* defensive capacities are thus, as it were, suspended; no energy is left for them" (EH Zarathustra 5).

However, risking one's life is not the only possible consequence of this conflict between self-preservation and creation. The excessive activity of the strong could lead to this type becoming reactive if it results in damage to the faculty of forgetting. The will to power of the creative type always looks for new dangers and unexplored horizons. Nietzsche notes that, "a *preference for questionable and terrifying things* is a symptom of *strength*" (KSA 12, 10[168]). A dormant power becomes a sort of vice and a symptom of weakness. The healthy, creative power needs to bestow, grow, explore and widen its sphere of influence. However, undertaking this challenge means to be "destructive also towards oneself" (KSA 12, 10[114]). This can happen, perhaps, by desiring dangerous challenges for which one's prowess is inadequate, or by desiring enemies one would have been prudent to avoid. These dangerous desires are the result of the "lust to rule," because of which the higher type "compels itself down to the low" (Z III 10:1). Such desires are indications of excessive forgetting where the strong forgets the "pathos of distance" essential to its nature as the creator of values. The pathos of distance, as Nietzsche argues, is what allows the noble type to "maintain[] an overview and keep[] looking down on subservient types and tools" (BGE 257). Therefore the forgetting of this pathos because of which the noble soul compels itself down to the lower type imperils creativity. It may be the case that the strong is interested in the weak since it is curious about the degree of its own strength and courage (KSA 13, 11[44]). It is not content with a self-satisfied life that is happy in the safety of its own convictions and victories. It seeks new spoils and it sacrifices itself for the sake of the future. It has always wanted to glimpse the limits of its strength by discerning "how much of the 'truth' [it] could withstand," and how much it could push itself to the limits without destroying itself (BGE 39).

Hence Nietzsche calls "virtue" in the form of "truthfulness," the "noble and dangerous luxury" (KSA 12, 5[49]). The weak represent the perilous limit because of which they appear "malicious" and "interesting" (KSA 13, 14[182]). The strong person "takes an interest in the people, the weak, the poor, the poetry of the petty, etc.," since this interest brings with it new challenges, which opens up new avenues and paths untraveled heretofore (KSA 11, 25[200]). Comprehending the interesting weak types might just represent the ultimate challenge for the will to create, even though, or precisely because, this challenge is fraught with the greatest dangers. The danger here is precisely that the noble type's active forgetting forgets too much, that is, it forgets the necessity to preserve a certain distance from the weak. We may say that a certain recklessness belongs to the creative impulse of the strong as a kind of sickness, even though this sickness is a sign of excessive health (KSA 12, 10[145]). Thus the reckless search for new spoils reveals another way in which the strong type becomes vulnerable to decadence.

(d) *Corruption*

Corruption of instincts is another factor in the disintegration of the strong. Corruption is "an expression of the fact that anarchy threatens inside the instincts and that the foundation of affects, which we call 'life', has been shaken" (BGE 258). Corruption might mean that an aristocratic race "throws away its privileges with a sublime disgust and sacrifices itself to an excess of its moral feeling" (BGE 258). For Nietzsche, one of the essential traits of the noble type is a certain awareness of its wealth, which this type does not want to preserve but wants to expend, as a sign of its strength. When it helps the unfortunate, it is not out of pity but from an impulse, which is a result of overabundant power (BGE 260). But how does the instinct for giving and bestowing turn into a kind of squandering, even at the expense of the disintegration of the self? To answer this, we must note that for the strong person to be creative, she must harbor within herself an excessive tension of contradictory forces in mutual strife. As Zarathustra says, "One must have chaos within, in order to give birth to a dancing star" (Z Prologue 5). Nietzsche often uses the metaphor of *"the bow with the great tension"* to describe the great human (KSA 11, 35[18]). The strong person possesses great virtues *and also their opposites* which form a creative tension. But this blessing of having an excessive tension is also a kind of curse, which makes the strong vulnerable to corruption of instincts, and perhaps even to decadence. How?

In *Thus Spoke Zarathustra*, Nietzsche writes that the greatest evil to grow out of the strong ones is "the evil that grows out of the conflict among [their] virtues" (Z I 5). This conflict of virtues is the reason behind the corruption of instincts. The many virtues that the strong "body" possesses are in constant mutual struggle for dominance and for the highest place. Each virtue wants the strong person's "whole spirit" and "whole strength," such that it can announce itself as the only virtue which expresses itself in the passions of "wrath, hatred and love" (Z I 5). Hence Zarathustra declares, "if you are fortunate you will have one virtue and no more: thus you go more easily across the bridge" (Z I 5). Each virtue is jealous of other virtues. However, the struggle between virtues is not an unfortunate situation, which must be avoided. Rather, this "evil" is necessary; "envy and mistrust and calumny" are necessary among the virtues since this evil essentially defines the strong type (Z I 5). But it is precisely envy and calumny between the virtues that results in the corruption of strong type's instincts. The strong individual, who is the battlefield of virtues, may grow "weary" of the battle. Indeed, he may go to the "desert and kill[] himself" (Z I 5). Zarathustra warns the healthy one: "therefore shall you love your virtues – for by them will you finally perish" (Z I 5).

However, the danger here is not necessarily that the strong will finally perish as a result of the struggle between virtues. There is also the possible danger that corruption results in excessive forgetting, thus signifying vulnerability to decadence. To see this possibility, we must consider some consequences of the corruption of instincts. On the one hand, I would like to suggest that one main implication of the corruption of the instincts is the development of "pity" for the base type. Nietzsche speaks of pity as Zarathustra's ultimate "temptation" and "final sin" which will lead him astray and distract him from his tasks (EH Wise 4).[299] There is a great peril that the "cry of need" of the "superior humans" – whom Nietzsche portrays in the figures of the "kings," "soothsayer," the "ugliest man," the "sorcerer," the "shadow," etc. in the final part of *Thus Spoke Zarathustra* – will lead the strong person away from himself such that he believes that he can find refuge in the safety of "pity for the suffering" and "selfless" actions, as a way of relieving himself of the great tasks assigned to him. It is almost as if the strong soul, in its vulnerable moment, wishes that it were "like" the weak. This tendency indicates excessive forgetting in the sense that the strong forgets its "distance" from the weak.[300] The development of pity for the suffering signifies forgetting in a unique way. The battle between the virtues essentially defines the active nature of the strong type. But if the strong grows weary of the battle, it is not able to "suppress" or "forget" the struggle such that the traces of the struggle enter the level of consciousness, indicating the onset of corruption. The strong type ends up forgetting its distance from the weak, misjudging and developing pity for the latter, leading itself away from its tasks.

On the other hand, instead of an attempt to renounce one's tasks, there is the tendency to squander the noble privileges as a consequence of corruption. The extreme tension between virtues gives rise to a "spiritual disturbance," which in turn leads to wastefulness, adventurousness and thirst for power (KSA 13, 14[182]). Through these excesses the strong take revenge for "some inner corruption" (BGE 269). These excesses may be shown to result in the same kind of indulgences that we saw in the previous subsection with respect to the strong type's need for challenges, and hence leading to similar instances of excessive forgetting. In these ways, corruption not only reveals the conflict between the strong type's creative will and its will to self-preservation, but also its vulnerability to decadence.

The analysis of each of the above four characteristics reveals a deep conflict between the creative and the self-preserving instincts of the strong type. The greatest challenge for this type is to continue exerting its creative impulse, while at the same time, preserving itself. The submission to the creative instinct at the expense of the self-preserving one is evidence of the spoiling (*Verderbniss*) of the strong. I have shown that the conflict between the two instincts may lead to a lapse in the faculty of forgetting, signaling the onset of decadence. This conflict may result in the active force of forgetting exceeding itself. Too much forgetting implies that the will to create exceeds the limits of self-preservation, endangering creativity itself. With respect to the traits of solitude and the bestowing virtue, excessive creativity was shown to lead to misjudgments of the weak – as evidence of a kind of excessive forgetting – which

---

299 Also, see Z IV 2.

300 Nietzsche writes: "the healthy should remain *separated* from the sick, should even be spared the sight of the sick so that they do not confuse themselves with the sick" (GM III 14). The development of pity may be seen as an instance of such confusion.

in turn results in a series of reactive repercussions culminating in the decadence of the strong. And with respect to the need for challenges and corruption, excessive forgetting manifests directly as the inability of the strong to maintain its distance from the weak. These lapses in the faculty of forgetting result in a displacement of reactive forces, which in turn ensures that the reactive forces are not acted upon. In short, the damage to the faculty of forgetting is not due to a struggle in the reactive apparatus, as Deleuze suggests, but is a consequence of the dominant strong type's excessive activity. The possibility of decadence is given by the very principle of growth and creation, which belongs to the will to power. These conclusions establish my broader thesis that the strong and the weak are not pure, fixed types and that the distinction between them is, at bottom, ambiguous.

Until now, our investigation into the decadence of the strong has remained at a general level, where we have shown the different ways in which the strong can spoil or be vulnerable to decadence. In the next chapter, we shall explore how mere vulnerability turns into actual decadence of a strong culture like that of the Ancient Greeks. By relying on Nietzsche's early writings and lecture courses on Greek politics, art and philosophy, we will examine what constituted the glory and disintegration of the Ancient Greek culture and what led to the birth of Socratic philosophy. The reader should bear in mind that the argument of the current chapter is incomplete without the analysis to follow. The case study in the next chapter will rely on the analysis carried out here, in order to examine how the characteristics peculiar to the strong type manifest themselves in different aspects of Greek culture, and how they might have come together, as it were, to actualize the decadence of that culture.

Chapter Five
Greek glory and decadence: a case study

Facets of Greek nobility: the state, art and philosophy

The previous chapter demonstrated that the very qualities that bring out the great-est strength of the strong type also expose this type to decadence. This point sub-stantiates my broader argument that, despite the typological differences, the strong and weak are not fixed, pure types, and that there is a gray area on the topological scale where the difference between two types becomes indiscernible. But so far our inquiry into the decadence of the strong has remained at a general level. The analysis provided in the fourth chapter must be brought to bear on the particularities of the decadence of a strong culture like that of the Ancient Greeks. In this chapter, with the help of Nietzsche's insights into Ancient Greek culture, I consider the question of how it is that this noble culture actually underwent decadence. We will then conclude the present study by reflecting upon what the irreducible equivocalness of the distinction between the two types of wills implies about Nietzsche's ambiguous critique of meta-physics, which is grounded in his meta-existential approach.

The following analysis will proceed with an eye towards addressing the following two considerations: first, how are the four general characteristics peculiar to the strong type, which we have isolated in the previous chapter, manifest themselves in different aspects of Greek culture (in the unique characteristics of their art and philosophy) constituting this culture's glory? And second, in *which domain* of the Greek culture do these four traits come together, in order to reveal that threshold point where mere vulnerability turns into actual decadence? We will see that this critical point is also the point of inescapable ambiguity, where a kind of excessive health appears absolutely indiscernible from a sort of sickness, signifying the inception of decadence. This threshold point, where the differ-ence between strength and weakness, between health and sickness, appears equivocal, is characterized by the loss of the strong Greek culture's creative instinct to its will to self-preservation. I shall argue that the fundamentality of the ambiguity of the threshold point implies that the source of metaphysical oppositions, as the quality of will to power that entails a denial of life, is ultimately elusive. We cannot clearly delineate this source as either belonging to the strong Greek type, in which the creative instinct is dominant, or to a weak type, in which self-preserving instinct is dominant.

I will discuss three distinctive features of Ancient Greek culture: state, art and philosophy. These are not arbitrary selections, but they constitute the main headings under which Nietzsche persistently meditated upon the Ancient Greeks, especially in his earliest unpublished lectures, essays and his published writings.[301] In one of

---

301 For the arguments to be made in this chapter, I will rely heavily on Nietzsche's early writings. I have argued so far that the ambiguity central to Nietzsche's meta-existential approach and this ap-

these lectures on pre-Platonic philosophy, Nietzsche declares that he intends to probe into the history of Greek philosophy, not for the sake of philosophy, but "*on behalf of the Greeks*" (*The Pre-Platonic Philosophers* 3). Nietzsche sought to investigate Greek philosophy, not for the sake of philosophical scholarship, but to better understand the Greek character, since he considered their philosophy as a window to their character. Similarly, in the discussion to follow, I want to consider Greek state, art and philosophy, from Nietzsche's point of view, only insofar as they shed light on Greek nobility. This methodological decision will also help me maintain a relatively narrow and precise focus on a broad range of topics. Moreover, dividing our discussion of the Greeks into these three main headings has a very useful structural advantage in that it allows us to precisely demarcate the domain in which we must locate the threshold point of decadence.

We shall begin with a consideration of the Greek state. For Nietzsche, the state has a hierarchical pyramid-like structure, with the "laborers" at the bottom and the "artists" at the top. While among the laborers the self-preserving instinct is dominant, with the artists it is the creative will that prevails. The functions of the Greek concept of "agon" ("contest" or "competition") and the Greek myths in maintaining the overall health of the state will also be analyzed. The former determines the relation among the laborers and also among the artists, and the latter provides an overarching meaning for the members of the state. However, I will argue that the Greek state (especially through the work of the laborers), considered in relation to the overall structure of the Greek culture, had a self-preserving function. On the other hand, Greek art as a whole performs a creative function. The discussion of Greek art involves analyzing the Apollonian and Dionysian impulses as the two strongest impulses of the Hellenic culture, and showing that their mutual strife culminates in the highest form of Hellenic art: Attic Tragedy. Within the domain of Greek art, it is the Apollonian impulse which is self-preserving, compared to the Dionysian force, which is more of the creative impulse. With respect to Greek art, we will explore the relation between art and myth, and also the role of the agonistic instinct in furthering art.

These two discussions of Greek state and art will set the stage for the final investigation into pre-Platonic philosophy. My argument will be that it is in the domain of philosophy that we must locate the threshold point of Greek decadence. By interpreting Nietzsche's writings on pre-Platonic philosophy, I will suggest that philosophy is a peculiarly Greek phenomenon that is *both* a sign of this culture's excessive health and also of its sickness. While the state and art seem to have clearly designated roles to play in the overall structure of the healthy Greek culture (in their capacities as preserving and creative forces respectively), philosophy does not have a properly delin-

---

proach itself is central to his mature writings beginning with *Human, All-Too-Human*. However, as we shall see below, his early works on the Greeks already anticipate his later writings, especially with regard to the problem of decadence. Hence, based on a meta-existential interpretation, one could make a strong case for a greater continuity in Nietzsche's philosophy than is usually acknowledged.

eated function to perform, although philosophy grew out of this very noble culture, as a glorious extension of it. Thus the domain of Greek philosophy reveals that active forces which determine this strong culture go beyond the mere functional role of "acting out the reactions" (this role corresponds to the two levels of state and art) to a more uncertain terrain, which is simultaneously an expression of a greater strength of the culture than the one expressed at the two lower levels, and also the beginning of this culture's decadence. The battle between the will to self-preservation and the will to create which sustains every stratum of Greek society reaches its ultimate and decisive phase in the domain of Greek philosophy. My study will be guided by the following background questions: Why such a phenomenon called "philosophy" among the Greeks? What is its meaning and its cultural function? What is its relation to the agonistic instinct and the myths in general? What do some of the basic tenets of Socratic philosophy tell us about the meaning of Greek decadence?

The Greek state

Oh, those Greeks! They knew how to live... (GS Preface 4)

In a short essay, written in 1871 as one of the "Prefaces" to an "Unwritten Work," Nietzsche contrasts the Greek state to the modern state. Unlike the former, in modernity, the individual is fragmented, and is "flamboyantly pieced together" (*The Greek State* 176). The reason for this lack of directionality is to be found in the absence of an overarching myth that lends unity and purpose to existence. While giving his account of the death of Greek tragedy in *The Birth of Tragedy*, Nietzsche argues that the degeneration of the Hellenic culture goes hand-in-hand with the destruction of the myth. Only a horizon surrounded by living myths "encloses and unifies a cultural movement" by securing it a sacred place of origin (BT 23). The images of myth are the "daemonic guardians under whose tutelage the young soul grows up and by whose signs the grown man interprets his life and his struggles" (BT 23). Without the guidance of myth, "all cultures lose their healthy, creative, natural energy," and a mythless culture is a culture of "abstract education, abstract morality, abstract law, the abstract state" (BT 23). Although, in this section, Nietzsche is mainly concerned with the importance of myth in relation to Greek tragic art, his argument also entails its significance for the Greek state. Indeed, as we shall see, it is precisely the importance of myth for a noble state that also shows its peculiar need for art. In other words, it is the very presence of myth which indicates the necessary connection between Greek state and art. But what was the unique configuration of the Greek state such that it could allow itself to be guided by the horizon of living myths?

In contrast to modernity, which gets anxious about the mere mention of the word "slavery," and would rather talk about the "dignity of man" and the "dignity of labor"[302] than confront its own impoverished spirit, the Hellenic state admitted to itself with astonishing frankness that labor is indeed a disgrace (*The Greek State* 176–177). The insight behind this admission is the wisdom that "existence has no inherent value" (*The Greeks State* 177). This wisdom, instead of casting a pessimistic spell on existence, actually provides a genuine space for art, thus making it possible. Art is precisely that phenomenon, which, through its aesthetic embellishments, justifies and affirms existence. But for art to exist there must be artists. And for the birth of artist, it is necessary that the concerns and occupations of at least some of the members of the state go beyond the mere struggle for bare existence, which constitutes the realm of labor. The birth of the artist presupposes the luxury of an excess that goes beyond mere preservation of existence. A culture must be genuinely rich enough to afford this excess that gives birth to the artist and her art. At the same time, existence is not worth preserving for its own sake, since existence itself has no value. Existence must be preserved only insofar as its preservation makes possible something (i.e. art) that goes beyond preservation into creation and affirmation. Art is therefore essentially related to the creation of myths. If the role of myth is to act as the overarching horizon providing a unified space of meaning for a culture, art creates exactly those images of the myth in its affirmative function.

The peculiar organization of the Greek state allowed for the creation of art and myths. For Nietzsche, the Greek state was intricately hierarchical with a pyramid-like structure. Just as the Hellenic culture as a whole can be examined under three main headings (state, art and philosophy), the structure of the state itself can be analyzed in terms of three different levels. At the bottom of the edifice is the hoard of common "laborers" or "slaves" who earn their livelihood by performing menial jobs that concerned with everyday existence. This bottommost level has the greatest number of representatives belonging to it, as it is represented by commoners and "practical" people. For the most part, as these laborers perform just those functions that meet the everyday demands of brute existence, and since existence itself has no value, all labor involves a feeling of "shame" (*The Greek State* 178). However, there is redemption associated with the work of labor. It consists in the fact that it is precisely when the laborers perform their assigned tasks properly, can the state afford the luxury of having the artists. The artists – who belong to the second level in the state-hierarchy – are by nature the "exceptional" ones, the privileged few who are exempt from contributing to the total labor force of the state, as it is required that they reserve their energy and genius for nobler purposes. The labor class, thus, can be seen as providing a solid foundation, a firm basis, generating a sphere of excess and freedom for the artists to engage in their creative endeavors. In this sense, the labor class performs a self-

---

302 Nietzsche's phrase is *Würde der Arbeit*, which Carol Diethe has translated as "dignity of work." But, in this context, I prefer the term "labor" for *Arbeit* than "work" since it brings out the menial, repetitive nature of a particular task better than the latter term.

preserving function for the state as a whole, specifically so that the state can exercise its creative will through the guise of the artists.

Labor in itself is disgraceful and full of the feeling of shame. This feeling is also derived from the fact that the laborer is "just a tool of infinitely greater manifestations of will than he considers himself to be, in his isolated form as individual" (*The Greek State* 178). He is merely a means to an end that is greater than him, and he would have fulfilled his function if he sacrificed himself for the promotion of that end. And only this mythology of a higher and overarching purpose that lends meaning, unity and goal to the individual's existence. Therefore the laborer's sacrifice for the sake of the artists is not done in vain. The laborer gets something indispensible in return: a sense of purpose, a *telos* for his life. The common individual must take comfort in the fact that a higher form of existence is inaugurated through him, and that he is a stepping-stone to an altar he himself may not enter. What Nietzsche calls "culture" is chiefly this "real hunger for art" as a higher, creative function that justifies existence (*The Greek State* 178). Culture, therefore, rests on a terrible basis, and on the cruel fact that "slavery" belongs to its very essence (*The Greek State* 178).

Without shame and labor there is neither culture nor the artist. The masses must remain oppressed and they must sacrifice themselves, so that the privileged few do not have to worry about the basic struggles of existence, and are free to create and satisfy a new world of necessities. Nietzsche further claims that the more the masses are subjected to life's struggle, beyond the measure that their own wants necessitate, in the service of a minority, the broader, deeper, and more fruitful is the soil for the development of artists and art (*The Greek State* 178). The majority, through the surplus of their labor, generates that space of luxury for the artist to thrive. The "morality" that the state must legislate to produce a culture of artists is what Nietzsche describes in *Daybreak* as the "morality of custom." It is through the commandment of the morality of custom that the "hegemony of custom, tradition, shall be made evident in spite of the private desires and advantages of the individual: the individual is to sacrifice himself" (D 9). Thus, through the morality of custom, the Greek state sets up a solid foundation for the production of art and artists, in order to say "yes" to itself: an ability that is distinctive of the noble mode of evaluation.

Given this order of things, one can define the state as the objectification of that instinct, which subjugates the interests and lives of the masses for the sake of a social and cultural process, which finds its highest justification in the work of art. Nietzsche writes: "nature, in order to bring society about, uses pitiless inflexibility to forge for herself the cruel tool of the state – namely that *conqueror* with the iron hand" (*The Greek State* 180). Through imposing its morality of custom, the state ensures that the majority of its people exhibit hardness, uniformity and simplicity of form. It fosters only those virtues that *discourage* excesses and functional devia-tions among its laborers. The state guarantees cultural unity. It ensures uniformity and the "herd-like" existence of the masses precisely to let the few artists do their creative work.

But what are these creative functions that the artists carry out? The artists deliver "in appearance [*Schein*], in the mirror of genius," and by doing so, they justify the *pudenda origo* of the state, and thereby affirm existence (*The Greek State* 181). They create the realm of art, of overarching myths and mythical gods, which I identify as the third and highest level in the Greek state. The artists' deliverance happens through one or both of the following ways: first, their art, in its "mirroring" capacity, provides a novel expression of the prevailing myth, recasting the latter in a new light; second, through their art, the artists interpret the existing myth, bettering it by introducing variations and distinctions to it in such a way that the new myth not only reflects more clearly the existing condition of the people, but also hints at new directions in which the state and its people could grow and progress. In this way, both art and myths are created to affirm and further the overall health of the people and the state. On their part, the state and its rulers are themselves guided by the presentiment of a myth, "of an invisibl[e] deep intention" (*The Greek State* 181). And this presentiment gives the state and its rulers an indefinable greatness and power, due to which the common individuals feel that they are just the means of an intention, manifesting itself through them and yet hiding itself from them.

It is through the herd individuals that the state preserves itself; but this self-preservation is not done for its own sake, but for the more noble sake of artistic and mythical creation. Therefore the will to self-preservation of the healthy Greek state is subordinated to its creative will. However, there is also a back-and-forth correspondence between the labor class and the highest realm of art and myth, with the artists acting as the "mediators." The mythical realm "gives back" to the labor class (and to the artists too) by providing them with a sense of purpose to their lives. This correspondence shows that the health of the state rests on a delicate balance between its creative will and its self-preserving impulse.

Besides maintaining the cultural unity by ensuring that the oppressed laborers remain oppressed and they do not turn rebellious, the state also preserves the culture by protecting itself against its hostile neighbors. Nietzsche justifies the Greeks' need for periodic wars along the same lines as he justifies their need for slavery. Because the state tempers the natural instincts of people and channels them in such a way that they are domesticated and are transformed to serve the greater cultural purpose, the stored up war-like and barbaric instincts and energies of the people must be released every now and then in other ways, so that the state may go on performing this very function of compelling the social process. Nietzsche poses the following question about the bellicose nature of the Greeks:

> This bloody jealousy of one town from another ... this murderous greed of those petty wars, the tiger-like triumph over the corpse of the slain enemy, in short, the continuous renewal of those Trojan battle-scenes and atrocities which Homer, standing before us as a true Hellene, contemplated with deep *relish* – what does this naïve barbarism of the Greek state indicate? (*The Greek State* 181–182).

The justification for all these atrocities is twofold: first, these wars are a way of discharging the state's stored up energies; however, secondly, this discharging is not done for its own sake, but so that the state's inner elements (its subjects and laborers) are refreshed and re-unified for the task of a higher culture which is its highest justification. Nietzsche expresses this when he writes, "the concentrated effect of that *bellum*, turned inwards, gives society time to germinate and turn green everywhere, so that it can let the radiant blossoms of genius sprout forth as soon as warmers days come" (*The Greek State* 182). War is as necessary to the state as slavery is to society. And both of these are necessary for the birth of an artistic culture. Hence we may conclude that the proper aim of the Greek state was to ensure the "Olympian existence and constantly renewed creation and preparation of the genius [of art] – compared with which all other things are only tools, expedients and factors towards realization" (*The Greek State* 185). Thus we see a close and necessary connection between Greek state and art, political greed and artistic creation, battlefield and the work of art.

The Hellenic need for war reveals this strong culture's need for challenges. The latter is grounded in the Greek state's necessity to "refresh" it subjects and their energies, for the sake of the ever-renewed preparation and production of the artistic genius. But war alone is not sufficient to ensure that the common subjects go on performing their laborious tasks. They need something else which would compel them to their destined tasks even when there were no wars. According to Nietzsche, this other ingredient is the spirit of agon or the competitive instinct. In another unpublished essay, *Homer on Competition,* Nietzsche remarks that the finest Hellenic principle is that of "competition," which by inducing envy, jealousy and the agonistic spirit in people plays a major role in preserving the health of the state (*Homer on Competition* 194).[303] It is the competitive instinct in the Greeks, which accounts for their traits of cruelty, "of [their] tiger-like pleasure in destruction" (*Homer on Competition* 187). It also acted as the instigating factor compelling the ordinary Hellene to overcome his personal boredom and perform his designated labor.

Nietzsche points to the account of the myth of the two Eris-goddesses in Hesiod's *Works and Days* as the most remarkable of Hellenic ideas. According to this account, one of the Eris goddesses promotes the cruelty of war and feuding, and the other goddesses, who resides among common people, has the intention of driving the unskilled person to skilled labor (*Homer on Competition* 189). The latter goddess goads the commoners to action by instilling envy and jealousy among them. The poor envies the rich, and it motivates them to "[hurry] off to sow and plant and set [their] house in order" (*Homer on Competition* 189). Thus the neighbor bears grudges against neighbor, carpenter against carpenter and beggars against beggars. Grudge and envy pushes people to excel in their individual works in a bid to overtake their competitor.

---

303 The agonistic spirit itself is the product of Homeric art, which transforms the horrors and barbarism of pre-Homeric world through extraordinary artistic precision, the calmness and purity of lines (*Homer on Competition* 188–190).

It also ensures the uniformity of the people, and keeps them away from a revolting desire for variation. The promotion of a healthy competition among laborers is necessary, since most of them are not in possession of the conscious knowledge that they are merely a tool for a higher purpose to which they do not have direct access. The state needs the common people to continue to labor even in this condition of ignorance. It is precisely a myth (that of Eris-goddesses), which comes to the relief of the state by instilling the spirit of agon among commoners, so that they are challenged to perform their labors, in turn ensuring the possibility of continued creation and renewal of myths. Again, we see a back-and-forth interaction between the commoners and the mythological realm, reflecting a struggle between the self-preserving and the creative will of the state.

Furthermore, it is interesting to note that the agonistic spirit determines the works not only of the laborers, but also of the artists and geniuses. For the Greeks, the artist's work "falls into the same category of undignified work as any philistine craft" (*The Greek State* 178). Nietzsche here is not contradicting what he asserted earlier about the exclusivity of the artists, but rather alluding to the profound depth of the hierarchy of the Greek social structure. Just as the laborer is only a means to get to the artist, the artist himself is a means to affirm the myth, that invisible deep purpose which secures the meaning and justification of the culture. Hence Nietzsche writes, "However, when the compelling force of artistic inspiration unfolds in him, he *has* to create and bow to the necessity of work" (*The Greek State* 178). Just as the one who gives birth sacrifices himself for the sake of his creation, the creative artist sacrifices himself for the sake of his art. The artist is not greater than the myth, but rather he submits himself to it in order to reinterpret, renew and reaffirm the myth. In the end, even the artist's interests are sacrificed to the "well-being of the whole, of state society" (*Homer on Competition* 192). The second level comprised of artists is subordinated to the highest level of myths, just as the level of laborers is subordinated to that of the artists. In establishing this order of subordination, the agonistic instinct plays an indispensible role.

Nietzsche writes: "Every great Hellene passes on the torch of competition" (*Homer on Competition* 191). The great artists incite and trigger each other into greater feats and transformative tasks by either inspiring each other with their artworks or by pointing out the fallacies in others' works. It is only several geniuses who can incite each other into action, and prevent each other from transgressing the limit between genius and corruption: the "*protective measure* against genius – a second genius" (*Homer on Competition* 192). Jealousy and envy again play a vital role in the mutual struggle between the artists. As Dale Wilkerson remarks:

> [T]he spirit of competition [inspired] poets and philosophers to seek out weaknesses in their works of their predecessors, to discover newly formed crevasses in the intellectual landscape, and to fill these voids with newly developed and more suitable standards of measure.[304]

---

304 Dale Wilkerson, *Nietzsche and the Greeks* (London: Continuum, 2006) 80.

The agonistic instinct shared by the Hellenes is thus a "drive for variation, for trans-formation, for alterity, for becoming."[305] But also, it must be observed that the ago-nistic instinct fosters a kind of uniformity among the artists, despite acting as a drive for variation, since it cultivates a community of artists, none of whom are greater than the overarching myth, which they strive to interpret and renew. Hence in the realm of the Greek state, this instinct has a very specific role to play; its application has a very specific "directionality" and a clear intention corresponding to the preservation of the hierarchical structure of the state. It oversees the structural formation and functional-ity of the Greek state.[306]

Greek art

[A]rt is... the true metaphysical activity of this life (BT Foreword)

Since the principal function of the Greek state is to subjugate the instincts of the laborers so that their repetitive labor frees up the sphere of art and artists, I suggest we view the state as a whole as performing a self-preserving function in the cultural geography of the Hellenic world. Through its "iron hand," the state ensures that the culture "persevere in constant struggle with neighbors or with the oppressed who are or threaten to be rebellious" (BGE 262). In contrast, art, broadly construed, must be seen as performing a creative function in this landscape. This follows from the above analysis, since the realm of art in general corresponds to the domain of excess, gener-

---

305 Wilkerson 80.

306 The absence of an active agonistic spirit among the artists or laborers entails not only their inner corruption, but the corruption of the state itself. As an example of the corruption of an Athenian ge-nius, Nietzsche discusses the ultimate fate of Miltiades, an Athenian general, who went beyond every fellow competitor due to his great success at Marathon. Miltiades found himself in a "lonely pinnacle" with a "base lust for revenge" (*Homer on Competition* 190). He was unable to bear the fame and the solitude his genius brought him, especially since it isolated him from the world of competitors. This situation has an adverse and corruptive effect on Miltiades who now, to satisfy his lust, "misuse[d] his name, the state's money and civic honor, and disgrace[d] himself" (*Homer on Competition* 190). He entered into a secret godless relationship with Timo, priestess of Demeter, and during night time entered the sacred temple from which every human being was banned. But when he was approaching the shrine, he was overcome by a panic-stricken dread that made him almost collapse and become un-conscious. With anxiety he jumped back over the wall, and in doing so, fell down, paralyzed and was badly injured (*Homer on Competition* 194). Unable to live in a world, where he cannot compete with his fellow humans, Miltiades enters a path of debauchery and corruption, and thereby commits the great-est of blunders by invoking challenge with the gods. He thus became a victim of the envy and wrath of the gods: "he only has the gods near him now – and for that reason he has them against him" (*Homer on Competition* 194). Miltiades was tried in the people's court. A "disgraceful death stamp[ed] its seal on the glorious heroic career to darken it for all posterity" (*Homer on Competition* 194). Nietzsche also notes that the finest of Greek states decayed and perished in the same way as Miltiades: through "*acts of hubris*" (*Homer on Competition* 194).

ated through the labor of the slaves and the transformative endeavors of the artists.[307] A further proof that art belongs to the realm of excess lies in the fact that in contrast to the Hellenic culture, many previous Oriental cultures, according to Nietzsche, never really got beyond the mere execution of their animalistic and preserving functions to affirm something more that does not just respond to the brute necessities of life. "Art" precisely stands as the elevated expression of this "something more." While the analysis of the state introduced us to the general schema of the Hellenic landscape, the following analysis of Greek art is more particular in that it will separately scrutinize one of the aspects (corresponding to the highest level in the hierarchy discussed above) introduced in the discussion of the state. However, the form of the following discussion will more or less remain the same, in that it will isolate that force *within* Greek art, which represents the self-preserving impulse and that which represents the creative impulse. Similarly, in the domain of art we will also investigate the roles played by the agonistic instinct and the myths.

In my consideration of Greek art, I will not specifically investigate the significance of earlier art forms of Homer and Hesiod for the development of the Ancient Greek culture.[308] Instead, I will limit my analysis to Greek tragedy, since Nietzsche's own interpretative efforts, for example in his first book, *The Birth of Tragedy*, were more focused on comprehending the unique glory of Hellenic life in terms of the origin and meaning of tragic art. In *The Birth of Tragedy*, Nietzsche also maps the death of tragedy and of Greek art in general on to the actual decadence of Greek culture. While the origin of tragedy consists in the strife and struggle between the two gods, Apollo and Dionysus, the death of tragedy, which would account for the "very striking but hitherto unexplained degeneration of the Hellenic world" would consists in the "disappearance of the Dionysian spirit,"[309] or rather in the disappearance of the very strife between the Apollonian and Dionysian (BT 19).

In the 1886 preface to his first book, Nietzsche summarizes the main question posed by the book: is there a pessimism of strength, or is pessimism always necessarily a sign of weakness, "of decline, decay, malformation, of tired and debilitated instincts"? (BT Attempt 1). The ambiguity in the meaning of pessimism is the interpretative problem, to which Nietzsche provides a solution in his book. Nietzsche's answer is that there is in fact a pessimism of strength which originates in an abundance of existence, rather than its deprivation. A suffering that originates in the superabundance of existence seeks out precisely "the hard, gruesome, malevolent and problem-

---

307 Hence, as we shall see below, the "Dionysian" drive (which is the drive of "excess") plays a central role in Greek tragedy.

308 For an interpretation of the importance of Homer and Hesiod for defining what it means to be Greeks, see Tracy B. Strong, *Friedrich Nietzsche and the Politics of Transfiguration* (Berkeley and Los Angeles: University of California Press, 1975), 135–185.

309 Ronald Speirs translates the terms *"Apollinischen"* and *"Dionysischen"* as "Apolline" and "Dionysiac" respectively. I prefer, instead, "Apollonian" and "Dionysian."

atic aspects of existence ... [and] *demands* the terrifying foe, as a worthy foe against which it can test its strength" (BT Attempt 1). Such pessimism of strength is expressed in Hellenic art; the former constitutes the latter's tragic nature. It is exactly here that the questions about the meaning of the tragic myth amongst the Greeks and also that of the phenomenon of the Dionysian are posed. The subtlety of Nietzsche's interpretation also involves an attempt to locate the threshold point, at which the pessimism of the great Hellenic art is transformed and re-interpreted as the other kind of pessimism, which is that of the smugness and "optimism" belonging to Euripidean artform and Socratic dialectics. I suggest that the birth of the Socratic pessimism, which is a "sign of decline, of exhaustion, of sickness, of the anarchic dissolution of the instincts" (BT Attempt 1), presupposes the prior disintegration of tragic art on its own terms. The question then is how the transition between these two kinds of pessimism takes place or how the Ancient Greek tragedy dies.

In a short essay, *The Dionysiac World View (Die dionysische Weltanschauung)*, written in the winter of 1870, Nietzsche argues that the force of the Dionysian god was initially foreign to the Hellenic soil, and Apollo was the only Hellenic god of art. It was the spirit of Dionysus which "came storming in from Asia," where previously it had effected "the crudest unleashing of the lower drives, a panhetaeric animality which sundered all social ties for a certain period of time" (*The Dionysiac World view* 121). The Apollonian world of Homer and the Olympians ruled the Hellenic world after gaining victory over the dark age of the "Titans and the slave monsters," in which the terrible "wisdom of Silenus" had become the "popular philosophy" (BT 3–4).[310] Apollo had gained victory over the Titanic sensitivity to suffering through creations of powerful and intensely pleasurable illusions, and had taught the Hellenes to discover joy in appearances. This was Apollo's myth and art.

Against the new Dionysian intruder, the Hellenic Apollonian drive initially puts up a brave resistance. Resistance, however, becomes more and more improbable when "shoots [of the Dionysian impulse] sprang from the deepest root of the Hellenic character" (BT 2). The best alternative at this point for the Delphic god was to take the "weapons of destruction out of the hands of his mighty opponent in a timely act of reconciliation" (BT 2). The glory and the highest point of Hellenic culture, for Nietzsche, consist in how this terrible Dionysian force interacts with the already-present Apollonian art, and how the contest between the two gods – Apollo and Dionysus – is reconciled such that both gods emerged victorious. Nietzsche's argument is that it is only the Greek Attic tragedy of 5th century B.C., which plays out the greatest reconciliation between the two artistic drives, making this period the highest expression of artistic culture ever known. Unlike in Asia, where the Dionysian intoxication had more adverse effects on the culture than positive ones, in Greece, the Apollonian

---

310 The wisdom of Silenus pronounced a horrific truth expressed as follows: "The very best thing is utterly beyond your reach not to have been born, not to *be*, to be *nothing*. However, the second best thing for you is: to die soon" (BT 3).

drive contested in such a way with the new alien god that, both the Apollonian and the Dionysian elements developed through a process of mutual struggle. These two drives stimulated each other alternatively producing various different art forms, culminating in the greatest form of Hellenic art, Attic tragedy, which is "Dionysian and Apollonian in equal measure" (BT 1).

The Apollonian drive, which denotes the *principium individuationis*, is the drive towards limitation, individuation and discreteness. It promotes an ethics of self-moderation and temperance. Individuality promises a refuge from the chaotic, primordial being, into which one is otherwise hurled. Accordingly, the Apollonian artist deifies individuality by presenting glorious images of individual persons or events. The chief art of Apollo, the god of light, is that of image-making. Beauty is the element in which Apollo reveals itself. Hence, in its very revelation, it hides itself in the brilliance of semblances: "[Apollo] governs the lovely semblance produced by the inner world of fantasy" (BT 1). The self-limiting imperatives "Know thyself!" and "Not too much!" belong to this aesthetic necessity of beauty, since an excessiveness of the image-drive would lead to a confusion about the very distinction between reality and semblance leading to pathological effects. Semblance would not be beautiful if it were not accompanied by the impulse for "measured limitation, that freedom from wilder impulses" (BT 1). For Nietzsche, the highest expression of Apollonian art is to be found in Greek epic poetry, especially that of Homer.

The Dionysian drive, on the other hand, is the opposing drive towards transgression of limits. It is the drive of *excess*, which dissolves all boundaries of individuation and ethical constraints. It is the sexual orgiastic drive of ecstasy that not only reconciles the bond between human beings (which may have been compromised due to individuation) but also that between nature and human beings. Nature that was previously "alienated, inimical, or subjugated celebrates once more her festival of reconciliation with her lost son, humankind" (BT1). In the Dionysian state, every human being stands naked before the primordial unity of all things. Having forgotten how to talk or walk, one is on the "brink of dancing, up and away into the air above" in mystical self-abandon (BT 1). Unlike in the Apollonian state, where humans are chiefly artists, in the Dionysian-narcotic state of drunken revelry, human beings are works of art themselves. For Nietzsche, music, especially dancing and choral singing, symbolizes Dionysian art.

If the Apollonian drive alone had determined the Hellenic culture, then it would have been a rather timid culture, whose people would have been more or less satisfied with the relative stability and safety that this culture would have secured for itself in its own image of itself. Its art would not have reached the pinnacle that Nietzsche claims for Greek attic tragedy. Alternatively, if Dionysus alone had dominated the Ancient Greek culture, we would have had some dire results such as the brutal and unhindered release of all animalistic drives, which Nietzsche associates with Asiatic cultures. Only in a contest and struggle with the Apollonian drive is the Dionysian impulse transformed to bring about "a festival of universal redemption, a day of transfiguration" (*The Dionysiac World view* 121). What Nietzsche seems to be suggesting is that the agonistic instinct is not only the driving force among the common laborers and the exclusive artists, as members of the different strata of the healthy Greek state, but that it determines the very nature of tragic art itself. The mutual struggle between the Apollonian and the Dionysian drives is a kind of agon, which constitutes the essence of Greek art.

What is at stake in this struggle between the two drives? Nietzsche's response is that the agonistic strife between the two drives had significant "metaphysical" implications.[311] The dictum that "the existence of the world is *justified* only as an aesthetic phenomenon," signifies Nietzsche's view that this it is art, not morality, which is the "true *metaphysical* activity of man" (BT Attempt 5). Tragedy consoled and seduced the Hellene to go on living. But why does the Hellene need consolation? Consolation from what? And why does existence need to be justified? Without getting caught up too much in the quasi-Schopenhauerian conceptual snares with which Nietzsche was operating in these early works, we may say that his description of Greek tragedy is governed by a basic assumption that what truly exists is the "eternally suffering and contradictory, primordial unity" (BT 4). The empirical, phenomenal world in which we live is fleeting and constantly becoming. It is the world of space and time, in which things come into being and pass away: a world of semblance, which is insulated from the terrible truth about the primordial and mysterious unity of all things by the veil of *maya*. This world is the Apollonian dream-world of images, the sphere of individuation. Every human being shows herself to be an artist as she creates and lives in the world of dream, "and the lovely semblance of dream is the precondition of all the arts of image-making" (BT 1). Within the world of semblance resides the illusion of culture, and the "cultured man ... generally thinks of himself as the only reality" (BT 8).

However, the more artistic the cultured man is, the more he is capable of seeing the phenomenal world of semblance precisely *as* a world of semblance. At this point, he may either wish to go on dreaming knowing that he is in fact dreaming, or he may be overcome by that Dionysian impulse that tears him away from the *principium individuationis*. For Nietzsche, Dionysian music has the power of sound "to shake us to our very foundations"; it destroys the veil of *maya* through the highest intensification of symbolic powers, and the oneness (between human beings and between humans and nature) as the "genius of humankind, indeed of nature itself" is expressed through it (BT 2). In this state of intoxicating ecstasy, one feels a member of a higher and a more

---

311 Nietzsche's use of the term "metaphysics" in these early works was significantly different from his use of the same term in the later works. In the early writings, especially in *The Birth of Tragedy*, as we shall see, the term "metaphysics" is used mostly in connection with the aesthetic justification of existence. Existence needs to be justified because, in itself, it has no meaning. By establishing a mythical unity for culture as a whole, art performs a "metaphysical" function, and lends meaning and purpose to life and culture. This use of "metaphysics" does not have a direct implication for the main arguments regarding Nietzsche's critique of metaphysics made in this work.

ideal community, and one moves to the rhythm of a universal harmony. One gazes into the eternal contradiction of the primordial unity of all things. One now fathoms, ever so slightly, that mysterious ground of our being of which we ourselves are an appearance. Dionysian excess "reveals itself as the truth; contradiction, bliss born of pain, spoke of itself from out of the heart of nature" (BT 4). I suggest that this ascent, this transformation from the Apollonian to the Dionysian world, should be understood as the achievement of a *creative* will which tears one away from and overcomes the sphere of individuation within which one existed, however painful this process might be. It challenges one to break free from the safety net of beauty and semblance in which one has lost oneself. It reveals the Dionysian truth of eternal contradiction, which terrifies and horrifies us. The will to create dictates the necessary movement from the Apollonian to the Dionysian. It reveals to us that our phenomenal world, governed by its "principle of sufficient reason" harbors an exception, which, in fact, is the more real ground of this very phenomenal world. Furthermore, there is a feeling of nausea associated with the removal of the veil of ignorance, and with the attainment of an insight into the knowledge about the true essence of all things. This unsettling experience leads to an abhorring of all action; knowledge finds action repulsive, since "action requires that one to be shrouded in a veil of illusion" (BT 7). In this sense, the artist with the Dionysian vision needs a kind of solace, a justification to go on living.

Precisely here, Nietzsche argues that "pain[ful experience] awakens pleasure" (BT 2). With the Dionysian insight one is now privy to a greater wisdom – of a new Dionysian myth – that despite the transitory nature of all changing appearances, "life is indestructibly mighty and pleasurable" (BT 7). And this wisdom provides a "metaphysical solace" for the one who is hurled into gazing the eternal chaos of all being (BT 7). It reveals that it is in fact individuation, which is the cause of all of life's suffering. What other revelation could be a greater consolation for the one who has been denied the safety of individuation? Through this teaching, the creative-Dionysian will justifies existence.[312] The unique quality of the Greeks is that, for them, the Dionysian transformation of the everyday world finds expression as an artistic phenomenon, especially in the form of music. The chorus of satyr in Greek tragedies symbolizes a metaphysical solace, since it appears as a "chorus of natural beings whose life goes on ineradicably behind and beyond all civilization, as it were, and who remain eternally the same despite all changes of generations and in the history of nations" (BT 7).

We have now traced only that movement which leads one from the Apollonian world of semblance to the Dionysian gaze into eternal being. But there is an equally compelling movement that leads one from the Dionysian truth to its Apollonian symbolization in an image, the latter being a sensual expression of the horrific Dio-

---

312 The new Dionysian myth and wisdom which have been extracted, so to speak, from the prior effects of Apollonian mythical transformations are not the same as the old terrible wisdom of Silenus (which declared that the second best thing one can do is to die soon), since the earlier wisdom spoke of a world not yet interpreted by the Homeric-Apollonian images.

nysian truth. The latter movement shows the Dionysian need for the Apollonian, an "original desire for semblance" (BT 4). Whence comes this desire? Nietzsche's answer is that the artistic drives in nature themselves long for their "redemption and release in semblance"; the primordial unity itself "simultaneously needs, for its constant release and redemption, the ecstatic vision, intensely pleasurable semblance" (BT 4). The world of appearance in which we live is, as it were, created and summoned forth by the primordial unity for its own release and salvation; the world and our existence itself are justified in this way, since we are episodes and projections of the primordial unity. The primordial unity creates the phenomenal world in order to *preserve* and conserve itself. Release and redemption are self-preserving impulses. Through this preserving act, the existence of the phenomenal world is justified. Thus the tendency in nature towards Apollonian semblance is the primordial instantiation of the "will to self-preservation."

To use a Kantian expression, it is not possible to bear the Dionysian truth and the gaze into primordial unity, as this truth and unity are in themselves. One needs to gain a certain "distance" from the primordial unity, so that one is not completely destroyed and torn apart from the terrible nature of its truth. The experience of the sublime requires, ever so slightly, an Apollonian beautification to complete it. This is not to say that in the revelation of the Dionysian truth, the veil of individuation is not shattered. But rather, notwithstanding the shattering of individuality, one still needs, to a minimal degree, an Apollonian dream-image in order to gaze at this very truth. The presentation, the reflection of the original primordial unity in the world of semblance, is what guarantees that vital distance, without which the human being would be crushed by the infinite suffering of the primordial truth. One just cannot view the latter pure, naked and simple. In this sense, the release and redemption of the primordial unity in pleasurable semblance may be seen as another kind of "metaphysical solace," which seduces and enables one to go on living, even if by reflecting this very terrible truth. The beauty of the reflected truth justifies the existence of human beings, since existence itself is shown to be the appearance or semblance of the ground of all things. Through the creation of images and symbols, the human race preserves itself in the face of a horrific Dionysian truth.

The transformation of the Dionysian truth into an Apollonian image is the "highest symbolism of art" in which we see the "Apollonian world of beauty and the ground on which it rests, that terrible world of Silenus, and we grasp, intuitively, the reciprocal necessity of these two things" (BT 4). The necessity of these two things implies the necessity both of the tearing away of the individual and the ascent to Dionysian unity, and also the necessity of the release of the Dionysian truth into Apollonian semblance. These two contradictory movements – which involve, as we have seen, two instances of metaphysical solaces and two corresponding justifications for existence – reflect the very essence of the eternally suffering and contradictory primordial unity itself. Hence they are not dispensable; they form the eternal to-and-fro of existence, the fundamental strife between being and becoming, between the will to create and the will to self-preservation. For Nietzsche, Apollonian art gets its highest justification only in reflecting its Dionysian ground; this reflection is the "primal process of the naïve artist and also of Apollonian culture"; "Apollo could not live without Dionysus" (BT 4). Apollo, the deification of the *principium individuationis*, shows us with sublime gestures that "the whole world of agony is needed in order to compel the individual to generate the releasing and redemptive vision and then, lost in contemplation of that vision, to sit calmly in his rocking boat in the midst of the sea" (BT 4).

Given his artistic metaphysics, Nietzsche interprets various kinds of Hellenic art, especially of the sixth and fifth century B.C., to be products of the mutual strife between the Apollonian and the Dionysian drives. For example, Doric art and Doric state were the result of the Apollonian Delphic god resisting with all his might the onslaught of the imposing Dionysus. Doric art was the "permanent military encampment of the Apollonian ... [in a state of] unremitting resistance to the Titanic-barbaric nature of the Dionysian" (BT 4). Apollonian art reaches a high expression precisely in resisting the Dionysian drive to collapse all individuation; and in turn, the Dionysian overcoming of the set Apollonian imagery, makes possible a further enhancement of art. The entire Hellenic world, during its greatest period, was dominated by this mutual struggle, this agon between the two gods, involving a "succession of ever-new births" and a "process of reciprocal intensification" (BT 4). The Apollonian and the Dionysian mutually transform one another in a process of endless and contradictory struggle, thus creating the varying forms of Hellenic art and dictating the various transformations of Greek culture itself. Ultimately, it is only in the Greek Attic tragedy and the dramatic dithyramb that these two drives are mostly clearly seen to exist side by side, "in equal measure" and "mostly in open conflict, stimulating and provoking one another to give birth to ever-new, more rigorous offspring" (BT 1). The union and strife of the two drives, their eternal contradiction expressed in Greek tragedy, is the highest form of art.

Nietzsche traces the germs of Greek tragedy in his interpretations of various forms of Greek art. The lyric poet (who is also a musician, like Archilochus) is the Dionysian artist, who interprets the original "music" at the heart of the contradiction and pain of the primordial unity. His interpretation proceeds through images and symbolic representations that precisely grow out of the Dionysian "mystical state of self-abandonment and one-ness" (BT 5). Hence, even though he is a Dionysian artist, he is also an "Apollonian genius" (BT 6). But unlike the epic poet, who is more of an Apollonian artist, the lyric poet is not content in living within the images he creates. The images of the lyric poet are "nothing but *the poet himself*, [they are] various objectifications of him, as it were, which is why he can say 'I' as the moving center of that world" (BT 5). In the folk song of Archilochus, for example, we see a "*perpetuum vestigium* of a union of the Apollonian and the Dionysian," which can be regarded as a "musical mirror of the world, as original melody" (BT 6). The original melody begets lyric poetry by undergoing several objectifications in several texts, giving birth again and again in ever-new ways, in brilliant "sparks of imagery" (BT 6).

In contrast, epic poetry is "lost in the pure contemplation of the images" (BT 5). An epic poet, such as Homer, is joyfully content in living in the images he creates, and becomes one with his figures. The Apollonian epic artist transforms the original Dionysian truth into an object of contemplation by taming and somewhat neutralizing the original contradiction through his creative images. He thus enjoys the dream-pleasure that is derived in the beauty of semblances and individuation. However, this Apollonian art still has and serves a Dionysian purpose insofar as it is precisely the Dionysian excess of the primordial unity that summoned forth the realm of semblance for its own salvation. Apollonian beauty and moderation rests "on a hidden ground of suffering and knowledge which is exposed to [its] gaze once more by the Dionysian" (BT 4).

When the strife between the Apollonian and Dionysian elements develop to such an extent that they exist side by side as reciprocal forces stimulating each other to greater and greater degrees, Greek art itself develops, resulting in tragedy. Tragedy begins with satyr, in which nature is seen in its raw excesses, untouched by the framings of culture. But the great peculiarity of the Hellenes, Nietzsche observes, is that they did not see in raw nature merely animalistic drives. Instead, they saw in it the "original image of mankind, the expression of man's highest and strongest stirrings" revealing man's proximity to his god; man as "a sympathetic companion in whom the sufferings of the god are repeated" (BT 8). It is as if the highest expression of humankind and of Greek culture is reached only when all the representations of popular culture are wiped away or overlooked, but still the primary Apollonian ability to create and behold images is retained in the most economical way only in order to reflect the primordial suffering. Without this reflection, one could imagine the Greek state to resemble a barbaric one. An integral part of tragedy is the chorus of satyrs, which is "first and foremost a vision of Dionysian mass," a "self-mirroring of Dionysian man" (BT 8). The chorus consists of the agitated mass of Dionysus' servants shouting in jubilation as they are seized by moods and insights so powerful that they see themselves as geniuses of nature. Chorus is the artistic imitation of the original phenomenon of nature. In chorus, the highest peak of Dionysian excitement is reached, as individuality is surrendered by way of entry into another nature. Dithyrambic chorus is a "chorus of transformed beings who have completely forgotten their civic past; they have become timeless servants of their gods" (BT 8).

Nietzsche argues that the tragic chorus is the original phenomenon of drama, since here one has the experience of "seeing oneself transformed before one's eyes and acting as if one had really entered another body, another character" (BT 8). Although drama is entirely dream-appearance (and hence Apollonian), it is originally this process of Dionysian transformation. Not only the members of chorus, but even the audience or spectators of the Greek tragedy were enchanted by the process of transformation, and imagined themselves as members of chorus. In the enchanted condition, one sees oneself as a satyr, and as a satyr one sees the god. But with the Dionysian transformation, one posits and sees a "new vision outside [oneself] which is the Apollonian perfection of [one's] state" (BT 8). Thus the Apollonian and Dionysian exist side-by-side in Greek tragedy, and drama, as the embodiment of Dionysian insights and effects, reveals this fact. It is in the vision of drama that the primal ground discharges itself in a succession of radiances; but this vision is also the tearing away of the individual and the latter's unison with primal being. Thus we define Greek tragedy as a "Dionysian chorus which discharges itself over and over again in an Apollonian world of images" (BT 8).

In tragedy, the old Olympian myth undergoes transformation expressing a new, deeper myth. Homeric epic and its myth, which spoke clearly through the Olympian culture by suppressing the Dionysian-Titanic force, is now reborn to a new life under the "overwhelming influence of tragic poetry" (BT 10). Similarly, the "Olympian torturer" makes a timely alliance with Prometheus, and in Aeschylus we see that the terrified Apollonian Zeus makes a pact with the Titan (BT 10). The new tragic myth is a result of the "metempsychosis" of the Apollonian gods and the transformation of myths of the old Apollonian culture under the influence of the Dionysian god, and also the latter's transformation within the representative power of the Apollonian Greek world. The Apollonian and the Dionysian urge each other on, challenging each other to reach ever- deeper truths, and to represent these truths in more sublime symbolic images.

Only through a reconciliation between the two forces in contest is the relative stability of a new myth secured, which can act as the overarching guiding force for the Hellenic culture, providing it a unity and a horizon of meaning. But this reconciliation does not amount to stagnancy, but only to a relative stability and calm. The strife between the Dionysian and the Apollonian is never resolved in a final act of reconciliation in tragedy. There is no end to the struggle between the Hellenic will to create and its will to self-preservation. Rather, the never-ending struggle is to find an optimum "balance" between the two drives so that Hellenic culture finds its most adequate expression, even though one can imagine this ideal of adequacy to be only a "regulative ideal" (in the Kantian sense of the term) that can never really be fulfilled.[313] There is a furthering of myth in ever-grander reconciliations of the two drives signifying the highest points of the tragic Hellenic culture. Greek tragedy and its myth had the enormous power to "stimulate, to purify, to discharge the entire life of the people"; they are the essence of all "prophylactic healing energies, as a mediator between the strongest and inherently most fateful qualities of a people" (BT 21).

A new and greater myth is born only out of reciprocal intensifications and deeper struggles between the two drives. The tragic myth comes into being, for the first time, when the old and dying Olympian myth is re-invoked by the "re-born genius of Dionysian music" (BT 10). But formerly, the Homeric world and its myth were themselves the result of the Apollonian-Homeric transformation of the pre-Homeric world of "night

---

313 Such a paradoxical situation belongs to the essence of the self-contradictory nature of the primordial unity, and the struggle between the Apollonian and the Dionysian that results from it.

and horror," of "purely material fusion" by means of artistic deceptions involving "extraordinary artistic precision, calmness and purity of the lines" (*Homer on Competition* 188).[314] Through this transformation, the brute "struggle-to-the-death" was transformed into the spirit of "competition" proper (*Homer on Competition* 190). What then constitutes the continuing health of the Greek people is a series of artistic transformations (from the pre-Homeric to the Homeric, from the Homeric-Olympian to the tragic-Dionysian). These transformations produce greater and greater art forms, and the corresponding re-interpretations of the overarching myths, in the process producing exceptional artists and statesmen such as Homer, Hesiod, Archilochus, Aeschylus, Sophocles and Miltiades.

As we saw in the previous section, for these transformations to occur, there must exist a solid basis provided by laborers, with shared instincts and goals, at the bottom of the state's rung. Only this presupposition will allow for the freedom of transformation and experimentation at the top tier and for the birth of exceptional types. So there is a balance between the bottom sphere comprised of laborers, and the kind and number of exceptional ones that can be produced at the higher sphere. As Wilkerson puts it, there is a "measured appropriation of genius and madness as counterweights to normality."[315] The health of the Greek state depends on this delicate balance. This must be so because the variations in myth introduced by the artistic transformations are not arbitrary, since the transformed myth still has to produce that relative stability of meaning so crucial to the worldviews of the laborer class. The variations of myth effected by art is a kind of re-casting and re-interpreting of the instincts already shared by the culture, such that the new myth may appeal to the same class of people. The transformations in myths are not random but they occur in constant comparison with existing myths, just as the exceptional types are always grounded in the culture that produced them. Although with Greek art, we are already dealing with the realm of excess, there is still a clear directionality and purpose to the function of the agonistic instinct, just as in the realm of Greek state. The transformations of myths brought about by the different forms of art also have a proper rationale, since they are based on the struggle between the two artistic drives. Hence art, like the Greek state, has a *definite* function (a "creative" one, as opposed to "self-preserving" one) to play in the Greek cultural landscape.

If this is true, whence comes the decadence of the Greek culture? How does Nietzsche explain the "hitherto unexplained degeneration of the Hellenic world?" If tragic art represents the apex of the Greek world, then the death of tragedy must help us understand the decadence of the Greeks. Nietzsche makes an enigmatic remark in BT 11: "Greek tragedy perished differently from all the other, older sister-arts: it died by suicide"; these sister arts, in contrast, died the "most beautiful and peace-

---

314 Therefore, according to Nietzsche, it is art that created religion among the Greeks by way of giving birth to and renewing myths. See *Philosopher* 13.
315 Wilkerson 46.

ful deaths, fading away at a great age." The death of tragedy was itself tragic and terrible, which left behind a vast emptiness felt deeply everywhere. Tragedy died by suicide. I argue that, by these words, Nietzsche is implying that the noble Greek culture decayed on its own terms, and only because this happened first, there was a birth of the decadent Socratic culture, which foreshadows the decadent history of the West. It is not as if Socratism or Euripidean art form *caused* the death of tragedy, but rather these two are, more correctly, symptoms or expressions of a prior decadence,[316] or of a decadence that was already well underway.[317] Generally, commentators tend to under-emphasize or altogether miss this crucial point. David Allison, for example, suggests that Nietzsche clearly held the view that the death of tragedy comes about with "Euripides' reform."[318] Under the spell of the new demon, Socrates, Euripides destroys tragedy through the "sober pronouncements of natural language," by introducing to drama the "rationally explicative prologue," merging the "chorus with the actors themselves."[319] Julian Young, too, insists that, "Nietzsche thinks that Greek tragedy died at the hand of Euripides."[320]

Such readings are based on Nietzsche's own seemingly unequivocal suggestions in *The Birth of Tragedy* that "in league with Socrates, Euripides dared to be the herald of a new kind of artistic creation [which] caused the older tragedy to perish"; "aesthetic Socratism is the murderous principle"; "the Dionysian versus the Socratic, and the work of art that once was Greek tragedy was destroyed by it" (BT 12). Apart from the fact that this interpretation attributes to Socrates a somewhat superhuman and unbelievable power to singlehandedly defeat the entire Hellenic culture, there is evidence that Nietzsche, at several places in his text, also suggests the contrary position, for which I am arguing. For instance, Nietzsche contends that the new branch of Euripidean art that blossomed after the old tragedy had already died, like "wasted epigones," did not "bear the features of its mother, but only those which she had shown during her long death-struggle" (BT 11). More explicitly, he says "an anti-Dionysian tendency was already at work even before Socrates and [it] was only expressed by him with unheard of grandeur" (BT 14). This view is echoed by Nietzsche even in his final works when he writes that when Socrates came on to the scene, "degeneration was everywhere silently preparing itself: the old Athens was coming to an end ... Everywhere

---

316 With his claim that Socratism is not the cause, but the expression of an ongoing decadence, I think the early Nietzsche was already on his way to his later critique of causality, which, as we have seen, introduces us to his concept of will to power.

317 In accordance with this reading, Nietzsche argues that Plato, the "typical Hellenic youth" comes on to the scene when the old Hellenic culture has already completely disintegrated (BT 13). Hence he characterizes Plato, unlike Socrates, as a "mixed type," both with respect to his personality and his philosophy (*Philosophy in the Tragic Age* 34–35).

318 David Allison, "Musical Psychodramatics," in *Why Nietzsche Still?: Reflections on Drama, Culture, and Politics*, ed. Alan D. Schrift (Berkeley and Los Angeles: University of California Press, 2000) 75.

319 Allison, "Musical Psychodramatics" 75.

320 Julian Young, *Nietzsche's Philosophy of Religion* (Cambridge: Cambridge University Press, 2006) 27.

the instincts were in anarchy; everywhere people were but five steps from excess" (TI Socrates 10). Socrates was but "another expression of *decadence*" (TI Socrates 11). He was an "instrument [not the cause] of Greek disintegration" (EH The Birth 1). Furthermore, Nietzsche held the view in *The Birth of Tragedy* that the first indications of the demise of Greek tragedy were already evident in Sophocles' tragedy (not Euripides'), where we see a "change in the position of the chorus ... [which is] the first step towards the *annihilation* of the chorus" (BT 14).

It appears, then, that the roles played by Socrates and Euripides in the death of Greek tragedy, and in Greek decadence in general, are more ambiguous than is usually acknowledged. Socrates is neither the cause nor simply the effect of this decadence. Already in his first book, Nietzsche acknowledged the complexity of "the problem of Socrates" by calling the teacher of Plato "the most questionable phenomenon in Antiquity," who was "enigmatic, unclassifiable, [and] an indissoluble mystery" (BT 13). He urges us to ask ourselves "what a phenomenon like Socrates points to, for the Platonic dialogues do not permit us to view him solely as a disintegrative, negative force" (BT 14). With my suggestion that Socrates is more of a symptom or expression of Greek decadence, rather than its cause or effect, I do not mean that Socrates was simply an innocuous, outward manifestation of an inner decadent process. Rather, he was both a symptom of a prior process of disintegration and an active contributor to this very decadence, who interprets and recasts this process in novel way that leads to the ultimate "suicide" of Greek tragedy and culture. Socrates fits the role of the ambiguous "ascetic priest," who, for Nietzsche, is both a decadent and an original innovator and cultural force. He was original because "he touched on the agonistic instinct of the Hellenes – he introduced a variation into the wrestling-matches among the youths and young men" (TI Socrates 8). For this reason, Nietzsche includes the Socratic "daimonion" as the third original force, in addition to the two forces of Hellenic culture, Apollo and Dionysus (BT 18). And this is also the reason for Nietzsche's early lectures on "pre-Platonic philosophers" (not "pre-Socratic"), since he considered Socrates to be one (albeit the last) of the original thinkers in Greek philosophy, before Plato heralds the era of the "mixed types."

The genius of the daemon that spoke through Socrates recognized that the old Hellenic culture was well and truly degenerating, and that "no one was any longer master of himself, that the instincts were becoming mutually *antagonistic*" (TI Socrates 9). Socrates' originality consists in his recognition that "all the world had need for him – his expedient, his cure, his personal act of self-preservation" (TI Socrates 9). In asking obsessively for "reasons" why the world is the way it is, through his excessive rationality, he taught how to combat one's instincts. He taught that through the permanent daylight of reason, one could attain ultimate truth free of all errors. However, Nietzsche argues that, in the pretext of providing a cure for the prevalent decadence, Socrates, the cultural physician, merely managed to "*alter its expression*," and ironically, quickened the inevitable death of the culture that bore him (TI Socrates 11).

Socrates represented the "archetype of a form of existence unknown before him, the archetype of *theoretical man*" (BT 15). He was the "theoretical optimist" providing the "panacea" of knowledge against the "practical pessimism" of his time, who convinced his fellow Athenians to understand error and illusion as inherently evil (BT 15). In contrast to the Greek artists of the previous generation, in Socrates, it is instinct that "becomes the critic and consciousness the creator" (BT 13). He thus opposed art through his optimism, which gradually penetrated the Dionysian regions, and drove tragedy out "of necessity, to self-destruction by taking a death-leap into domestic tragedy" (BT 14). Through his doctrines – "virtue is knowledge; sin is only committed out of ignorance; the virtuous man is a happy man" – Socrates unwittingly expressed the death wish of tragedy, although he did not cause this death. In the new Euripidean *New Attic Comedy* "tragedy lived on in degenerate form, as a monument to its own exceedingly laborious and violent demise" (BT 11). Socrates became the pied piper of the Hellenic youth; the latter, Nietzsche remarks, "sought refuge *after* the shipwreck [that is, after the old art forms have already disintegrated]; crowded together in a narrow space, and anxiously submissive to the one helmsman, Socrates" (BT 11, my emphasis).

Socrates is indeed "the first genius of decadence," as Deleuze notes,[321] but Socrates himself is a symptom of a decadent condition already prevalent in the Hellenic world. His genius merely provided a novel expression and orientation to this decadence. In other words, the Socratic way of evaluation (consciousness rather than instincts) corresponds to a point that is "further down" in the topological scale of the process of Greek decadence. So there is a prior threshold point, which simultaneously represents the pinnacle of the noble Greek culture as well as the beginning of its decline. Both the summit and the decline are a result of an inner necessity peculiar to Greek culture, and one must resist the impulse to simply "blame" Socrates, as though he was the singular cause of this downfall. The basic tenets of Socratic philosophy indeed become crucial for us as they provide a moral interpretation of decadence, and thereby, bring this decadence to completion. Nevertheless, our initial question about the precise point at which Greek culture "breaks" and the suicide, the exceedingly laborious and violent demise of tragedy, begins still remains unanswered. What really led to the disappearance of that mutual struggle between Apollo and Dionysus that glorified Greek tragedy and sustained a unifying myth for the entire culture? What does Nietzsche mean when he claims that Greek tragedy died by suicide? To answer these questions, we must turn to Greek philosophy.

---

321 Deleuze 13.

Greek philosophy

Among the Greeks alone, he [the philosopher] is not an accident.

(*Philosophy in the Tragic Age* 33)

There is a disastrous simultaneity of spring and autumn (BGE 262)

The problem of the death of Greek tragedy, and thereby of Hellenic culture, cannot be resolved from within the domain of art. For this, we must turn to the third realm, that of Greek philosophy, specifically pre-Platonic philosophy. My goal is not to establish that it is in fact the entirety of Greek philosophy, not just Socrates, which is the "cause" of the decadence of Hellenic art and culture. Rather, my thesis is that it is only the domain of Greek philosophy, which is the symptom or expression of both the highest achievement and pinnacle of Ancient Greek culture and also the first traces of this culture's decadence. In this sense, Greek philosophy goes "beyond" art, and is something different from the other two functional domains, Greek state and art. Moreover, it is not the case that, in Greek philosophy, we see the highest achievement of this culture and this culture's disintegrative features existing side-by-side. I will rather argue that Greek philosophy reveals that the greatest achievement of this culture (what this might be, we will see below) is *indiscernible* from an inception of this culture's decadence. Here, the utmost strength of the Hellenes and their weakness are sharply juxtaposed, signifying the threshold point of decadence. Philosophy grew out of that very noble soil that gave birth to the Greek state and the tragic art form, as its highest glory, but it is also the expression of Greek culture's disintegration. This is a testament to the through-and-through ambiguous status of philosophy with respect to the Hellenic culture.

The argument presented here is not invalidated by the observation that a fair amount of early Greek philosophy predates the tragedies of Aeschylus, and that the innovations introduced into the intellectual landscape by the pre-Socratic philosophers is presupposed by tragedy. Strong, for instance, has observed that the pre-Socratics "made possible the use of the intellect in determining the relation of the individual to the world around him."[322] In particular, the conscious use of intellect, with the aid of categories and concepts, was the main factor in countering the mythological world of Homer and Hesiod. The earlier poets also determined the relation of the individual to the world, but in a "non-reflective" manner; however, the "scientific orientation of the pre-Socratics forced the development of consciousness and explanation."[323] According to Strong, tragedy retains the development of consciousness and intellect, and following the efforts of philosophy, it seeks to "consciously educate and remind a people of its foundations and grounding"; thus the "pre-Socrat-

---

322 Strong 161.
323 Strong 161.

ics provide[] the means that make tragedy possible."[324] Assuming this observation is accurate, it does not take away from the thesis advanced here that early Greek philosophy goes beyond the realm of tragic art, in that philosophy, unlike tragic art, does not play a strictly delineated functional role within the Hellenic cultural landscape. We are here interested in what philosophy itself represents, from the cultural point of view, irrespective of what art form it makes possible; and, as we shall see, pre-Platonic philosophy's use of conceptual thinking to "resolve the problems of the relation of the knowledge of the world with a form of life"[325] implies a much more ambiguous sense and function for philosophy than what is suggested by the phrase "development of consciousness."

Our task now is to investigate why there was philosophy among the Greeks. How does one understand the Greek need for philosophy? Did philosophy, like art and state, have a designated cultural function to perform? What cultural role did philosophy and philosophers execute? What roles do the agonistic instincts play among the "tragic" philosophers of sixth and fifth century B.C., from Thales to Socrates? What is the philosopher's relation to myth?

Nietzsche raises similar questions repeatedly in his early works and in the unpublished notebook entries of the early to mid-1870s. For example, he writes: "What is a philosopher? What is a philosopher's relation to culture? In particular, to tragic culture?" (*The Philosopher as Cultural Physician* 69). Nietzsche tirelessly reflects on these themes in his two lectures on pre-Platonic philosophy, and also in some of the *Nachlaβ* material such as "The Philosopher as Cultural Physician," "The Philosopher: Reflections on the Struggle between Art and Knowledge" and "The Struggle between Science and Wisdom." In these writings, Nietzsche analyzes the meaning of philosophy in general (and its application to modern culture), relying on his interpretation of pre-Platonic philosophy.

To the question whether early Greek philosophy (or philosophers) had a designated cultural place, the answer is both "yes" and "no." This view brings us closest to Nietzsche's own complex interpretation of Hellenic philosophy. Philosophy had a legitimate place among the Greeks insofar as it is an extension, an overflow of their health and nobility. But at the same time it lacks a definite cultural place, unlike art, insofar as it does not perform a clearly delineated function: whether one of self-preservation or creation. Philosophy, thus, represents the symptom of a peculiar kind of a Greek sickness, a "neurosis of health" (GM III 10). (We will see below some features of Greek philosophy that make it both a symptom of strength and of weakness). Therefore, philosophical contemplation appears in "disguise, with an ambiguous appearance" (GM III 10). Due to its irreducible ambiguity, philosophy has no definite place in the cultural context, although it still has an essential, non-accidental meaning for Greek existence. Philosophy reveals the volatile, abysmal domain of the Greek landscape, where the final scenes of the struggle between the self-preserving will and the creative will

---

324 Strong 161.
325 Strong 153.

are played out. The complex interpretative predicament that Nietzsche mentions in the 1886 preface to *The Birth of Tragedy* – whether there is a "pessimism" and "madness" of strength and overabundant life as there is of degeneration (BT Attempt 2, 4) – captures most pertinently the problem of the meaning of Greek philosophy. Philosophy in the tragic age is symptomatic of a Greek pessimism, which is simultaneously the greatest affirmation and the beginning of the death of Hellenic culture.

We must emphasize, at the outset, that philosophy is a phenomenon unique to the Greeks. For Nietzsche, the spiritual or intellectual speculations of other cultures such as the Orient do not share some of the distinctive attributes that belonged to Greek thinking. And there are some other cultures, like that of the Romans who "during their best period lived without philosophy" (*Philosophy in the Tragic Age* 27). The type of health that defines the Romans was such that it did not require something like philosophy to express itself; and even if the Romans did philosophize moderately, one could imagine that their philosophy would have been quite different from the basic tenets of that of the Greeks. Nietzsche argues that it belonged to the characteristic health of the Greeks (the same health which articulated itself through the Greek state and art) that it summoned forth something like philosophy in a very unique way, precisely as an expression of this health: "Philosophy is dangerous wherever it does not exist in its fullest right, and it is only the health of a culture – and not every culture at that – which accords it such fullest right" (*Philosophy in the Tragic Age* 28). Only because the Greeks had a fully healthy culture, did they justify philosophy by engaging in it. This is revealed in the fact that the Greeks began philosophizing at the right time, at the pinnacle of their cultural glory (the age of Persian wars and tragedy). They demonstrate more than any other people "how one must start out in philosophy," that one must not "wait until a period of affliction" (*Philosophy in the Tragic Age* 28). Their philosophy began as a "pursuit springing from the ardent joyousness of courageous and victorious maturity" in the "midst of a good fortune" (*Philosophy in the Tragic Age* 28). This is the reason why Nietzsche thought that among the Greeks the philosopher was not an accident. The Greeks are "Greeks" not because of their artistic or mythical drive, but because of their philosophical drive: "The drives which distinguish the Greeks from other people are expressed in their philosophy" (*Philosopher* 5).

Hence we must expect that Greek philosophy had its own distinctive features, not shared by other cultural attempts at philosophy. Not only this, even from within the signposts of Hellenic culture (the state, art and religion) their philosophy is still something entirely different, even as it grew from within this very same Greek soil. Philosophers are people who are essentially different from the laborers, the practical people and also from the creative artists. Nietzsche makes this point very clear:

> Whoever conceives of them [the pre-Platonic philosophers] as clear, sober, harmonious, practical people will be unable to explain how they arrived at philosophy. And whoever understands them only as aesthetic human beings, indulging in all sorts of revelry in arts, will also feel estranged from their philosophy (*The Pre-Platonic Philosophers* 3).

So if Ancient Greek philosophy is an original and unique phenomenon, whose roots cannot be traced back to Asia or Egypt, and Greek philosophers are necessarily different from the class of laborers and artists, we have a profound problem of locating the cultural place of Greek philosophy.

Philosophy has an essential relation to its culture. It indicates the "vitality of a culture" (*The Struggle* 132). Like the artist, the philosopher "does not stand completely apart from the people" (*Philosopher* 5). Only when a philosopher is born in a genuine culture like that of the Greeks (which has a "unity of style"), is he not a vagabond, a "chance random wanderer": "There is a steely necessity that binds a philosopher to a genuine culture" (*Philosophy in the Tragic Age* 33–34).[326] However, this necessity cannot be the same as that which binds an artist or (art in general) to culture. The Greek philosopher performs a very curious and different function than the artist or the man of religion or science, and therefore has a very special relation to his culture. As noted earlier, Nietzsche finds a third divine voice determining the Hellenic culture – the Socratic daemon – something that is neither Apollonian nor Dionysian. I suggest that the Socratic daemon represents not just the voice of Socrates, but also the force of the entire philosophical spirit – from Thales to Socrates – that constituted pre-Platonic philosophy. The ambiguous relation of Greek philosophy to its culture must be sought in all of these philosophers, not only in Socrates.

In contrast to the artistic drive of the Hellenes, which we have described as the drive of excess, I argue that the philosophical drive is one of *excessive excess*. By using this term, I mean to suggest that from a certain perspective, Greek philosophy was *not* necessary for the Hellenic culture, in the same way art was necessary. (Therefore, earlier in our general introduction to the Hellenic landscape and in our discussion of the Greek state, we did not mention philosophy, although we discussed art). Even though art belongs to the realm of excess, it has a preset function to perform for the culture: the creative one of reinterpreting and renewing myths. Philosophy has no such preset function, not even an unambiguously creative one. Philosophy "has no existence at all of its own" (*The Philosopher as Cultural Physician* 71). However, philosophy *is* necessary in that, it is what stamps the identity of Greeks as such. It is the expression of that very dangerous health that could not have remained satisfied with the achievements of art, religion or science. Philosophy is "higher, finer, rarer" (BGE 262). It is as if the peculiar health of the Hellenes was not exhausted with the neat structuring of society into laborers, artists and myth; it still had something more to bestow, something overflowing in its energy and spirit. It still had the "means of life, even of enjoying life, exist[ing] in abundance" (BGE 262). At this crucial juncture, if

---

326 The above insight is the cause of Nietzsche's frequent lamentations in his earlier works that the "philosophies" of his time were like limbs without a body, lacking any genuine culture to back them up. They lacked justification (they were "dangerous") since modernity, for Nietzsche, unlike the Greek society does not represent a cultural unity, a unity of style.

the Greek culture "wanted to continue, it could do so only as a form of *luxury*, as an archaic *taste*" (BGE 262).

Although in BGE 262, Nietzsche does not directly mention Greek philosophy, but only the Greek polis, in the context of its growth and decadence, I contend that his remarks are very relevant for our understanding of early Greek philosophy. The latter is precisely this overflowing luxury, this "taste" for the excessive excess. It is a unique drive for variation, which accumulates the tremendous amount of force stored up so far within the breeding factory of culture in order to give a "threatening tension into the bow" (BGE 262). It is the highest risk and wager of the noble culture. The arrow of variation could either bring about a "deviation" into the "higher, finer, rarer" *or* "degeneration and monstrosity, [which] suddenly comes onto the scene in the greatest abandon and splendor" (BGE 262). This particular crossroads of Greek culture is the most "dangerous and uncanny point"; Nietzsche calls it the "turning point[] of history" in which a "magnificent, diverse, jungle-like growth and upward striving, a kind of *tropical* tempo in the competition to grow [appears] alongside (and often mixed up and tangled together with) an immense destruction and self-destruction" (BGE 262).[327] Either way, the quest that is expressed through Greek philosophy is the quest for the "most diverse, most comprehensive life [to] *live[] past* the old morality" and customs (BGE 262). In this most incredible passage, Nietzsche clearly alludes to the inescapable ambiguity surfacing at the twilight and turning points of Hellenic culture. This ambiguity takes us to the very core of the meaning of Greek philosophy, where we may locate the threshold point of decadence.

What is the philosophical drive? Nietzsche's answer is clear: it is the drive for knowledge. The pre-Platonic philosophers had an "insatiable thirst of knowledge" (*Philosophy in the Tragic Age* 31); "they mastered the knowledge drive" (*Philosopher* 9–11). However, the drive for philosophy must not be confused with the Dionysian-tragic drive, which reveals the Dionysian truth about the primordial unity of all being. As we shall see, the philosophical drive is something peculiar, and is different from the artistic drive. One might be inclined to protest that there is nothing special about the knowledge-drive; all philosophers and scientists possess it. But Nietzsche means something very specific about the Greek drive for knowledge: it is contextually based on the peculiar cultural unity of Greek existence. The mastery of the knowledge drive was lost after Socrates, since European culture lacked the cultural unity, which Ancient Greece had (*Philosopher* 9). For the Greek philosophers, "'knowing' is *creating*, their creating is a legislating"; philosophers are commanders and legislators (BGE 211). Knowledge as legislating and commanding is possible only for a healthy people, who have an "excess of intellect" (*The Pre-Platonic Philosophers* 6).

However, Nietzsche's view is not that the pre-Platonic philosophers had some extreme intelligence that people who came after them lacked. Rather, the "excess

---

327 Ahern expresses the above point by noting that the emergence of Greek philosophy indicates the "chaos" which is typical of the "apex and bloom" of Hellenic culture (Ahern 56–57).

of intellect" refers to the excessive excess, the stored-up, extra health of the unitary culture of the Greeks that has been accumulated over generations, which takes them even beyond the artistic need. Furthermore, for Nietzsche, the ancient philosophers are the only ones who came close to attaining a sort of "objectivity" in their philosophical attitude, since only they were able to go beyond merely "personal, individual purposes" (*The Pre-Platonic Philosophers* 6). To go beyond the latter is possible only for the excessively healthy, since when the sick seek truth and knowledge they are only "seeking *cures* for themselves," which is a sort of "personal" quest (D 424). Knowledge or truth "exists only for souls which are at once powerful and harmless, and full of joyfulness and peace" (D 424). It is no surprise, then, that such knowledge is extremely rare, which makes the philosopher the "rarest of the great," and "also the highest type of man" (*Philosopher* 45–46).

But what is the "object" of knowledge (truth)? What did the pre-Platonic philosophers seek when they sought truth? Before we answer this question, and as a way of leading us to an answer, we must say a bit about these pre-Platonic philosophers as solitary, individual thinkers. Indeed, according to Nietzsche, Greek philosophy cannot be understood without reference to these individual philosophers. We must "observe how 'the philosopher' appeared among the Greeks, not just how philosophy appeared among them" (*The Pre-Platonic Philosophers* 3). This necessary connection between philosophy and the individual philosophers becomes apparent when we observe that, although Greek philosophy had the virtue of objectivity, the latter does not entail an access to a "pure, objective, disinterested realm," out of which the will of the individual philosophers would be banished. Even though their philosophy is a result of going beyond personal, individual purposes of the philosophers, these philosophers were knowers and legislators since they left the mark of "their personality, their behavior," their "type" in their individual philosophies (*The Pre-Platonic Philosophers* 4). In terms of Nietzsche's later language, we might say that these philosophers' will to truth was their particular will to power. The stamp of the individual philosopher's personality is not detrimental to the objectivity of philosophy, but is essential to it.

The Greek philosophers from Thales to Socrates were "*archetypal philosophers*" (*The Pre-Platonic Philosophers* 4); they invented "*archetypes of philosophical thought*" (*Philosophy in the Tragic Age* 31). They were originals, who lived in grand *solitude*, who lived "*only* for knowledge" (*The Pre-Platonic Philosophers* 4). They were similar to each other as products of the same culture, but at the same time, each of them was uniquely different; each one of these pre-Platonic philosophers is "entirely hewn from one stone," although as individuals "each is the first-born son of philosophy" (*The Pre-Platonic Philosophers* 4). They were "precursors and as it were the precocious *firstling instances of individuals*" (GS 23). Even though all of these philosophers were products of the same glorious culture, they never worked together to form a community of philosophers or a school of philosophy. Since there was rigorous necessity between their characters and their thoughts, there were as many different original philosophies as there were characters (*The Pre-Platonic*

Philosophers 4). For Nietzsche, philosophers in general are champions of diversity, of "magnificent, diverse, jungle-like growth," who surface as diverse individuals at the apex of culture. The more the diversity of the philosophers, the more is the originality and variety of philosophies, and the greater is the testament to the grand health and the unity of the culture that produced these philosophers. Nietzsche often uses the metaphors of trees and fruits to express this point: Philosophers, as firstling instances of individuals, are like the "fruit of fruits hang[ing] ripe and yellow on the tree of people" (GS 23). Culture, the tree of a people, "existed for the sake of this fruit!"; the individual fruits are "the seed-bearers of the future, the spiritual colonizers and shapers of new states and communities" (GS 23).

There is a necessary link between the philosopher's drive for knowledge and the fact that the philosopher is a solitary type, an individual figure. It is precisely the special kind of knowledge that the philosopher aims for (in contrast to the scientist, the religious leader or the artist) that makes him the solitary. Nietzsche underlines this vital insight when he writes, "Knowledge *isolates*. The early philosophers represented in isolation things which Greek art allowed to appear together" (*Philosopher* 16). Nietzsche is here making an astonishing connection between Greek philosophy and art. What appeared in a more unified form at the cultural level of art appears in an isolated form in the individual will of the philosopher, at the rarer level of philosophy. Art, Homeric or tragic, represents reality, the mythology of meaning, by unifying disparate elements of culture into a whole, even though this unity is only a relative and conditional one. Nevertheless, philosophy employs the isolated elements which art had brought together in order to master the knowledge drive; its contents, therefore, "are the same [as in] art" (*Philosopher* 16). From this suggestion, it would appear that philosophy just tears apart those cultural elements that art had unified, thereby performing a purely negative function. Is the stored-up strength of the culture simply squandered by subjection to the knowledge drive, which disperses and diversifies what was contained as a unit?

Undeniably, Greek philosophy has a negative moment of dispersion. Philosophers, therefore, stand in isolation from the rest of the people in the culture. They are "anomalies" who "*do not exist for the people's sake*"; "Philosophy is *not something for the people*" (*The Philosopher as Cultural Physician* 74). The pre-Platonic philosophers were strangers to their own culture. If "culture is a unity...the philosopher only seems to stand outside of it" (*Philosopher* 54). The philosopher is someone who works outside of the frame of culture; he is someone who seems to be exempt from the cultural conditioning and ethos into which the laborers are subject. But he is also different from the artist in that he does not just create and interpret an overarching myth for the culture. The philosopher appears to be a strange parasite, who presupposes and relies on a healthy culture and its stored up energies, in order to fritter them away for some unknown ideal of knowledge. At times, Nietzsche's words seem to suggest this: "[The philosopher] acts as a *solvent* and a *destroyer* regarding all that is positive in a culture or a religion," and that he is "most useful when there is a *lot to be destroyed, in terms of chaos or degeneration*" (*The Philosopher as Cultural Physician* 71–72).

However, this is not the complete picture. In addition to these negative roles, Nietzsche attributes the most positive function to philosophy. Philosophy does not merely scatter away the isolated elements that art had previously united. It subjects these elements into the knowledge drive, only in order to subdue the knowledge drive itself into another kind of unity. Only in doing so, philosophy shows its highest worth: *"Philosophy reveals its highest worth when it concentrates the unlimited knowledge drive and subdues it to unity"* (*Philosopher* 9). Through this subjugation, philosophy accomplishes a mastery of the knowledge drive (*Philosopher* 11). And the new unity is the "truth" that the knowledge drive of philosophy seeks. But what kind of unity is it that philosophy provides? Surely, it is not the artistic unity, since the latter is, in a way, already compromised by the knowledge drive. Nevertheless, philosophical unity or "mastery works to the advantage of an artistic culture" (*Philosopher*11). The Greek philosopher, like the artist, emphasizes the "problem of existence," and "empathize[s] to the utmost with the universal suffering" (*Philosopher* 8). "The earlier philosophers ... are governed in part by a drive similar to the one which created tragedy" (*Philosopher* 21). This positive relation between art and philosophy, however, does not really capture the positive role of Greek philosophy.

We recognize this role only when we note that the mastering unity of the philosophical drive has an *eternalizing* function. Nietzsche argues that Greek philosophy taps into a peculiar character present in all the drives of the Greeks, which is precisely the trait of "mastering unity." The mastering unity captures the essence of "Hellenic will" (*Philosopher* 16). The peculiar trait of the Hellenic will is that it "endeavors to exist to eternity" (*Philosopher* 16). The ancient philosophers, then, – each in their own way – "attempt to construct a world from these drives" by personifying the Hellenic will. Their individual will (their "will to power") is an original expression of the deeply rooted Hellenic will. The various expressions form the different unique philosophies of the pre-Platonic philosophers: whether it is Thales' theory that "all is water," or Anaximander's principle of the "Indefinite" or Parmenides' "One." For this reason, Ancient Greek philosophy must be seen as an extension and further expression of the Greek strength and vitality. It *"grows* from [life] like a rare blossom. It utters its secret" (*The Struggle* 133).

In its eternalizing mode, the pre-Platonic philosopher's drive for knowledge takes up in isolation an aspect or a unique ingredient of Greek culture, which has attained a relative or conditional unity (at the level of art) with other aspects of the culture, and then eternalizes it in concepts as if it reflected the unity of all things. The philosopher seeks *"ultimate knowledge"* and relies *"upon himself,"* his own individual will to furnish this knowledge (*The Struggle* 129). He stands outside the sphere of culture, in order to reflect Greek life. The philosopher's fundamental stance is that of reflection, of mirroring the whole of the cultural life in his individual will. In the philosopher, "what is unique in a people ... comes to light in an individual" (*Philosopher* 6). He is the "self-revelation of nature's workshop" (*Philosopher* 6). He "strive[s] to understand that which [his] fellow men only live through" (*The Struggle* 141). Hence Nietzsche calls the Greek philosophers "witnesses concerning that which is Hellenic," and in their reflective abilities, the different "philosophies are the underworld shades of the Greek nature" (*The Struggle* 142). The philosopher isolates himself and his own will from that of the rest of the people – whether laborers or artists – in order to claim a universality to his own will, as if it spoke the truth of all the will of his people: "the drive of the people is interpreted as a *universal* drive and is employed to solve the riddle of the universe" (*Philosopher* 6). The philosopher is therefore a legislator, a commander, an archetype, an exemplar.

In other words, the truth the philosopher seeks is the knowledge of the unity of the whole existence. In order to express his intuition about the unity of all existence, he may often employ some isolated things and concepts such as "water," "air," "the One," "numbers," etc., in order to recast the latter thing as the "principle" of all things. In any case, by such a representation of the universal in the individual, he puts a seal of eternity on the latter, as if this individual thing (his own will) does not just stand for a unique quality of Greek culture, but the "in itself," the truth of all things. He fixates, trying to reveal the being of becoming; he finds "repose in the restless current, for becoming conscious of the enduring types of disdaining multiplicity" (*Philosopher* 6). "The philosopher seeks to hear within himself the echoes of the world symphony and to re-project them in the form of concepts" (*Philosophy in the Tragic Age* 44). The philosopher seeks a world-picture. If Greek culture is the body, which has attained a relative, healthy unity, Greek philosophy is the consciousness of this body. It is an "understanding of the world with self-consciousness" (*Philosopher* 52). It is an "art that presents an image of universal existence in concepts" (*The Pre-Platonic Philosophers* 7–8).

But there is an inevitable risk of disintegration in philosophy's wager to reflect the truth of all existence. For, the philosopher must necessarily disrupt the unity gained at the level of culture and art. He wagers that he will find a higher eternal unity in reflection, which would compensate for the earlier loss of unity. But this variation introduced by the philosopher may not find its desired goal, the desired unity. It might just turn out to be a "*labyrinthian aberration*" (*The Struggle* 130). Philosophical reflection involves an inescapable danger, since the unity sought by the philosopher has no immediate, solid cultural backing or foundation in contrast to that sought by the artist. Hence there is no preset cultural place or function for philosophy. There are no groups of laborers who work directly for the sake of the philosopher and his creations. The philosopher's existence is precarious. With the philosopher, the culture is shooting in the dark, as it were, and the chances of success are quite low. But it is a risk the Greek culture had to take, in keeping with its own excessive health. Nietzsche sums up this point: "Nature propels the philosopher into mankind like an arrow; it takes no aim but hopes the arrow will stick somewhere" (SE 7).[328]

---

328 Ahern also expresses the above point nicely when he writes, "[the philosophers] are only a promise; anything can happen in the garden of life; and the seeds may sprout or die" (Ahern 49).

It is apparent to see – given the juxtaposition of the negative and positive functions of philosophy – that the status of philosophy is much more ambiguous within the domain of Hellenic culture than that of art. The ambiguity is expressed in the fact that Greek philosophy has no preset, designated cultural place: "There is no appropriate category for philosophy" (*Philosopher* 19). Greek philosophy "has no common denominator: it is sometimes science and sometimes art," and that it has "no existence at all of its own" (*The Philosopher as Cultural Physician* 70–71). The philosopher is "contemplative" like the artist, "compassionate" like the religious man, and "is concerned with causes" like the scientist, but he is not identical to any of them (*Philosopher* 22). Like an assimilator, he allows the multifarious sounds of culture to resonate within himself in order to present a total unified "sound outside of himself by means of concepts" (*Philosopher* 22). Against art he opposes a conceptual language, against religion he de-deifies and de-mythologizes, and against science he dematerializes. We see a parallel schema of "identity and difference" with respect to the Greek philosopher's relation to his people, and to the society at large. Although the great ancient philosophers are part of the general Hellenic life, they were also anomalies to their people. Every philosopher from Thales to Socrates was "*timeless*" in contrast to his people. But as Nietzsche repeatedly insists, although these philosophers have "nothing to do with the accidental political situation of a people," they are nevertheless not "merely accidental" people with respect to their culture (*Philosopher* 6). These seemingly contradictory statements of Nietzsche can be understood only when we recognize the completely ambiguous appearance of the Greek philosopher within this culture's landscape.

Finally, we must highlight another important sense and function of Greek philosophy. Because philosophy had no definite cultural place, and was different from art, religion, science and from the ethos of culture at large (although it was similar to these things in many respects), it had an essentially critical role to play. In his lectures, Nietzsche emphasizes the critical stance of philosophy by translating "philosophy" not as "love of wisdom" as it is usually done. He argues that etymologically "*sophia*" is related to "*sapio*," which can be translated as "taste" (*Philosophy in the Tragic Age* 43; *The Pre-Platonic Philosophers* 8). The philosopher is the one with the keenest taste: "A sharp savoring and selecting, a meaningful discriminating ... makes out the peculiar art of the philosopher" (*Philosophy in the Tragic Age* 43). Science, for instance, lacks this principle of selectivity since it strives to know everything at all costs. Philosophy does not just seek knowledge blindly, but judges what kind of knowledge is worth seeking. It emphasizes the divine, the great and also the practically useless. Nietzsche sums it up: "Philosophy is distinguished from science by its selectivity and its discrimination of the unusual, the astonishing, the difficult and the divine, just as it is distinguished from intellectual cleverness by its emphasis on the useless" (*Philosophy in the Tragic Age* 43). With its selective and discriminating power, Greek philosophy opposes scientific dogmatism, and as a cultural critic, it demonstrates the "*dangers*" inherent within the Greek culture (*The Struggle* 131). But what kind of dangers are these?

In answering this question, we finally come to understand philosophy's relation to cultural myth. According to Nietzsche, pre-Platonic philosophy saw the mythical unity, the horizon of meaning, guaranteed by the joint efforts of both the laborers and the artists as a kind of a "*constraint*" and a "*barrier*" (*The Struggle* 134). Early Greek philosophy was "opposed to myth" (*The Philosopher as Cultural Physician* 71). It saw in these myths possible dangers, confusions and superstitions. Using conceptual thought, the tragic philosophers "deprive[d] themselves of myths" (*The Struggle* 129). No amount of cultural conditioning could contain the peculiar taste for freedom that the philosopher has. It is as if the unique excessive strength of the Hellenic soil itself gave birth to the philosopher, who is the critic and transgressor of the very myth and morality of custom that harbored his growth. Nietzsche identifies some possible harmfulness in the critical stance of philosophy when he writes that there is a danger that philosophy may "dissolve[] the instinct, culture and customary moralities," which have been developed with great difficulty (*The Philosopher as Cultural Physician* 73). If the life of Greeks is comprehensible only where the ray of myth falls upon it, how do the philosophers endure the darkness? Nietzsche's answer is that they rely on themselves, the strength of their individual will, and on their hope of finding ultimate knowledge to compensate for this darkness (*The Struggle* 129). Nietzsche claims that philosophers of no other culture had the amount of "confidence in one's own knowledge" like the early Greeks had (*The Struggle* 129). Their harshness and arrogance regarding their right to universe knowledge is unparalleled.

Hence Nietzsche describes the pre-Platonic philosophers as "tyrants [of the spirit]" (*The Struggle* 129).[329] For the philosophers, the myth was not pure, not lucid enough; they were seeking a "*brighter* sun" in the realm of knowledge, although this path was full of "perils and difficulties" (HH I 261). With one leap, they wanted to solve the riddle of the universe. They discovered this new "light in their knowledge, in that which each of them called his 'truth'" (HH I 261). In this quest, they competed against their own contemporaries and predecessors, in a bid to trump the other philosophers' intuition with their own. "Each of them was a warlike brutal *tyrant*" who wanted to exercise his own individual will to power and severe interpretation to create a world in his own eyes (HH I 261). So it is the agonistic instinct, which is active among these philosophers, albeit in a different form than it is evident among artists or laborers. This instinct instilled a need for challenges in each of them as they tried to dominate the other philosophers and non-philosophers with their incredible thirst for knowledge; in doing so, they tried to be the source of light in place of the displaced myth. Each one of them tried to "settle all questions with a *single* answer" (D 547). There was no doubt that only one person could achieve this feat, but each one of them fancied themselves to be that one. Hence Greek philosophy was a "supreme struggle to possess the tyrannical rule of the spirit" (D 547). The agonistic drive among the phi-

---

329 Also, see HH I 261 and D 547.

losophers was employed for this tyrannical purpose, although unlike among artists and laborers, this drive was not used to secure the mythical unity of the culture. On the contrary, it is precisely with the aid of the spirit of agon that philosophers combated and repudiated myths, in the quest for finding the ultimate unity of knowledge. Hence in the domain of philosophy, the agonistic instinct lacks a clear-cut directionality that was evident in the domains of art and state.

The fight against myth defines early Greek philosophy. The latter begins distinctively with Thales, whom Nietzsche describes as *"unmythological"* (*The Pre-Platonic Philosophers* 7). By thinking conceptually, Thales opposes the mythical preliminary stage. His insight that "all is water" was meant "non-mythically and non-allegorically" (*Philosophy in the Tragic Age* 41). Nietzsche also traces the unmythological orientations in all the pre-Platonic philosophers who came after Thales (*The Struggle* 131, 135, 146). But already in Thales, the opposition of conceptual thought to myth must be seen as philosophy's opposition to art and religion. Philosophy separates or isolates what art has brought together under a mythical unity. The opposition to myth by concepts achieves nothing but this isolation of some constituent of artistic unity. Nietzsche sometimes refers to philosophical conceptual thinking as the work of a scientific mode of thinking: "In Thales for the first time the man of science triumphs over the man of myth" (*The Struggle* 145).

Because philosophers oppose both art and the culture in general, Nietzsche hints that they "lack something in their nature," perhaps to suggest that philosophy's critical stance is a kind of a compensation for this lack (*The Struggle* 134). However the negative, opposing, critical mode of Greek philosophy is only one side of its essence. On the other side lies philosophy's grand vision, its very greatness. For, although philosophy's scientific impulse opposes myth, philosophy's impulse for "wisdom" opposes this very scientific drive (*The Struggle* 145). What is the impulse for wisdom? It is the very same impulse, which seeks to comprehend or know the unity of all things. This impulse seeks the whole. By the virtue of the fact that Thales sought to comprehend or create a unified view of the world – in his proposition "all is water" – he goes beyond all the various sciences (*The Pre-Platonic Philosophers* 7). He sought to grasp in one sweeping intuition the knowledge of the universal essence and core of all things. He then expressed this intuition in words. Thales, the philosopher with taste, legislates greatness by this act of name-giving. In effect, by announcing, "This is a great thing," he not only checks the scientific drive for knowledge (and therefore induces taste by determining what is worth knowing), but he also elevates this individual thing to the principle of all things (*Philosophy in the Tragic Age* 43). And only because of his lofty apprehension and unitary expression can Thales be called the first Greek philosopher. In his positive flight into a higher unity, the philosopher expresses his mastery of knowledge. Thus Greek philosophy is the work of "creative imagination," of an "alien, illogical power" (*Philosophy in the Tragic Age* 40; *Philosopher* 22). The philosopher's knowledge drive, the need to isolate what art has united, the mastering unity of universal knowledge, the critical stance against art and culture, and the opposition to myth all belong to pre-Platonic philosophy as its essential aspects.

However, it is absolutely crucial to acknowledge that the ultimate flight of the imagination is not without its dangers. In fact, we encounter here the un-canniest of all dangers, since with the philosophical propulsion, the very health and vitality of the culture hangs in balance. In seeking the highest unity of all things, philosophy aims for a "*higher form of existence*" (*Philosopher* 17). Unlike science, the value of philosophy is therefore not strictly to be found in the sphere of knowledge, but in that of life (*Philosopher* 17). With the Greek philosophers, the Hellenes were on the point of "discovering a *type of man still higher* than any previous type" (*The Struggle* 134). The pre-Platonic philosophers were necessarily future-oriented as the "*forerunners of the reformation of the Greeks*" (*The Struggle* 134). Philosophy is a perilous wager that puts the already-attained unity of Greek culture on the line for a higher and unheard-of greatness. It represents a reckless challenge to which the great health of Greeks subjects itself. This wager is perilous because the universal essence and unity of all things, which philosophy aims for, is not given beforehand from within the domain of culture. Rather, it must be posited or created. Hence the individual will of the legislator-philosopher is indispensible for the success of philosophy. The knowledge drive forces the philosopher to "again and again leave the inhabited lands behind and venture forth into the unknown" (*The Struggle* 143). The drive for knowledge is the drive into the unknown; it is the creative drive of an excessive health that wants to venture into the unknown after it has outlived the victory it gained at the cultural level. It wants to surpass the latter in search of a higher, hitherto unknown greatness. But knowledge is only a means for the best life. The tragic philosopher is not "satisfied with the motley whirling game of the sciences. He cultivates a new *life* (*Philosopher* 11–12). He envisions new "*possibilities of life*" in search of "great happiness and strength" (*The Struggle* 143). Since the philosophers are "circumnavigators of life's most remote and dangerous regions," everything here is "sensible, daring, desperate, and hopeful" (*The Struggle* 143).

But the philosopher cannot venture into the unknown blindly and insensibly. He cannot simply take both his feet off the ground, and hope to be blown away into another terrain, because such misadventure would only destroy him. He must be grounded in his culture as much as he can, *while at the same time*, in his creative mode, he must fight against his culture, standing outside it, in the search for the great, unknown destination. Every time the knowledge drive risks the leap into the unknown, it must "grope its way back to an approximate secure place on which it can stand" (*The Struggle* 143–144). The philosopher needs a secure place of a relative cultural unity, perhaps as a temporary resting place or also perhaps to refurbish his own exhausting energies, before he submits to his experimental knowledge drive again. He cannot be too removed from his people and the artists that unite his culture. Nietzsche, here, is emphasizing the importance of the will to self-preservation for the philosopher. The philosopher's will to create that aims for a higher life cannot completely ignore the self-preserving demands of his present life. In the philosopher is played out the struggle between these "two hostile drives, which press in opposite directions, under a *single* yoke" (*The Struggle* 143). And as the struggle between these two drives increases, the "struggle between life and knowledge" becomes greater, and therefore, "the rarer it is for them to remain under a single yoke" (*The Struggle* 143). As the struggle increases, "unity becomes rarer as life becomes more full … and knowledge in turn becomes more insatiable and impels one more covetously toward every adventure" (*The Struggle* 143). With struggle, the stakes increase and the chance of success, correspondingly, diminishes. Like the tightrope walker in *Thus Spoke Zarathustra*, the philosopher is involved in a delicate balancing act. An imbalance on either side (creative or self-preserving) may lead to the philosopher's eventual downfall. If this downfall occurs, the strength of the whole culture, not just of the philosopher, is at risk, since the philosopher is gambling the former in the quest to find an expression for a greater health. The problem of the success or failure of the philosopher's project, therefore, makes it possible for us to locate the threshold point of Greek decadence.

One could argue that with respect to the Greeks, the "excessive" movement from art to philosophy, for the sake of a different kind of unity than what art had provided, is not really needed. But that would be to misunderstand the peculiar health of the Greek spirit that creates, out of itself, the need to engage in something like philosophy, which has all the traits we have described above. The Greeks were faithful to this need even if that meant endangering the very structural unity previously achieved at the cultural level. One could say that the birth of Greek philosophy, beyond art, denotes a topological possibility unique to the Greek existence. The pre-Platonic philosophers actualized this possibility by giving expression to some of the distinguishing features of the strong type, analyzed in the previous chapter.

The magnanimous solitude of their existence and the strong individuality of each of their wills; their bestowing virtue, which seeks to repay in a greater fashion the prior opposition and disruption of existing myth, by comprehending in one sweeping intuition the knowledge of the universal essence of all things, and then recasting this intuition in conceptual terms, thereby anticipating a brighter sun, a higher form of existence, a new life, a new higher type of human being hitherto unknown; their need for challenges expressed in the very kind of philosophy they practiced (which sought the questionable knowledge of the essence of all things, wagering the health of the cultural unit in doing so), and in the agonistic instincts of the individual philosophers, because of which they competed against one another in order to solely possess the tyrannical rule of the spirit. But these very characteristics entail certain "weak" sides of philosophy, which may be inferred based on the discussion in the previous chapter. Furthermore, a kind of corruption is noticeable in the early Greek philosophers since their agonistic instincts lack a clear directionality, which we noticed in the case of artists and the laborers. These four traits, therefore, indicate the four salient ways in which the early Greek philosophers are susceptible to undergo spoiling or rotting. With Greek philosophy, we enter the domain of the thoroughly ambiguous, in which the two hostile drives of creation and self-preservation wage the most spectacular battle, vying to gain control over the same single yoke. Hence the distinction between strength and weakness, health and sickness, becomes ever more indiscernible.

Philosophy is essentially reflection. But reflection is equivocal. Reflection is shown in the philosopher's ability to view himself "coldly as a mirror of the world," by "seeking within himself the echoes of the world symphony," and then creatively reinterpreting and re-projecting them in the form of concepts (*Philosophy in the Tragic Age* 44). It is reflection understood in this sense – in which the creative instinct is more dominant – to which the pre-Platonic philosophers aspired. However, reflection might also be indicative of the last resort of a type of being, the creative instinct of which has lost its battle with the self-preserving instinct, and in which, therefore, the latter instinct has become dominant. Reflection, in this sense, would be associated with the fanaticism of excessive rationality, the final expedient of a decadent state, which does not want to perish at any cost. In the chapter "The Problem of Socrates" in *Twilight of the Idols*, Nietzsche argues that the latter kind of reflection is dominant in Socratic dialectical philosophy. Here reflection is closer to a kind of "spectatorship," which imagines itself to have gained a perspective independent of all life. Reflection, abstractly and passively, seeks to comprehend the whole. It is indicative of an active forgetting that forgets too much, especially the necessity of preserving the distance from the base class. This is revealed in the fact that Socratic rationality is a universal rationality; Socrates taught that, in principle, anybody can employ reason to penetrate the deepest abysses of being, and using thought, one can both understand and correct existence. Reason and thought, are not the prerogative of the few, but they ultimately have a utilitarian purpose concerning human happiness. Knowledge and understanding are now given the power of panacea with the Socratic equation, reason = virtue = happiness (TI Socrates 10; BT 15).

Note that this type of reflection is different from the former kind, which although seeks to grasp the whole with a single intuition, still tries to maintain one foot in the ground of culture. The pronouncements of the former kind of reflection, therefore, emerge from the realm of cultural unity. Although it disrupts the latter, it strives to give another higher unity back to culture. On the other hand, the idea of reflection, as found in Socrates, aims for pure abstraction. Hence Nietzsche suggests that Socrates was un-Hellenic and anti-Greek since his dialectics tried to create an abode in a "beyond" completely independent of the culture that bred him.[330] In art, the Socratic tendency to appeal to the public and misjudge their place and worth was seen in Euripidean plays. Euripides wrote his comedies for the sake of the consumption of the spectator, and therefore first "brought the *spectator* on to the stage" (BT 11). The spectator was now deemed capable of judging drama, and the artist accommodated himself to the taste of the public. In these plays, everyday life pushed its

---

330 See BT 13 and TI Socrates 3.

way out of the audience and on to the stage, whereas previously the audience had to elevate themselves in order to partake in the glorification of life that was staged in tragic plays. There is a clear shift in the concept of reflection: "the mirror which once revealed only great and bold features now became painfully true to life" (BT 11).

However, despite these aspects of Socratic thought, I contend that the more self-preserving variety of reflection, in some nascent form, is already in play at the very inception of Greek philosophy – even before Socrates – intricately bound up with the other, more creative, type of reflection. All the dangers and harmfulness associated with Greek philosophy – such as its opposition to cultural unity and mores, and also to myths, and the lack of any unitary direction to the agonistic drive – allow room, so to speak, for this second type of reflection to be irreducibly bound up with the first type. Greek philosophy is nothing but the seat of a struggle between these two kinds of reflection. With this struggle a new type of human being was born – the philosopher – who is thoroughly ambiguous at first, but then mutates gradually along the topological scale, as the struggle unfolds, to finally generate the Socratic type, in which the self-preserving type of reflection is clearly more dominant. The very possibility of philosophy in Ancient Greece shows its internal need for a variation of a type of being who has hitherto existed at the cultural level. The need for variation of type is possible only for a people that have already achieved a sort of completion and unity of its content at the cultural level. For such an excessive culture of tremendous health, the means of life, even of enjoying life, exist in abundance, and therefore it challenges itself to seek a new type of being, hitherto unknown. This new type might be a deviation into a higher type or a degeneration and monstrosity, and both these possibilities are initially bound up with each other.

At these turning points in history, Nietzsche writes, there is the birth of the "individual" – such as the Ancient Greek philosopher – with all the traits of the tyrant who submits to the agonistic drive (BGE 262). The ambiguity of the new individual type is revealed in the fact that, during these threshold points of history, the competition to grow appears alongside, often mixed up and tangled together with, an immense destruction and self-destruction. Because there is a compulsion to break free from the preset cultural mores, there is nothing but "new whys and hows... misunderstanding is allied with disregard" (BGE 262). Nietzsche argues that in such a "disastrous simultaneity of spring and autumn," in such times of "corruption," "decay [*Verfall*], ruin [or "spoiling," *Verderb*] and the highest desires are horribly entwined; the genius of the race overflows from every cornucopia of good and bad" (BGE 262).

Nietzsche is here pointing out the kind of highly indiscernible, completely uncertain and un-anticipatable events that occur at the critical stage of the development of a culture like that of the Greeks. The higher the stakes, the greater is the possibility of genuine creation; however, at this very limit point, the risk of falling into the abyss is also enormous. In the battle between the culture's will to create and will to self-preservation, as it is played out in the philosopher, the greatest challenge is to keep exercising the former instinct while still ensuring self-preservation. Balance is priceless, but it is also very hard to accomplish. There is a very small margin of error, if there is a margin at all, and accordingly, the distinction between great health and degeneration becomes more and more indiscernible. Reflection could simply be the mirroring of the universal truth of culture in a single intuition, as the ultimate conquest of the philosopher's will to create, *or* reflection might turn out to be the first step taken toward a decadent, life-denying philosophy, which has lost the battle against the will to self-preservation, and which passively seeks a spectatorship to view "universal truth" from nowhere. There is an essential ambiguity here, and an intricate, inseparable entanglement of these two possibilities.

Another way to express this ambiguity is as follows: at some critical point in the gray area of transition, the submission to the will to create results in the latter, more decadent variety of reflection, whereas previously, at less critical points in the topological scale, this very submission resulted in the former, more healthy kind of reflection. Therefore the onset of decadence is not the "fault" of Greek philosophy; one cannot simply blame the philosophers in general or Socrates or Euripides for initiating the decadent type of reflection. Nietzsche insists that, "there is a gap, a breach in evolution"; what we can observe is that the "quarrelsome and loquacious hordes of the Socratic schools" follows the era of the glorious, pre-Platonic philosophers (HH I 261). But what actually happens at that threshold point of decadence forever "remain[s] a secret of the [cultural] workshop" (HH I 261). All we can say is that the submission to the creative will appears as a blind, reckless one at the threshold point, signifying that the creative will has been exerted at the expense of preservation. But exercising the will to create at the expense of self-preservation precisely results in the *loss* of the creative instinct to the preserving one.[331] That is, paradoxically, submitting to the will to create at the threshold point implies not the victory of creation over self-preservation, but the loss of the former to the latter. Therefore the very activity, health, strength and growth of the strong Hellenic culture result in the decadence of this culture. As Nietzsche sums it up, "Life itself, its eternal fruitfulness and recurrence, creates torment, destruction, the will to annihilation" (KSA 13, 14[89]).

The fundamentality of the ambiguity at the threshold point also implies that the origin of metaphysics as the origin of life-denying evaluation cannot be clearly isolated as belonging to one type or the other, to either the strong, creative Hellenic type or to the new Socratic type dominated by the instinct of self-preservation. Since it is submission to the very creative will, which previously constituted the health of the Hellenic will, which now results in the decadent type of reflection, the strong Hellenic type cannot be blamed for the onset of decadence. At the same time, Socratic philosophy and reflection, Socratic rationality and dialectics, and the dominance of the will to self-preservation too result from submission to the Hellenic will to create. As such, they are symptoms or expressions of a life-denying decadent state, but not its cause.

---

331 In terms of our analysis in the previous chapter, this loss is signified by a lapse in the active faculty of forgetting.

Subsequently, these symptoms become the typological characteristics of a newly emerged weak type (which later modifies into the *ressentiment* type with the advent of Christianity) only "further down" in the topological scale. This weak type does not exist as a fixed type at the threshold point initiating decadence or the metaphysical mode of evaluation. It is as if one is bound to arrive either too early or too late to interpret the threshold point. The "breach in evolution" at this point contains a "secret" that cannot be totally exposed. No doubt, one could (and should) use the different traits of Socratic philosophy and Christian morality, as symptoms of decadence, to interpret the metaphysical mode of evaluation, as Nietzsche does throughout his writings. But these symptoms must not be confused for the essence of metaphysics or its origin. The source of metaphysical oppositions as the particular life-denying quality of will to power is forever elusive. It is always open for interpretation, since it cannot be settled in a final, definitive way.

With respect to the Hellenic culture, and in the secret workshop of its possibilities, the four different ways in which the strong type could undergo *Verderbniss* come together in unique ways as revealed in the various features of Hellenic philosophy from Thales to Socrates. The supreme challenge for Greek philosophy and philosophers was to submit to this highest point of the creative instinct and still conserve or preserve itself. Nietzsche calls it the "greatest test of independence" of the "rich souls of a higher type, who spend themselves extravagantly, almost indifferently, pushing the virtue of liberality to the point of vice ... *to conserve* [themselves]" (BGE 41). At the threshold point, either the genetic spark of the will to create is lit up and the philosopher achieves the highest moment of intuitive creation without destroying himself or his culture in the process, or the creative will loses its battle against the self-preserving instinct. The loss entails the dominance of the latter instinct, and hence of the decadent variety of reflection, leading to the emergence of the Socratic type as an independent type. Only with the actualization of this loss, do the possibilities given in *Verderbniss* actualize into the *Zugrundegehen* (destruction) of the philosopher, and hence, of the entire Greek culture.

Nietzsche's interpretation of the Hellenic age implies that, it is only when we get to Socrates that the conversion of *Verderbniss* into *Zugrundegehen* completed. The threshold point of decadence is abysmal and equivocal, and one needs to gain a certain distance from it in order to interpret it. This distance provides the space for the clear emergence of a new type of human being. For Nietzsche, it is the Socratic daemon, which announces the surfacing of the new weak type – the philosophical type which comes to dominate the rest of Western history – and which provides the most profound interpretation of the ongoing decadence, in the pretext of providing a cure to this very decadence. The appearance of the Socratic type indicates that the creative instinct of the Hellene has already lost its struggle against the self-preserving one. It is almost as if the Greek culture was in a state of pregnancy from Thales up until the time of Socrates, and the product of this pregnant culture was Socrates. The sixth and fifth centuries, for Nietzsche, remained a workshop of only a "promise and proclamation" of the "hitherto undiscovered highest *possibility of the philosophi-cal life*" (HH I 261). Hence the philosophers from Thales to Democritus are "hard to discern" (HH I 261). But what this promise produced was a Socrates, as if these glori-ous philosophers had lived in vain, as if their higher moments in the end amounted to nothing once the threshold was crossed. The pre-Socratic philosophers never com-pletely realized that new higher type of human being; all they "managed to found were sects" (GS 149).

With the onset of Socratic dialectical philosophy, the *Zugrundegehen* of Greek culture and philosophy is thoroughly realized. Socratic philosophy provides, what Nietzsche describes as a metaphysical-moral interpretation of the ongoing deca-dence, in which the "instincts" had already become "mutually *antagonistic*" (TI Socrates 9). Socratic philosophy does not initiate the decadence but lends a novel expression to it. The genius of Socrates lies in his intuition that everywhere dec-adence was already rampant. He provided a novel interpretation, a new direction to this ongoing "anti-Dionysian tendency," and completed the "suicide" and "self-destruction" of the old Greek existence (BT 14). As a helmsman, who promised a refuge after the shipwreck, Socrates offered his apparent "cure," which was nothing but a moral expression of the ongoing decadence. This cure took the form of the belief in a "real" world governed by the principles of pure reason (reason = virtue = happiness), which is opposed to an "apparent" world, which is contradictory to reason and logic. Through the employment of reason, Socrates taught that existence can not only be understood but also be corrected, whereas previously the purpose of art (and the inner intent of early Greek philosophy) was to justify and affirm exis-tence. But the Socratic remedy only betrays the emergence of a new weak type, which is dominated by the self-preserving instinct.

For Nietzsche, the Socratic belief in the real world and excessive rationality is only a novel moral expression of an ongoing decadence, not the cause of the latter. It is not the origin of metaphysics, but is complicit with the prevalent metaphysics of decadence. In the face of the Socratic cure, the old tragic culture had to drive away whatever Apollonian-Dionysian element that still remained in its nature and sought refuge in the safety provided by the pincers of excessive rationality: "The fanaticism with which the whole of Greek thought throws itself at rationality betrays a state of emergency: one was in peril, one had only *one* choice: either to perish or – be *absurdly rational*" (TI Socrates 10). The decadent Greek culture had a desperate need for Socrates' art of self-preservation (TI Socrates 9). Faith in rationality was the sup-posed panacea, the antidote against the ongoing sickness, since Socrates taught that, by dialectical reason, one could separate true knowledge from illusion and error, and thus attain a viewpoint from which one can watch the spectacle of existence in accor-dance with divine reason. However, this Socratic faith in the "beyond" of rational reflection thoroughly achieves the *Zugrundegehen* of Hellenic culture, through a re-evaluation of its old values.

Nietzsche highlights various aspects of the Socratic inversion of values by which the weak morality comes to dominance. For example, with Socrates the roles of instinct and consciousness are interchanged ("instinct becomes the critic and consciousness the creator" (BT 13)). There is a reversal of the evaluating glance. Thus the new type of morality anticipates the morality of *ressentiment*, which begins with a "no" as its first creative deed (GM I 10). Also, in Socratic thought, virtue is linked with knowledge and faith with morality (BT 14); myth is dissolved, and in "place of metaphysical solace a form of earthly harmony" is substituted as an optimistic solution to the problem of existence (BT 17).

These characteristics of Socratic thought betray a prior lapse in the active faculty of forgetting, which occurs at the onset of decadence when the will to create loses its struggle against the self-preserving instinct. Socratic reflection is symptomatic of the emergence of a type in which the self-preserving instinct has become dominant. With this lapse, the key functions of the active faculty – especially the filtering function that makes it possible for the healthy unit to be done with any particular experience, thus making room for new experiences – are compromised. Therefore the primary trait of such a self-preserving will is that it is unable to be done with an experience, which is the most basic meaning of decadence. The self-preserving will is not able to perform a genuine action, which involves allowing the instincts to discharge themselves outwardly. Hence, at bottom, this will is incapable of bestowing or squandering. Instead, it seeks a firm ground to hold on to. It endlessly ruminates, since it fails to get rid of an impression.

In moral terms, this implies seeking a meaning and justification for one's suffering through the attempt to correct existence. It means seeking some sort of permanence that can redeem the apparent world and its contradictions and change. Thus an opposition is set up between the real and the apparent world. But the desperation to hold on to something pure and permanent, not infiltrated or corrupted by becoming and change, must be seen as a consequence of the prior condition of decadence. Socrates' art of self-preservation, as an interpretation of decadence, only "*alter[s]* its expression, [but does] not abolish the thing itself" (TI Socrates 11). The Socratic cure is like a traumatic reaction to a pre-existing trauma, the sound of an echo, which repeats itself indefinitely, bleeding to death interminably, but never really dying, never perishing, since dying itself would be a genuine action.

Conclusion

The final two chapters demonstrate, at a general and at a particular level, that the distinction between the strong and the weak types of wills is ultimately equivocal. If we consider the two types as actual cultural types, we see that they undergo real transformations during the course of history. They either disintegrate or become healthier, thus going through topological displacements. The process of the disintegration of the strong type reveals a threshold point of decadence where it becomes impossible to unambiguously differentiate between the highest glory of a noble culture and the first steps of its decadence. With the eventual proliferation of the disintegrative influence, a new weak type is born, which dominates the future course of history. Thus topological variations affect the typology of wills.

The fundamental ambiguity of the threshold point of decadence shows that the source of metaphysical, life-denying evaluations is, in the final analysis, absolutely elusive. The particular quality of the will to power, which is "behind" the oppositional schema or the life-denying evaluation, cannot be settled in a definitive way, and it is always open for interpretation. In this sense, I have argued that Nietzsche carries out a thoroughly ambiguous critique of metaphysics. My argument undercuts the debate between the internalists and the externalists. Both of these groups of commentators are mistaken about the precise relation of Nietzsche's philosophy to metaphysical thought, although, as we have seen, they do grasp vital aspects of this relation. Just because the concept of will to power implies a non-foundationalism – in which the will cannot be conceived as a given, self-identical unit – it does not mean that Nietzsche exceeds the boundaries of metaphysics. To make the latter claim, the internalists had to subscribe to something like a pure typology of wills. However, ironically, this strategy would commit Nietzsche to a kind of "metaphysical" position, which I have argued does not quite escape the Heideggerian interpretation. On the other hand, just because Nietzsche puts forward the will to power as the essence of all existence, it does not confine him within the limits of metaphysics. The key to the Heideggerian metaphysical reading is the attribution of an oppositional stance to Nietzsche's critique, which is simply not present in it. I have argued that Nietzsche aims precisely at the source of the oppositional schema; and in doing so he offers an open-ended critique of metaphysics.

The reader might find this inconclusive and open-ended solution to the issue of the distinction between the two types (and hence that of metaphysics itself) somewhat unsatisfactory. In our reading, the concepts of real and apparent worlds and truth and falsity were re-interpreted and made sub-ordinate to the more basic issue regarding the distinction between the two types, and therefore, the problem of Nietzsche's relation to metaphysics entirely depended on the interpretation of the two types of wills. However, this dissatisfaction is not warranted. For, even though the qualitative source of metaphysical oppositions or of life-denying evaluations remains elusive, Nietzsche does not give up pursuing it. And in his relentless quest for this source, he depicts a radically differential philosophy, which consistently resists the temptation to set up oppositions of its own. Indeed, Nietzsche's differential philosophy illustrates an open terrain of incessant criticism, where no concept or distinction is privileged or presupposed in such a way that it is immune from radical re-interpretation. The ultimate intention or goal of this Nietzschean philosophy is the affirmation of existence, although what the definitive quality is that makes this affirmation possible is itself open for interpretation and revision. What life-affirmation exactly consists in is something that Nietzsche grapples with as he undertakes his critique of metaphysics.

The only presupposition that Nietzsche's thought does make is the realm of existence or the existential distinction. Nietzsche presupposes the latter in the sense that he does not first discover it as a basic concept through a prior distinction or opposition. However, the givenness of the existential realm does not imply that existence is a foundational ground or a noumenal realm, which has a reality independent of its phenomenal manifestations. Nor does it mean that existence can be explicated or determined "directly." Nietzsche's interpretation of existence unfolds radically indirectly through varying, evolving viewpoints, which I described in the first two chapters as the subjective and the objective interpretative perspectives. Nietzsche's indirect, meta-existential method not only preserves the ambiguity of the existential distinction, but also affirms it thoroughly by alternatively switching between the subjective and the objective perspectives. This affirmation acknowledges the elusiveness of the existential distinction.

Treating existence as the basic presupposition precisely allows Nietzsche to inaugurate a differential philosophy, which undertakes an unrelenting criticism of metaphysical concepts. Hence the ambiguity and the open-endedness of Nietzsche's critique of metaphysics are grounded in his meta-existential approach, which radically affirms the ambiguity of the existential distinction. In other words, Nietzsche can demonstrate that the source of metaphysical oppositions is elusive, precisely because, at the methodological level, he affirms the elusiveness of existence and of the existential distinction. His critique of metaphysics is complemented by his meta-existentialism and vice versa.

There are, of course, many problems that still need to be explored. In this study, I have merely hinted that the becoming of existence is revealed in the interaction between the typological and the topological aspects of wills, without directly dealing with the issue of existential becoming. This latter issue must be considered at the concrete level of historical and genealogical interpretation, which would bring into play the topological and typological concepts of the becoming and the emergence of the two types of wills. For this, we must investigate not only how a new weak (the Socratic and the *ressentiment*) type comes into dominance due to the prior decadence of the strong type, but also how a new, strong, free-spirited, "overhuman" type could emerge out of the modern, decadent, nihilistic humanity. Does the overhuman type come into being only after the total nihilism and destruction of the existing weak type is achieved? What roles do the current stronger, freer types play in this transformative stage? Nietzsche has plenty to say about these issues, as they are bound up with his own efforts at inaugurating a life-affirmative philosophy and also at showing a new path to the future development of humanity.

A further concern is the relation between Nietzsche's mature works and his earlier writings. Although I have argued that the meta-existential approach is at the very foundation of Nietzsche's philosophy of the middle and later periods, this does not preclude a meta-existential reading of some of the constant concerns of his early thought, which would establish a greater continuity between his early and mature philosophy than is usually acknowledged by scholars. In fact, we have already indirectly revealed this continuity in the final chapter, by relying heavily on Nietzsche's early published and unpublished writings to demonstrate the ambiguity that constitutes the threshold point of Greek decadence. But a more systematic inquiry into the continuity in Nietzsche's thought would involve showing the subtle conceptual shifts in his early thinking that led to the ideas published in *Human, All-Too-Human*, while, at the same time, demonstrating that something like the quest to affirm existence was already fundamentally determining Nietzsche's approach and the problems he targeted in his early philosophy.

Finally, our entire explication of Nietzsche's meta-existentialism has remained at a more abstract, methodological level, in which the main focus has been Nietzsche's critical evaluation of metaphysics. This present study has sought to provide the general conceptual framework and the basic methodological commitments of Nietzsche's thought, thus demonstrating how best to approach or read Nietzsche. One may certainly use the methodological lens provided here to interpret Nietzsche's multilayered analysis of art, religion, morality, science and culture that pervade his writings. Moreover, there are important stylistic issues, pertaining to Nietzsche's style of radical indirection, which are essentially intertwined with the methodological aspects of his philosophy. An in-depth consideration of these stylistic dimensions will introduce us to some of the unique existential themes of Nietzsche's philosophy such as "joy," "laughter," "play" and "dance," which are not usually emphasized by customary existential narratives that tend to highlight other themes such as passion, appropriation, anxiety, boredom, care and interestedness. These unique themes, which pertain to Nietzsche's attempt to affirm existence, are indispensible to his portrayal of the overhuman and the future free-spirited philosophers. This is a vast topic, however, which must be reserved for another occasion.

Bibliography

Nietzsche's works

The Anti-Christ. In *Twilight of the Idols and The Anti-Christ*. Trans. R.J. Hollingdale. London: Penguin, 2003. 123–199.

Assorted Opinions and Maxims. In *Human, All Too Human*. Trans. R.J. Hollingdale. Cambridge: Cambridge University Press, 1996. 207–299.

Beyond Good and Evil. Trans. Judith Norman. Cambridge: Cambridge University Press, 2002.

The Birth of Tragedy. In *The Birth of Tragedy and Other Writings*. Trans. Ronald Speirs. Cambridge: Cambridge University Press, 1999. 1–116.

The Case of Wagner. In *Basic Writings of Nietzsche*. Trans. and ed. Walter Kaufmann. New York: Modern Library, 2000. 609–648.

David Strauss, the Confessor and the Writer. In *Untimely Meditations*. Trans. R.J. Hollingdale. Cambridge: Cambridge University Press, 1997. 1–55.

Daybreak: Thoughts on the Prejudices of Morality. Trans. R.J. Hollingdale. Cambridge: Cambridge University Press, 1997.

"The Dionysiac World View." In *The Birth of Tragedy and Other Writings*. Trans. Ronald Speirs. Cambridge: Cambridge University Press, 1999. 117–138.

Ecce Homo. In *On The Genealogy of Morals and Ecce Homo*. Trans. and ed. Walter Kaufmann. New York: Vintage, 1989. 215–344.

The Gay Science. Trans. Josefine Nauckhoff. Cambridge: Cambridge University Press, 2001.

On the Genealogy of Morality. Trans. Carol Diethe. Cambridge: Cambridge University Press, 1994.

On the Genealogy of Morals. In *On The Genealogy of Morals and Ecce Homo*. Trans. and ed. Walter Kaufmann. New York: Vintage, 1989. 13–163.

"The Greek State." In *On the Genealogy of Morality*. Trans. Carol Diethe. Cambridge: Cambridge University Press, 1994. 176–186.

"Homer on Competition." In *On the Genealogy of Morality*. Trans. Carol Diethe. Cambridge: Cambridge University Press, 1994. 187–194.

Human, All Too Human: A Book for Free Spirits. Trans. R.J. Hollingdale, Cambridge: Cambridge University Press, 1996.

"The Philosopher: Reflections on the Struggle Between Art and Knowledge." In *Philosophy and Truth: Selections from Nietzsche's Notebooks of the Early 1870's*. Trans. and ed. Daniel Breazeale. Atlantic Highlands, NJ: Humanities Press, 1990. 3–58.

"The Philosopher as Cultural Physician." In *Philosophy and Truth: Selections from Nietzsche's Notebooks of the Early 1870's*. Trans. and ed. Daniel Breazeale. Atlantic Highlands, NJ: Humanities Press, 1990. 69–76.

Philosophy in the Tragic Age of the Greeks. Trans. Marianne Cowan. Washington D.C.: Regnery, 1962.

The Pre-Platonic Philosophers. Trans. and ed. Greg Whitlock. Urbana and Chicago: University of Illinois Press, 2001.

Sämtliche Werke. Kritische Studienausgabe. 15 vols. Ed. Giorgio Colli and Mazzino Montinari. Munich/Berlin/New York: dtv/De Gruyter, 1999.

Schopenhauer as Educator. In *Untimely Meditations*. Trans. R.J. Hollingdale. Cambridge: Cambridge University Press, 1997. 125–194.

Selected Letters of Friedrich Nietzsche. Trans. and ed. Christopher Middleton. Indianapolis: Hackett, 1996.

"The Struggle between Science and Wisdom." In *Philosophy and Truth: Selections from Nietzsche's Notebooks of the Early 1870's*. Trans. and ed. Daniel Breazeale. Atlantic Highlands, NJ: Humanities Press, 1990. 127–146.

Thus Spoke Zarathustra: A Book for Everyone and Nobody. Trans. and ed. Graham Parkes. Oxford: Oxford University Press, 2005.

"On Truth and Lies in a Nonmoral Sense." In *Philosophy and Truth: Selections from Nietzsche's Notebooks of the Early 1870's*. Trans. and ed. Daniel Breazeale. Atlantic Highlands, NJ: Humanities Press, 1990. 79–97.

Twilight of the Idols. In *Twilight of the Idols and The Anti-Christ*. Trans. R.J. Hollingdale. London: Penguin, 2003. 29–122.

Untimely Meditations. Trans. R.J. Hollingdale. Cambridge: Cambridge University Press, 1997.

On the Uses and Disadvantages of History for Life. In *Untimely Meditations*. Trans. R.J. Hollingdale. Cambridge: Cambridge University Press, 1997. 57–123.

The Wanderer and His Shadow. In *Human, All Too Human*. Trans. R.J. Hollingdale. Cambridge: Cambridge University Press, 1996. 301–395.

Werke. Kritische Gesamtausgabe. Ed. Giorgio Colli and Mazzino Montinari. Berlin/New York: De Gruyter (1967–).

The Will to Power. Trans. Walter Kaufmann and R.J. Hollingdale. New York: Vintage, 1968.

Secondary works

Acampora, Christa Davis. "Naturalism and Nietzsche's Moral Psychology." In *A Companion to Nietzsche*. Ed. Keith Ansell-Pearson. Oxford: Blackwell, 2006. 314–333.

Acampora, Christa Davis, ed. *Nietzsche's On the Genealogy of Morals*. Maryland: Rowman & Littlefield, 2006.

Acharya, Vinod. "Nobility and Decadence: The Vulnerabilities of Nietzsche's Strong Type." *PhaenEx* 7.1 (2012): 130–161

Ahern, Daniel R. *Nietzsche as Cultural Physician*. University Park: The Pennsylvania State University Press, 1995.

Allison, David B. "Musical Psychodramatics." In *Why Nietzsche Still?: Reflections on Drama, Culture, and Politics*. Ed. Alan D. Schrift. Berkeley and Los Angeles: University of California Press, 2000. 66–78.

Allison, David B., ed. *The New Nietzsche: Contemporary Styles of Interpretation*. Cambridge: MIT Press, 1985.

Ansell-Pearson, Keith, ed. *A Companion to Nietzsche*. Oxford: Blackwell, 2006.

Ansell-Pearson, Keith and Howard Caygill, eds. *The Fate of the New Nietzsche*. Aldershot: Avebury, 1993.

Benson, Bruce Ellis. *Pious Nietzsche: Decadence and Dionysian Faith*. Bloomington: Indiana University Press, 2008.

Blondel, Eric. *Nietzsche: The Body and Culture*. Trans. Seán Hand. Stanford: Stanford University Press, 1991.

Brobjer, Thomas H. *Nietzsche's Philosophical Context: An Intellectual Biography*. Urbana and Chicago: University of Chicago Press, 2008.

Clark, Maudemarie. *Nietzsche on Truth and Philosophy*. Cambridge: Cambridge University Press, 1990.

Clark, Maudemarie and David Dudrick. "The Naturalisms of *Beyond Good and Evil*." In *A Companion to Nietzsche*. Ed. Keith Ansell-Pearson. Oxford: Blackwell, 2006. 148–167.

Conway, Daniel W. "Life and Self-Overcoming." In *A Companion to Nietzsche*. Ed. Keith Ansell-Pearson. Oxford: Blackwell, 2006. 532–547.

Conway, Daniel W. *Nietzsche's Dangerous Game: Philosophy in the Twilight of the Idols*. Cambridge: Cambridge University Press, 1997.

Conway, Daniel W. "The Politics of Decadence." *Southern Journal of Philosophy* 37 (1999): 19–33.

Cox, Christoph. *Nietzsche: Naturalism and Interpretation*. Berkeley and Los Angeles: University of California Press, 1999.

Crowell, Steven. "Existentialism." *The Stanford Encyclopedia of Philosophy*. Ed. Edward N. Zalta. Winter 2010 Edition http://plato.stanford.edu/archives/win2010/entries/existentialism/ (11 March 2011).

Danto, Arthur C. *Nietzsche as Philosopher*. New York: Columbia University Press, 2005.

Descartes, René. *Meditations on First Philosophy*. Trans. Donald A. Cress. Indianapolis: Hackett, 1993.

Deleuze, Gilles. *Nietzsche and Philosophy*, Trans. Hugh Tomlinson. New York: Columbia University Press, 2006.

Derrida, Jacques. "Différance." In *Margins of Philosophy*. Trans. Alan Bass. Chicago: University of Chicago Press, 1982. 1–27.

Derrida, Jacques. "The Ends of Man." In *Margins of Philosophy*. Trans. Alan Bass. Chicago: University of Chicago Press, 1982. 109–136.

Derrida, Jacques. *Positions*. Trans. Alan Bass. Chicago: University of Chicago Press, 1981.

Derrida, Jacques. *Spurs: Nietzsche's Styles*. Trans. Barbara Harlow. Chicago: University of Chicago Press, 1978.

Evans, C. Stephen. *Kierkegaard's "Fragments" and "Postscript": The Religious Philosophy of Johannes Climacus*. New Jersey: Humanities Press, 1983.

Fink, Eugen. *Nietzsche's Philosophy*. Trans. Goetz Richter. New York: Continuum, 2003.

Haar, Michel. *Nietzsche and Metaphysics*. Trans. and ed. Michael Gendre. Albany: SUNY Press, 1996.

Hegel, G.W.F. *The Encyclopedia Logic*. Trans. T.F. Geraets, W.A. Suchting and H.S. Harris. Indianapolis: Hackett, 1991.

Heidegger, Martin. *Being and Time*. Trans. John Macquarrie and Edward Robinson. San Francisco: Harper & Row, 1962.

Heidegger, Martin. *Nietzsche*, vol. I: *The Will to Power as Art*. Trans. David Farrell Krell. San Francisco: Harper & Row, 1979.

Heidegger, Martin. *Nietzsche*, vol. II: *The Eternal Recurrence of the Same*. Trans. David Farrell Krell. San Francisco: Harper & Row, 1984.

Heidegger, Martin. *Nietzsche*, vol. III: *The Will to Power as Knowledge and as Metaphysics*. Trans. Joan Stambaugh, David Farrell Krell and Frank A. Capuzzi. San Francisco: Harper & Row, 1987.

Heidegger, Martin. *Nietzsche*, vol. IV: *Nihilism*. Trans. Frank A. Capuzzi. San Francisco: Harper & Row, 1982.

Heidegger, Martin. "The Word of Nietzsche: 'God is Dead.'" In *The Question Concerning Technology and Other Essays*. Trans. William Lovitt. New York: Harper & Row, 1977. 53–112.

Hill, R. Kevin. *Nietzsche's Critiques: The Kantian Foundations of his Thought*. Oxford: Oxford University Press, 2003.

Janaway, Christopher. *Beyond Selflessness: Reading Nietzsche's Genealogy*. Oxford: Oxford University Press, 2007.

Janaway, Christopher. "Naturalism and Genealogy." In *A Companion to Nietzsche*. Ed. Keith Ansell-Pearson. Oxford: Blackwell, 2006. 337–352.

Jaspers, Karl. "Existenzphilosophie." In *Existentialism: From Dostoevsky to Sartre*. Ed. Walter Kaufmann. New York: Meridian Books, 1956. 131–205.

Jaspers, Karl. *Nietzsche: An Introduction to the Understanding of His Philosophical Activity*. Trans. Charles F. Wallraff and Frederick J. Schmitz. Baltimore: The Johns Hopkins University Press, 1997.

Kant, Immanuel. *Critique of Pure Reason*. Trans. Norman Kemp Smith. New York: Palgrave Macmillan, 2003.

Kaufmann, Walter, ed. *Existentialism: From Dostoevsky to Sartre*. New York: Meridian Books, 1956.

Kaufmann, Walter. *Nietzsche: Philosopher, Psychologist, Antichrist*. Princeton: Princeton University Press, 1974.

Kierkegaard, Søren. *Concluding Unscientific Postscript to Philosophical Fragments*. Trans. and ed. Howard V. Hong and Edna H. Hong. Princeton: Princeton University Press, 1992.

Kierkegaard, Søren. *Philosophical Fragments*. Trans. and ed. Howard V. Hong and Edna H. Hong. Princeton: Princeton University Press, 1985.

Kofman, Sarah. *Nietzsche and Metaphor*. Trans. Duncan Large. Stanford: Stanford University Press, 1993.

Leiter, Brian. *Nietzsche on Morality*. New York: Routledge, 2002.

Lippitt, John. "Illusion and Satire in Kierkegaard's *Postscript*." *Continental Philosophy Review* 32 (1999): 451–466.

Löwith, Karl. *From Hegel to Nietzsche: The Revolution in Nineteenth-Century Thought*. Trans. David E. Green. New York: Columbia University Press, 1991.

Magnus, Bernd. *Nietzsche's Existential Imperative*. Bloomington: Indiana University Press, 1978.

Martensen, Hans Lassen. *Die christliche Ethik*. Berlin H. Reuther's Verlagsbuchhandlung, 1888.

Mooney, Edward F. *On Søren Kierkegaard: Dialogue, Polemics, Lost Intimacy and Time*. Hamphsire: Ashgate, 2007.

Müller-Lauter, Wolfgang. *Nietzsche: His Philosophy of Contradictions and the Contradictions of His Philosophy*. Trans. David J. Parent. Urbana and Chicago: University of Illinois Press, 1999.

Nehamas, Alexander. *Nietzsche: Life as Literature*. Cambridge: Harvard University Press, 1985.

Plato. *Phaedo*. In *Five Dialogues*. Trans. G.M.A. Grube. Indianapolis: Hackett, 2002. 93–154.

Plato. *Republic*. Trans. C.D.C. Reeve. Indianapolis: Hackett, 2004.

Richardson, John. *Nietzsche's New Darwinism*. Oxford: Oxford University Press, 2004.

Rumble, Vanessa. "To Be as No-One: Kierkegaard and Climacus on the Art of Indirect Communication." *International Journal of Philosophical Studies* 3.2 (1995): 307–321.

Safranski, Rüdiger. *Nietzsche: A Philosophical Biography*. Trans. Shelley Frisch. New York: W.W. Norton, 2002.

Sartre, Jean-Paul. *Being and Nothingness: A Phenomenological Essay on Ontology*. Trans. Hazel E. Barnes. New York: Washington Square Press, 1992.

Sartre, Jean-Paul. *Existentialism is a Humanism*. Trans. Carol Macomber. New Haven: Yale University Press, 2007.

Schacht, Richard. *Making Sense of Nietzsche: Reflections Timely and Untimely*. Chicago: University of Illinois Press, 1995.

Schacht, Richard. *Nietzsche*. London: Routledge & Kegan Paul, 1983.

Schopenhauer, Arthur. *Essays and Aphorisms*. Trans. R.J. Hollingdale. London: Penguin, 1970.

Schopenhauer, Arthur. *The World as Will and Representation*, vol. I. Trans. E.F.J. Payne. New York: Dover, 1969.

Schrift, Alan D. *Nietzsche's French Legacy: A Genealogy of Poststructuralism*. London: Routledge, 1995.

Schrift, Alan D. *Nietzsche and the Question of Interpretation: Between Hermeneutics and Deconstruction*. New York: Routledge, 1990.

Schrift, Alan D., ed. *Why Nietzsche Still?: Reflections on Drama, Culture, and Politics*. Berkeley and Los Angeles: University of California Press, 2000.

Solomon, Robert C. *From Rationalism to Existentialism: The Existentialists and Their Nineteenth-Century Backgrounds*. Rowman & Littlefield, 1972.

Solomon, Robert C. *Living with Nietzsche: What the Great "Immoralist" Has to Teach Us*. Oxford: Oxford University Press, 2003.

Solomon, Robert C., ed. *Nietzsche: A Collection of Critical Essays*. New York: Anchor Books, 1973.

Strong, Tracy B. *Friedrich Nietzsche and the Politics of Transfiguration*. Berkeley and Los Angeles: University of California Press, 1975.

Turnbull, Jamie. "Kierkegaard, Indirect Communication and Ambiguity." *The Heythrop Journal* 50.1 (2009): 13–22.

Westphal, Merold. *Becoming a Self: A Reading of Kierkegaard's Concluding Unscientific Postscript*. West Lafayette: Purdue University Press, 1996.

Wilkerson, Dale. *Nietzsche and the Greeks*. London: Continuum, 2006.

Wittgenstein, Ludwig. *Philosophical Investigations*. Trans. G.E.M. Anscombe. Oxford: Blackwell, 2001.

Wittgenstein, Ludwig. *Tractatus Logico-Philosophicus*. Trans. D.F. Pears and B.F. McGuinness. London: Routledge & Kegan Paul, 1974.

Young, Julian. *Nietzsche's Philosophy of Art*. Cambridge: Cambridge University Press, 1992.

Young, Julian. *Nietzsche's Philosophy of Religion*. Cambridge: Cambridge University Press, 2006.

Index

abstraction/ abstract thinking 2–4, 18–21,
    23–37, 46–47, 57, 131, 140, 174–175
Acampora, Christa Davis 13
action/ reaction 72–73, 79–83, 96, 99,
    119–127, 151, 179
Aeschylus 155–156, 160
aesthetic interpretation of Nietzsche 13–14, 23
affect 50, 72, 83–88, 96, 119–120, 135
agon 139–140, 144–156, 158, 161, 170–171,
    173, 175
Ahern, Daniel 113, 164 n.327, 168 n.328
Allison, David 157
ambiguity 20, 57–60, 107–109, 147, 158,
    160–164, 169, 182
– of the distinction between strong and weak
    types 100–101, 105–106, 109–116, 126,
    130, 137–138, 173–176, 180,
– of the existential distinction 3–4, 15, 25–37,
    45, 50–51, 181
– of Nietzsche's critique of metaphysics 5, 17,
    60–62, 67–68, 74–78, 103–106, 176–177,
    180–181
Anaximander 167
Apollonian 139, 147–155, 158–159, 163, 178
apparent world/ real world 4–5, 8–11, 62–65,
    91–93, 178–180
Archilochus 153, 156
art/ artist 9–10, 13, 21–23, 53, 59–60, 67–77
– Greek 117, 137–174, 178–179
ascending/ descending life 48–50, 96, 107, 111
ascetic priest 118 n.264, 130–131, 158
authentic/ inauthentic existence 2, 20–23, 32,
    34, 40, 49

bad type (of master morality) 117, 120–123,
    129–135, 140–146, 174
beauty 149, 151–154
becoming 7–9, 38–39, 62–65, 73–74, 90–93,
    111, 152, 168, 179, 181
– active 119
– as a subjective tendency 4, 27–34, 39–41,
    44, 52–53, 57–59, 67, 72–73, 86–87, 92
– of existence 19, 27, 39–41, 44, 50, 52,
    54–60, 77, 87, 90, 104, 181
– reactive of active forces 101 n.228,
    110 n.245, 118–127, 134–137

being 6–9, 27–28, 30–31, 38–39, 42–44,
    52–68, 72–75, 83–94, 102–104, 149–152,
    168
Benson, Bruce Ellis 115
bestowing virtue 130–136, 163, 173, 179
Blondel, Eric 10–11, 101–104, 111
body 10, 38–39, 52–62, 66, 119–127
Brandes, Georg 35
Brobjer, Thomas 35

Caesar, Julius 112 n.251
Camus, Albert 1, 18
cause and effect/ causality 117, 157–160,
    176–178
– Nietzsche's critique of 70–71, 79–91, 93,
    157 n.316
Christianity, Nietzsche's critique of 22, 57, 59,
    69–70, 108–110, 121, 177
Clark, Maudemarie 12–14
comic/ comical 26, 31, 33, 37, 40
commanding/ obeying 52–53, 83–88, 96–97,
    119–122, 164, 168
conscience 73, 81
– good and bad 59, 69, 71, 82, 116
consciousness/ unconsciousness 81–83,
    120–127, 136, 159–161, 168, 179
Conway, Daniel 108 n.239–240, 109, 114,
    118 n.265
Cornaro, Luigi 80
corruption 38–39, 135–137, 145, 173, 175, 179
Cox, Christoph 12–14, 43, 62–64, 91, 94–95,
    111
creation of values 70–73, 99, 107–108,
    112–113, 128, 131–134, 164–165, 170–173
creative will 15–16, 50, 53–62, 70–73, 75–89,
    93, 96–99, 112–117, 122–179
– See also self-preservation

Danto, Arthur 6
death 44, 133, 156–160, 162, 179
– of God 22, 40
decadence 96–97, 107–110
– Nietzsche's definitions of 121, 121 n.272
– of the Hellenic type 117–118, 138–140,
    156–182

– of the strong type 5, 16, 103, 105–128, 180–181
– strong type's vulnerability to 16, 110, 114, 126–137, 173
deconstruction, theory of 14, 68
Deleuze, Gilles 10 n.23, 61 n.152, 96–99, 101 n.228, 103 n.236, 110 n.245, 114, 116, 118–128, 137, 159
Democritus 178
Derrida, Jacques 10–11, 43 n.128, 49 n.146, 68–69
Descartes, René 9, 38–39, 42 n.127
despair 21, 75
destruction/ ruination (*Zugrundegehen*) 108–109, 114, 127–129, 175–179
differential relation/ differences in degrees 4–5, 38–39, 86–88, 98–99, 181
– between subjectivity and objectivity 3, 5, 32–39, 42–61, 67–78
Dionysian 107, 115, 117–118, 139, 147–159, 163–164, 178
direct/ indirect communication 3–4, 25–41, 43–51, 59–60, 77, 90, 94, 104–106, 181–182
directionality
– of the agonistic drive 140, 146, 156, 171, 173, 175
– of willing 58–59, 83–87, 96–100
dogmatism/ non-dogmatism 94–95, 101–103, 169
Dostoevsky, Fyodor 1

eternal recurrence 6, 8, 48 n.145, 63 n.157
ethical/ unethical 27–29, 33, 35, 37, 39–41, 49, 149
Euripides 148, 157–159, 174, 176
Evans, Stephen 26, 29 n.96, 30 n.97, 34 n.114, 40 n.125
existence 1–5, 18–63
– interpreting itself 43–45, 51–60
– justification of 19, 44, 141–145, 150–152, 178–179
– warped nature of 58–60, 77, 99
– *See also* becoming of existence
existential distinction 24–39, 49–52, 77–78, 181
– implications of drawing the 3–4, 15, 33–37, 39, 45, 49, 60–61, 104 n.237

existentialism
– Kierkegaard's (Climacus') versus Nietzsche's 1–5, 18–25, 35–42, 45–51, 68–69
experience, inability to cope with 121–124, 178–179
explanation (vs. description) 80–82, 85–86, 90
external/ outward 20, 26–32, 41, 121–122, 179
– *See also* inwardness/ inner
externalist reading of Nietzsche 6–9, 14–15, 24, 57, 62, 90, 96, 98, 103–104, 180
– *See also* Heidegger

Fink, Eugen 2, 18, 23 n.54, 24, 65
force
– active and reactive 88–91, 96–98, 114, 116, 118–127, 132, 136–137, 140
– *See also* becoming reactive of active force
forgetting
– active 56, 102, 120–127, 131–132, 174
– lapse in 124–127, 130, 132–137, 174, 176 n.331, 179
foundationalism/ non-foundationalism 11, 36, 65 n.170, 92–93, 98–99, 102, 180–181
free spirit 22, 40, 67, 70, 74, 181–182
free will 73, 79–82, 89, 93

genealogy 10, 22, 61 n.152, 96, 99, 101, 107, 111–114, 116–118, 181
god 22, 28, 40–41, 64, 81–84, 143–149, 153–155
Goethe, J.W. von 112 n.251
good type (of master morality) 16, 102, 112–113, 118, 120, 122
– *See also* strong type
gravity, spirit of 131–133

Haar, Michel 10–11, 64–65, 91–92, 96–98
health/ sickness 20, 22, 56, 76, 107–140, 143–145, 148, 150, 156, 161–168, 172–180
Hegel, G.W.F. 2–3, 20–21, 25–35, 37, 46–49, 51, 61 n.152, 98, 102, 125–126
Heidegger, Martin 1, 6–12, 14–15, 24, 42, 52–53, 57, 62–66, 68, 87, 90–95, 100, 102–104, 110–115, 180
– *See also* externalist reading of Nietzsche
Hesiod 144, 147, 156, 160

Hill, Kevin 12, 14 n.42
historical method (Nietzsche's) 67, 69–72
– See also genealogy
Höffding, Harald 35
Homer 76 n.188, 112 n.251, 143–144, 147–149, 151 n.312, 154, 154–156, 160, 166

illusion 5, 56–59, 62–63, 70–76, 80, 82, 148, 150–151, 159, 178
immanence 11, 65, 91–92, 95, 99
indirect communication/ indirection
– See direct communication
individual/ individuality 1–5, 18–23, 26–30, 35, 39–41, 49–51, 54–58, 88–89, 114, 140–143, 149–155, 160, 165–175
innocence 71, 73, 84
instinct
– for cleanliness 130
– internalization of 121
internalist reading of Nietzsche 10–12, 14, 24, 62–65, 68–69, 78, 91–92, 94–105, 126, 180
inwardness/ inner 20, 27–32, 40, 49, 86–87
– See also external/ outward
irony 26, 29 n.93, 33, 37, 40, 46

Janaway, Christopher 12–13, 111, 113 n.256
Jaspers, Karl 1, 2, 4, 18, 21–22, 23 n.54, 46, 48, 65
Jesus 28, 112 n.251
justice/ injustice 57, 73–75, 121, 128–129, 132

Kant, Immanuel 14, 19, 43, 46, 48–49, 52, 152, 155
Kaufmann, Walter 2, 18–19, 22, 65
Kierkegaard, Søren/ Climacus, Johannes 1–4, 15, 18–42, 45–51, 63, 68, 75, 83 n.196
Kofman, Sarah 10–11, 102–104, 111
knowledge 38–39, 56–58, 72–74, 80–86, 149–151, 161–174, 178–179

labor/ laborers 53, 139–147
Leiter, Brian 12
life
– and its relation to philosophy 18–22, 46–50
– affirmation and denial of 4–5, 9, 14–17, 22, 48, 57–66, 72–73, 91–93, 97–106, 110–112, 119–122, 141–143, 174–182

– Nietzsche's use of the term 44–45, 53
– See also existence
Lippitt, John 26
logic/ illogic 57, 75–76, 80, 92, 171, 178
love 21, 128, 131–132, 135

Magnus, Bernd 18
Martensen, Hans Lassen 35
masks 40, 48–49, 102
memory 123–124
metaphysical need 61, 66, 72–77, 91–93, 99
– Nietzsche's use of the term 70–71, 74–75
metaphysics
– as incompatible with or opposed to existential thought 1–2, 18–25, 35–38
– oppositional nature of 4–5, 38–39, 62–66
– overcoming of 4–5, 7, 10–12, 14, 61–62, 70–78, 91–94, 98–100, 103–104, 180–181
– source of the oppositional structure of 5, 15–17, 92–100, 104–106, 176–181
Miltiades 146 n.306, 156
Mooney, Edward 25–26, 31 n.99
morality 9 n.16, 22, 49–50, 70–77, 80–82, 107, 128, 179
– master/ slave 111–114, 116–123
– of custom 142, 170
Müller-Lauter, Wolfgang 10, 65 n.170, 92
music 149–155
myth 139–163, 166, 170–173, 179

naturalist reading of Nietzsche 12–15, 23, 43, 62–64, 66 n.171, 91, 94–95, 111
nature 12–13, 72–76, 81, 142, 149–154, 168
necessity
– of actions 73, 80, 82, 89
– of the effect 81–82, 89
need for challenges 133–134, 136–137, 144, 170, 173
negation, origin of 96–100, 104–105, 124–127
Nehamas, Alexander 13, 23
nihilism 22–23, 40, 107–111, 181
noumena 39, 43, 46, 52, 59, 181
– See also thing-in-itself

objective (or: objectivity) See subjective
optimism 148, 159, 179
order of rank 22, 53–55, 112, 128
overhuman (Übermensch) 22, 108, 181–182

Parmenides 167
passion 2–4, 18–19, 23, 31, 49, 76, 132, 135, 182
pathos 86–87
– of distance 128–137, 174
perspectives/ perspectivism 11–13, 36–46, 50–64, 67–78, 84–91, 94–96, 101–102, 134, 181
pessimism 20–21, 70, 108, 147–148, 159, 162
philosophy, pre-Platonic 16, 139–140, 158–179
pity 128, 135–136
Plato 7, 38, 43, 46, 48–49, 81, 102, 112 n.251, 113, 157 n.317, 158
Platonism 7–19, 52–53, 62–64, 108–110
poetry, epic and lyric 149, 153–155
power 53–62, 71–75
– See also will to power
– feeling of 56–57, 79 n.190, 82–84, 97
principle of identity 11, 65, 92
Prometheus 155
psychology (Nietzsche's) 48, 67–72

real world See apparent world
reason/ rationality 53–54, 81–82, 86, 119, 131, 151, 157–158, 174–179
reflection 26–32, 167–168, 174–179
Reformation 70
relational
– aspect between active and reactive forces 119–124
– aspect between strong and weak types 100–101, 113–114
– aspect of willing 83–88
Renaissance 70, 72
resistance 53–56, 84–91, 99, 121, 148, 153
responsibility 73, 82
ressentiment 22, 112, 116, 118, 122–123, 126, 128, 177, 179, 181
revenge 22, 79 n.190, 124, 130, 132, 136, 146 n.306
Richardson, John 12
Romans 162
romanticism 70, 115
Rumble, Vanessa 25, 32 n.110

Sartre, Jean-Paul 1–2, 18, 41
Schacht, Richard 12, 62, 64 n.163
Schopenhauer, Arthur 19–21, 39, 48, 67, 70, 76 n.189, 97, 112 n.251, 150

science 4, 12–14, 19, 47, 62, 66–78, 80, 85–86, 107, 163–172, 182
secret 29, 112, 122, 167, 176–177
self-overcoming 19, 50, 56–61, 75, 96–97, 133
self-preservation 15, 50, 55–56, 59–62, 70, 75, 84–86, 93, 96–97, 112, 117, 123, 127–159, 161, 172–179
– See also creative will
semblance 52–53, 59, 149–154
sickness See health
Silenus 148, 151–152
Socrates 17, 29–30, 38, 48–49, 107, 115, 117–119, 137, 140, 148, 157–165, 169, 174–179
solitude 128–130, 132, 136, 146 n.306, 165–168, 173
Solomon, Robert 2, 4, 18, 23–24
Sophocles 156, 158
soul 38, 52, 114–115
spoiling/ rotting (Verderbniss) 108, 114–115, 127–137, 173, 175
state, Greek 138–147, 154, 156, 160–163
Strong, Tracy 147 n.308, 160–161
strong type
– and its distinction from weak type 16, 66, 96–116, 119–129, 133, 173–180
– decadence of See decadence
subjective (or: subjectivity)/ objective 1–5, 15–16, 20–62, 66–78
– See also becoming as a subjective tendency
suffering 19–20, 62, 70, 73, 79 n.190, 81–82, 115, 128–132, 136, 147–154, 169, 179
style 2, 18, 40, 163
– Nietzsche's 4, 13, 19, 22, 42, 45–50, 69, 182
symptom 4, 30–31, 34, 48–50, 84–85, 95–99, 113, 117–118, 121, 134, 157–162, 176–179

taste 20, 48, 164–171, 174
Thales 161–167, 169–171, 177–178
thing-in-itself 14, 39, 49, 52, 92, 102
– See also noumena
Timo 146 n.306
topology 5, 16, 103–109, 114–128, 130, 138, 149, 173–181
– See also typology
tragedy, Greek 117, 139, 160–161, 166–167, 174–175
– birth of 147–156
– death of 140, 147, 156–160

truth 4–15, 22, 27–33, 38–40, 49 n.146, 53,
    63–64, 67–70, 86, 90–91, 101–103,
    110–113, 134, 150–155, 158, 165–176,
    180
– as anti-natural 75
– *See also* will to truth
Turnbull, Jamie 26
typology 5, 56, 96–107, 111–128, 138, 177,
    180–181
– *See also* topology
tyranny 170–175

values/ evaluations *See* morality; creation of
    values
– re-evaluation of 22, 107–111
virtues 21, 67, 69, 127–137, 142, 159, 173–174,
    177–179
– in relation to vices 69, 134, 177
Voltaire 70

Wagner, Richard 67, 76 n.189
weak type *See* strong type
Wilkerson, Dale 145–146, 156
will as multiplicity 83–84, 90–91, 93, 119
– *See also* will to power
will to power 5–11, 16, 44, 52–62, 63 n.157,
    71–106, 125–126, 133–134, 137, 165–170
– qualitative aspect of 5, 16, 55, 66, 78–92,
    96–97, 100, 102–106, 119, 128, 138, 177,
    180
– quantitative aspect of 53–62, 66, 78, 86–90,
    92, 96–97, 119
will to truth 13–15, 56–62, 66, 72–76, 82–83,
    91–96, 99, 165
– *See also* metaphysical need
– unconditional 66, 73, 93–96, 99
Wittgenstein, Ludwig 47

Zarathustra 79, 130–133, 135–136